A Woman's Place Is Everywhere

A Woman's Place Is Everywhere

*INSPIRATIONAL PROFILES OF FEMALE LEADERS
WHO ARE EXPANDING THE ROLES
OF AMERICAN WOMEN*

Lindsey Johnson

Jackie Joyner-Kersee

MasterMedia Limited
New York

Published 1994 by MasterMedia Limited

MASTERMEDIA and colophon are registered trademarks
of MasterMedia Limited.

Library of Congress Cataloging-in-Publication Data

Johnson, Lindsey.
    A woman's place is everywhere : inspirational profiles of female leaders who
are expanding the roles of American women / Lindsey Johnson, Jackie Joyner-
Kersee.
        p.   cm.
    ISBN 0-942361-97-0 (pbk.) : $9.95
    1. Women in the professions—United States—Biography.
  I. Joyner-Kersee, Jacqueline, 1962- II. Title.
HD6054.2.U6J64   1994
305.4'3'00973—dc20   94-5151
                                               CIP

Manufactured in the United States of America
Book design by Alan L. Marks
Production services by Lynn & Turek Associates, New York

10 9 8 7 6 5 4 3 2

Dedications

To Gertrude Lee, my grandmother and a pioneering woman who serves as an inspiration for us all. To my parents, who always told me I could be anything I wanted to work for; and to my sisters, who give me the strength to be the best person I can be.

—Lindsey Johnson

To my mother, who taught me the importance of self-reliance, self-respect, and self-discipline; in possessing these traits, I learned there is nothing in life I couldn't accomplish.

She inspired me to be a great person, instilled in me never to take anything for granted, and implanted the belief that life is a precious gift that should not be misused, but treasured.

To my mother, Whose Place Was Everywhere, but who will always have the Best Place of All—IN MY HEART.

—Jackie Joyner-Kersee

Contents

Foreword by Gail Blanke   *xv*
Introduction by Lindsey Johnson and Jackie Joyner-Kersee   *xxi*

Marin Alsop   *1*

Musician Marin Alsop is living proof that anything is possible when dreams are backed by determination. Despite numerous setbacks, including being rejected by Juilliard after she had already built a career as a violinist and band leader, Alsop refused to forfeit her desire to become a conductor. Today her award-winning work is expected to distinguish her as the first woman conductor to enjoy a world-class career.

Del M. Anderson   *10*

Once prized for her beauty, Del M. Anderson is now praised for her intellect and insightful leadership as the president of San Jose City College. Downplaying publicity that focused attention on her as the first woman and only the second black to hold the college's top post, Anderson has set an ambitious agenda that's proving she's a professional to be reckoned with.

Priscilla Beard   *17*

Ignoring conventional business wisdom, Priscilla Beard set her sights on a seemingly impossible goal—to create a company that combined profitable entrepreneurialism with a socially responsible conscience. Today Beard's $3 million enterprise, Message!Check, is tucked away on a scenic coastal island, but it's at the forefront of revolutionary corporate practices ranging from systematic support of worthy causes to innovative employment policies.

Elaine L. Chao   25

Raised on the American Dream by immigrant parents who sacrificed much, Elaine L. Chao seems to thrive on overcoming obstacles. After graduating from Harvard, she rose through the banking profession and the federal government to become the highest-ranking Asian-Pacific American ever appointed to the executive branch. Chao's reputation as a dedicated public servant—and her own belief in the "unique American spirit of voluntarism"—prompted her latest, and some say, toughest assignment: president and CEO of the United Way of America.

Linda Chavez   32

Her courage to express unpopular opinions and confront controversy head-on have guided Linda Chavez's career. An accomplished journalist and high-profile politico, she's often criticized by both Hispanics and liberals for her persistence in challenging widely accepted schools of thought. But on this much fans and foes agree: Chavez is one of the most influential opinion-makers of her time.

Elizabeth Dole   41

Mention the name Dole in D.C. and some people think of the Senate minority leader, Bob Dole. But others are just as apt to think of his wife. Armed with the good manners of the sorority house and the political instincts of the back room, Elizabeth Dole has become one of the nation's most powerful—and popular—female leaders. A two-time Cabinet member, she's currently president of the American Red Cross.

Rita Dove   48

Winner of the Pulitzer Prize and now the nation's youngest—and first black—poet laureate, Rita Dove has achieved a success she hardly dared dream of when she was growing up in Ohio. Today, with the eyes of the literary world upon her as never before, this new laureate is dedicated to making poetry more accessible to American society.

Marsha Evans   56

Throughout her twenty-five-year Navy career, Marsha Evans has worked within a male-dominated system to create an atmosphere in which people can be rewarded for their accomplishments. Now as the rear admiral in charge of all Navy recruiting, Evans has an unparalleled opportunity to break down barriers and end gender discrimination.

Helen Fisher   *63*

Plucky and personable, Helen Fisher defies stereotypical notions about anthropologists. Rejecting the traditional academic route favored by her profession, she has made a name for herself as a best-selling author and national TV personality who's sought after for her provocative views on romance and relationships.

Whoopi Goldberg   *72*

Once a member of the welfare ranks, she's now one of the country's highest-paid stars. Born Caryn Johnson and raised in a Manhattan housing project, Whoopi Goldberg's journey from poverty and drug abuse to the bright lights of Hollywood is the kind of story that movies are made of. Widely regarded as one of the most powerful women in her profession, Goldberg is using her success to help raise awareness about social issues such as homelessness and AIDS.

Cathy Guisewite   *79*

Not every girl is lucky enough to have a mother who tells her what to do with her life. But thank goodness Cathy Guisewite's mom recognized the potential of her daughter's doodling. Now *Cathy*, her namesake comic strip, is beloved by millions of American women and Guisewite's humorous insights have spawned everything from books and TV specials to novelty products such as calendars and coffee mugs.

Bernadine Healy   *87*

Her breakneck professional pace and her headstrong style prompted opponents to give Bernadine Healy the nickname "She Who Must Be Obeyed." As the first woman to head the National Institutes of Health, a traditionally male bastion, and now as a candidate for the U.S. Senate from Ohio, this feisty feminist is tackling the tough job of making medical care in this country live up to the American dream.

Charlayne Hunter-Gault   *96*

Determined to become a journalist, Charlayne Hunter-Gault did the unthinkable: She applied for admission to the University of Georgia and became the first black woman to break racial barriers at the tradition-ally all-white institution. That civil rights challenge, her first brush with fame, proved an auspicious beginning to a career that has earned her countless awards and a reputation as one of the most talented chroni-clers of contemporary history.

Mae Jemison   105

Growing up on the South Side of Chicago, Mae Jemison didn't set out to make history as the first black female in space—but she knew in her heart that she would someday travel among the stars. Nurturing scientific ambitions that emerged while she was in kindergarten, Jemison chose a career as a chemical engineer and medical doctor, a move that eventually helped open the door to NASA's astronaut program. Now she's making it her mission to help spread the message that space exploration is "the birthright of everyone who is on this planet."

Julie Krone   112

Julie Krone was born to race. As early as age two, she demonstrated an instinctive prowess for handling a horse. Two decades later, she was setting records that would earn her millions, not to mention a reputation as the most successful female jockey in the history of horse racing.

Amy Langer   120

By all appearances, everything was going Amy Langer's way: She was an Ivy League-educated, thirtysomething Wall Street workaholic earning a six-figure income. Then a doctor diagnosed her with breast cancer and Langer's world turned upside down. Deciding to invest her skills and energy to help other women fight this life-threatening disease, she's found a new—and more fulfilling—career as the executive director of the National Alliance of Breast Cancer Organizations.

Siri Marshall   130

Crises are almost an everyday occurrence when you're a lawyer. But somehow Siri Marshall, one of only three women in the country to serve as head counsel for a Fortune 500 company, manages to balance ten-hour days and high-level negotiations at the office with an equally full family life. All in all, it's quite an achievement for someone who never thought seriously about a career until her senior year in college.

Lynn Martin   139

Lynn Martin learned early about the harsh realities of politics when she lost an election in her eighth-grade class by one vote—her own. Martin's been voting for herself ever since, as she built a career that began with a board seat in Winnebago County, Illinois, and eventually landed her in Washington, D.C., as a representative and then secretary of labor. Known for her earthy style, quick wit, and willingness to take a tough stance, Martin is being eyed in powerful political circles as a potential candidate in the 1996 presidential election.

Marlee Matlin   *147*

After illness stole Marlee Matlin's hearing at an early age, she turned to acting as a way to express herself and cope with the painful rejection of kids who taunted her with names like "Deafo." Independent, outgoing, and self-assured, this aspiring star made headlines and Hollywood history when she became the youngest woman ever to earn the Oscar for Best Actress. Today, as she strives to find acceptance as an actress first, a deaf person second, she is using her fame and influence to help raise awareness about the rights of the hearing-impaired.

Terry McMillan   *154*

For years the publishing industry had maintained that blacks didn't buy books. But that was before legal typist Terry McMillan turned in her first novel and proceeded to launch a one-woman publicity campaign that made her a best-selling author seemingly overnight. Writing from her own struggles as a black woman trying to find love and happiness, a sense of self-worth and success, McMillan is making a fortune proving that a tale well told appeals to readers of all colors.

Josie Natori   *163*

Barely topping five feet tall and tipping the scales below the one hundred mark, Josie Natori is hardly an imposing figure—but she's a formidable force just the same. As a Wall Street banker, she was called "small but terrible," a joking reference to her business savvy. Now she heads her own company, a $35 million lingerie empire built on the premise that working women like herself, who've spent years climbing the corporate ladder and trying to conform, want to indulge themselves—to feel just as beautiful in the boardroom as they do in the bedroom.

Assunta Ng   *170*

The secret of publisher Assunta Ng's success has always been in not meeting expectations. As a girl, she was considered "least likely to succeed" among her Chinese peers because she was shy and didn't participate in extracurricular activities. Determined to be free of her culture's limiting expectations, Ng headed for America and for the first time in her life, felt at home—even though she had no money, friends, or family to turn to. Today she's highly regarded as a community leader in Seattle, where she started (against a lot of advice to the contrary) a Chinese-language newspaper that was the first of its kind in the Pacific Northwest.

Anna Quindlen   *177*

Whether she's writing about homelessness or abortion, grocery shopping or watching her son discover a lighting bug, award-winning columnist Anna Quindlen has a knack for expressing her own gut reactions in a way that touches readers and makes them think. Though her talent is unquestionable, and she has a career many would envy, Quindlen's greatest achievement may be making a convincing case that it's possible to balance professional satisfaction with a fulfilling personal life. As she puts it, "A good job doesn't warm you on Christmas Eve."

Janet Reno   *186*

Schoolchildren chant her name and fans line up for her autograph; Jay Leno invited her to be on *The Tonight Show* and she's been eulogized in a rap song. As the nation's first female attorney general, Janet Reno has a larger-than-life image that is making her perhaps the most popular member of the Clinton administration. Descended from a long line of fearless women, Reno cut her legal teeth in one of America's toughest cities, Miami, where she was known as a fierce opponent of drug dealers and deadbeat dads. Then the president called and offered her an even tougher assignment—as the nation's top crime fighter.

Ann Richards   *194*

The first woman governor of Texas in more than fifty years, Ann Richards has impressed fellow politicians and the public alike with her quick wit and warm, folksy style. Her rise to political prominence is all the more amazing, considering her life has been anything but a bed of yellow Texas roses. Raised with a belief that she ought to be perfect and that "a woman's greatest fulfillment is to get married and have children," Richards was forced to confront her lifelong fear of failure when her marriage fell apart, and again, when family and friends convinced her to seek treatment for alcoholism. Perfect or not, Richards is unquestionably one of the country's most admired public figures.

Martha Sloan   *203*

When Martha Sloan attended college, women were not allowed to wear slacks to class—a rule she couldn't abide, since one of her engineering courses required students to scale scaffolding. Getting permission to wear slacks was the first of many barriers Sloan has broken in her steady professional climb. Her latest achievement: becoming the first woman president of the Institute of Electrical and Electronics Engineers.

Marcy Syms   *212*

As the only Jewish girl in Bronxville High, Marcy Syms always felt like an outcast, but she refused to be a quitter. More importantly, she learned that strength is earned by confronting problems head-on and using them to your advantage. That lesson was never more valuable than when, at age thirty-two, she was named to head the company her father had founded—a move that made her one of the youngest women ever to be president of a New York Stock Exchange company.

Silvia Unzueta   *221*

When Silvia Unzueta was growing up in a poor Cuban neighborhood in Miami, a few empty soda bottles could mean the difference between eating and going hungry. It was a cruel existence for a girl born into a loving, wealthy family she was forced to leave behind when Fidel Castro took power of her homeland. Raised in a strange country without parents to nurture her not only made Unzueta resourceful, it taught her to appreciate the importance of giving people a chance to prove themselves. Today, as a Dade County official, Unzueta is distinguishing herself as a leader who's ensuring that women and disadvantaged people of all races have an opportunity to overcome obstacles of poverty and prejudice.

Wendy Wasserstein   *228*

"I'm someone who's always tried to become normal—it's just never worked out," says writer Wendy Wasserstein. Raised in a loving, though slightly wacky family, she revealed her keen eye for detail and off-the-wall humor early. Observing social change from the sixties to the nineties, Wasserstein has a talent for producing poignant musings, often about women's lives, that have made her an award-winning playwright.

Edith Weiner   *237*

Raised in foster homes from the time she was two, Edith Weiner was valued only as income-producing property for the people she lived with. Despite a straight-A average, an outgoing personality, and an aptitude for athletics, Weiner was told she was a problem child who would never amount to anything. Ironically, that lack of encouragement offered a sort of freedom that left Weiner open to follow whatever interested her. The result has been a widely successful career with accomplishments ranging from being a book author, to the youngest outside woman ever elected to a board of directors, to her current professional pursuit—a futurist whose clients include some of the nation's leading companies as well as the U.S. Congress.

Foreword

Look at the leadership ranks of almost any major organization—from America's leading companies to the U.S. military, universities to hospitals, nonprofit groups to political structures—and chances are you'll find a female face or two somewhere in the picture. By most measures, that's progress, the kind of social change tracked by the media and debated by feminists: Have we really come a long way, baby?

Certainly. But few of us breezed our way into the boardroom. I, for one, spent twenty years getting there.

As the senior vice president for advertising and communications for a worldwide cosmetics company, Avon Products, Inc., I am often asked to speak on and write about "women's issues," particularly the challenge of balancing professional success with a satisfying personal life.

The fact that such discussions are occurring in all kinds of public forums—and that many forward-thinking employers now are considering "work and family" policies—is encouraging. When I began my career in the early seventies, the workplace was a male-dominated world and there was very little awareness of the many demands and pressures on working women. It didn't matter what field we chose—business or education, banking or the law, public or private sector—women of my generation shared a common concern: how to take control of not only our careers but the nurturing of our families, our children, and in some cases, aging parents.

Two decades ago, there were few success stories about females in business, the arts, or politics. Women generally played a secondary role in the workplace, and those who did succeed in rising through the ranks usually found themselves alone at the top—the odd women out.

The rules of that work world, though rarely spoken, were clear: We were expected to be women first, successful careerists second. And there were many built-in reminders that the people in power still believed the old saw, "A woman's place is in the home." I remember early in my career interviewing for a job and being told I would be paid less than what a man would be paid for *the same exact job*. When I protested, I was told that my husband had a good job, so I really didn't need to be paid as much. Can you imagine anyone cutting a man's salary because he had a successful wife?

Thankfully, such discrimination—not to mention the petty injustices that women took for granted but rarely did anything about—is more visible today and therefore much more subject to criticism and change. But we shouldn't kid ourselves. The world can still be a very tough place for females.

Surveys consistently show that in many professions women don't yet make as much money as men, which would seem to prove that the old-boy network is still intact. And we can't overlook the very troubling issue of sexual harassment, which touches females of all ages. In a groundbreaking case in Minnesota, federal investigators found a pattern of "sexually hostile behavior" among elementary schoolboys. The most troubling revelation of the case wasn't that the boys were teasing their female classmates, using foul language and calling the girls names, but that school authorities treated these incidents as routine, disruptive behavior.

From a very young age, females learn that the world treats them differently than their male counterparts, and when those lessons are internalized, they begin to see themselves differently. Somewhere between elementary school and high school, girls encounter their first glass ceiling, figuratively speaking. More than one study has documented a gender bias in the classroom: teachers tend to call on boys more often, seem to value their opinions more highly, and in general, pay them greater attention.

As a consequence, girls start to lose their confidence, usually about age nine or so. Their self-esteem suffers and they lower their sights as they consider careers.

That's why *A Woman's Place Is Everywhere* is such an important contribution to contemporary writings on women. Though women unquestionably have come a long way, the journey is far from over. I expect my college-age daughter will have a much easier time of it than I did, and I hope by the time her younger sister, who's now eleven, starts working, stories like my being offered less money because I was a woman will sound so far-fetched they'll seem more like fairy tales than real-life recollections.

But if our daughters are to pick up the path where we leave off, we must point the way by showing them where we've been. *A Woman's Place Is Everywhere* does just that by sharing the stories of women who've broken new ground in their chosen fields and just as importantly, have succeeded in finding fulfilling careers without completely sacrificing their own personal satisfaction. Readers will recognize some of the women featured here, for their pioneering lives have become legendary. But there are an equal number of women whose names will not be familiar, because they're not widely known beyond their own professional circles.

That's what makes *A Woman's Place Is Everywhere* so special. Because the authors didn't want to do a book about famous women—but about women who are changing the future for all of us because they have the courage and determination to confront conventional thinking, defy stereotypes, and break down the barriers that threaten their success, however they choose to define it. Thanks to women like those featured here, the next generation, my daughters and yours, will have a better chance to take control of their lives, confident in the knowledge that anything and everything is possible for a woman. That no dream is too great and no career is beyond their reach, because in their world, *A Woman's Place Is Everywhere*.

—Gail Blanke
coauthor, *Taking Control Of Your Life:
The Secrets of Successful Enterprising Women*

Acknowledgments

A special thanks to the remarkable women who agreed to be profiled for this book. Their dreams shared can inspire many people.

To the publisher, Susan Stautberg, who cared enough to turn this idea into reality.

To editor Diana Lynn and her creative team—Christopher Turek, Sharon Overton, Mary Kim, Linda Morel, Fredda Rosen, and Alan Marks—our deepest appreciation. Many will reap the benefits of your work and dedication.

And to Serin S. Marshall, a young reader whose early reviews of the copy confirmed we were indeed creating the book we'd all envisioned.

Introduction

We are in many ways a most unlikely team. Although we grew up about the same time—we're both in our early thirties—we come from very different backgrounds and our careers have nothing in common.

Lindsey was raised in Connecticut, in a comfortably middle-class home. She's the oldest of four girls, which has always been something of a family joke since her father is an obstetrician; his wife and daughters love to tease him about the fact he's constantly surrounded by women. Lindsey's mother didn't work for much of her childhood—but she was always busy. Her mom's involvement in the community earned her a reputation as a leader, and eventually a career in politics. She's now serving her sixth term in Congress.

Jackie on the other hand grew up in East St. Louis, Illinois, a tough town where drugs and alcohol were a daily temptation. Although as a child Jackie never thought of herself as poor, her family often didn't have money for heat, and every stitch of clothing she wore was a hand-me-down. Her parents married young and were teenagers when Jackie, their second child, was born; she has two sisters and a brother.

As adults, we've lived equally distant lives. After graduating from college, Lindsey became involved in politics—initially to help her mother get elected to Congress—and served as a campaign manager for numerous elections, working at local, state, and national levels. From there, she took a job at a law firm as their director of legislative affairs. In 1988, she joined the Bush presidential campaign as the national director of the Coalition for Women.

After the election, she accepted the position of director of the Office of Women's Business Ownership with the U.S. Small Business Administration and undertook the implementation of policies developed during the campaign. Lindsey strongly believes that women's issues are economic issues and she felt the SBA job put her in a position where she could really make a difference. She resigned from that post in 1993 to go to Harvard, where she's working on an M.B.A.

Working in politics and public service often put Lindsey in contact with some of the nation's most powerful people, and as careers go, hers was pretty visible. But while Lindsey's name may be familiar in Washington circles, Jackie's is recognized the world over. (In fact, Jackie had been a strong role model for Lindsey years earlier when Lindsey was running long distance for the University of Chicago Track Club.)

Blessed with the talent to be a world-class runner, Jackie left East St. Louis and headed west to attend college at the University of California at Los Angeles. By the time she graduated, Jackie had already won her first Olympic medal. In the 1984 games in Los Angeles, she earned a silver medal in the heptathlon, a two-day, seven-event competition that includes running, long jumping, and javelin throwing.

Dubbed the "greatest athlete in the world" by Bruce Jenner, the famed 1976 decathlon champion, Jackie has set records only she can beat. To date, she has won three Olympic gold medals, three world titles, and set six world records.

Clearly, we move in different worlds. But our paths crossed when the publisher of this book approached each of us asking for our support on this project. We agreed because her idea for a book that would profile female role models struck a familiar chord in both of us—for as different as we are in some obvious ways, in other respects we're completely in sync.

We were both fortunate enough to have grown up in loving homes, with parents who believed in us and taught us how to believe in ourselves. They encouraged us to dream, and in doing so, gave us the confidence and courage we needed to fly as high

Lindsey Johnson   Photo by Ankers, Anderson & Cutts

and as far as our hearts desired.

Though we chose different professional paths, we share a common bond: our success is built on a solid foundation, thanks to our families. We also had the benefit of role models who helped us challenge our own stereotypes and set goals to reach our dreams.

Yet we recognize that in today's world, many children grow up without the benefit of supportive parents and role models. That's why this project appealed to us so much—we understand the importance of role models and we're painfully aware that many people must look far beyond their immediate environments to find the inspiration they need to live fulfilling lives.

This is particularly true for young girls; according to groundbreaking research, as early as grade school, girls begin to realize they are treated differently than boys. For instance, teachers tend to call on boys more often, seem to value their opinions more highly, and in general, pay them greater attention. The result: at about age nine, girls start to lose their self-esteem and confidence, which causes them to lower their sights as they consider careers.

That's a pretty discouraging outlook, but there is one bright spot: this same research reveals that the presence of one powerful role model can lift a girl's hopes and give her dreams.

Role models are important not only to young girls, but to women of all ages. For example, working women contemplating career changes often suffer the same constraints on assessing their options that young women just entering the work force typically feel. Nevertheless, today a growing number of women are infiltrating nontraditional fields—even boardrooms and executive suites; some are choosing to start their own businesses. Many of them credit the presence of a role model with helping them develop the vision and courage they needed to pursue their dreams.

That's what we hope to accomplish here, for you are about to meet thirty amazing women whose triumphs and trials will convince you that almost anything is possible when you set your mind and heart to it. Like Jackie, some of the women featured here are household names because they've set records, broken barriers, and made history as the "firsts" in their fields of endeavor. Others are people you've probably never heard of, but who are quietly, often behind the scenes, helping to shape the way our society views women and expand our ideas of what's possible for humankind.

Jackie Joyner-Kersee

Although we realize that reading about famous women may be more appealing to some readers, we purposely avoided that focus as many books of that nature already exist. We wanted to pay tribute to the many contributions contemporary women are making to our world. So we set out to find female leaders who we felt were changing the future—in ways large and small—for all women. Thus, our title, *A Woman's Place Is Everywhere.*

In this book, you'll meet women from all walks of life, because we didn't want to create the impression that there's only one path to success. These women come from different professions, cultural backgrounds, and even generations. No two stories are alike, which is why we think you're going to enjoy getting to know these dynamic women.

Like the two of us, as different as these women are in some respects, they are surprisingly similar in others. As they reflected on their successes, the lessons they've learned along the way, and the beliefs that guide their lives, some common messages emerged.

You've got to have a dream if you want to make a dream come true.

Success is rarely, if ever, an accident. That's why this line from a Rodgers and Hammerstein song so aptly sums up why many of the women in this book are living the lives they dreamed of. Even as kids, they knew, *really knew,* their answer to the question "What do you want to be when you grow up?"

When you know where you want to go in life, other choices and decisions just seem to come easier. As anthropologist Helen Fisher says in her profile, "Successful people have a plan for where they want to be a year from now, where they want to be five years from now, where they want to be ten years from now. Things happen to people who plan for it and dream about it and prepare themselves for it."

Yet it's all but impossible to explain why some people just seem to intuitively lock onto their dreams long before it's time to pick a college and plan a career. "I was always going to be a jockey—and a great one, too," says Julie Krone, the most successful female jockey in the history of horse racing. You'll find the same kind of conviction in the profile of Mae Jemison, the first female black astronaut. She remembers as a kid, "looking at the stars, wondering what was up there, knowing I'd go there someday, though I didn't know how." It didn't matter to her that at the time, the only astronauts were white men. Which leads us to another important lesson many of these women said they had to learn.

The only person who can stand in the way of your dreams is you.

Even when you know where you want to go in life—and many of us don't until adulthood—your path may be anything but smooth. As you will see, most of these women encountered obstacles, not the least of which were people who tried to discourage them with the argument that "women don't do that." Fortunately, they didn't listen; if anything, their determination to prove themselves only increased.

When Marin Alsop was rejected from Juilliard's conducting program—even though she was already an accomplished musician and had previously studied at Juilliard and Yale—she decided school officials must not have read her application, simply because she was a woman. But that didn't stop her from pursuing her dream to become a conductor: "I'm the kind of person who, when I couldn't get my foot in the door, I went around looking for the back door. And when I couldn't find the back door, I'd just punch a hole through the wall." Today Alsop is widely recognized as one of her generation's leading conductors and may very possibly become the first woman conductor to enjoy a world-class career.

Alsop's challenge was to overcome the barriers other people put in her path. But sometimes, the biggest obstacle you face is yourself. Personal doubts and fears can be a powerful force that will surely hold you back.

That was certainly true for Rita Dove, the nation's youngest and first black poet laureate. Despite her obvious success, Dove candidly admits that privately she struggled with her dream to become a writer: "My biggest obstacle has been myself—the nagging insecurities, the fear that I would be laughed at or misunderstood if I were truly honest in my writing...there's been a lot of wasted energy beating down these interior devils."

Surround yourself with people who share your dream.

If your dream is destined to take you someplace where no woman has been before, you can expect a lonely journey. Because no matter how many advances we've made, it's never easy to buck the system or defy conventional thinking. But the loneliness you face when striking out in a new direction can be eased if you surround yourself with people who share your dream.

We're not talking just about the obvious support of family and friends who love you. If you're lucky enough to have that kind of support system, as we did, by all means take advantage of it. What we're really suggesting is something more: Look for kindred spirits and role models.

When Martha Sloan, who is now the first female president of the world's largest technical professional organization, attended Stanford University, she was the only woman in her freshman class majoring in engineering. Her career choice was so unusual at that time (it was the sixties), she had to get special permission to wear slacks to class, so the men couldn't look up her skirt when she climbed on scaffolding. Sloan struggled with feelings of isolation: as a woman, she didn't fit in with the other engineering majors, but as an engineering major, she didn't fit in with other women. But she was smart—she sought the company of the few freshmen women who were science and math majors and began studying with them, which at least helped allay her feelings of being different.

Sometimes people you've never even met can help boost your spirits and give you the courage to keep pushing ahead. For example, Texas Governor Ann Richards, one of the country's most admired public figures, claims that in many ways she has modeled her life after Eleanor Roosevelt. Why? Because, Richards says, "She saw the human needs."

And when Jemison is lauded as the first African-American woman to explore outer space, she is quick to credit the white female and black male astronauts who went before her—because their accomplishments helped open the door for her career.

Similarly, Cathy Guisewite, the creator of one of America's most beloved cartoon strips, *Cathy,* claims she might not be the success she is today if Charles Schulz hadn't first introduced the world to Charlie Brown, Snoopy, and their gang. "I feel that *Peanuts* really paved the way...for a strip like mine," Guisewite says. "It was the first strip that dealt with real human feelings, real insecurities, and frustrations in the comic pages."

What all these women are saying, in one way or another, is that while your path may at times feel terribly lonely, in the end, none of us really succeeds alone. Which brings us to our final, and in many ways, most important lesson.

Success grows more rewarding every time you pass it on to someone else.

Many of the women in this book feel, as we do, that it's important to "give something back" to society, and that in doing so, your own life becomes richer—you reap the real rewards of success.

There are many ways of giving back. Some people, like Elizabeth Dole, choose a career in public service. Active in politics and currently the president of the American Red Cross, Dole says, "I've always been interested in making a positive difference in the lives of others. For me, the most rewarding times in my government service career were not spent in smoke-filled rooms exchanging political gossip. Rather, they were in classrooms, listening to at-risk youth and teen mothers who were turning their lives around; in the fields, meeting with migrant workers who needed a voice; and in far-flung corners of the world where people needed help."

Others choose to use the fame their success has brought them to draw the public's attention to issues they support. For example, actress Marlee Matlin is well-known as an advocate for the rights of hearing-impaired people. Similarly, Whoopi Goldberg has helped raise awareness about homelessness, AIDS, and racial issues. "I now have a voice that is heard above the din," says Goldberg, who, because she struggled for many years to make it, now takes the responsibility of her star status very seriously. "I believe I'm here for a reason...to throw little torches out to the next step to lead people through the dark."

Someone who's equally committed for many of the same reasons, but whom you've probably never heard of, is Silvia Unzueta. Growing up in a poor Cuban neighborhood in Miami, she scavenged empty soda bottles from other people's trash to keep from going hungry. Today she's a respected Dade County official who's using her influence to improve the lives of women, children, and minority groups in her community.

"Women have a bond that transcends who we are and where we came from," says Unzueta, who has a special interest in ensuring that women of color have a voice in the feminist movement. "Culturally, you have a double whammy," she says. "The system makes you choose if you're a woman or a Hispanic. I happen to be all of it. I don't want to be dissected into pieces."

With strong voices like these leading the way, how can women fail to find their rightful place in this world? We feel privileged to have been a part of this celebration of contemporary women. May their stories delight and inspire you as much as they did us, and when you have finished this book, may you truly believe, with as much conviction as they and we do, that a woman's place is indeed everywhere!

—Lindsey Johnson
Jackie Joyner-Kersee

A Woman's Place Is Everywhere

Marin Alsop

*⌒It's never too early to pursue a career you feel
a true calling for. Just do it. The key to success
is perseverance, so just don't give up.
It's that pure and simple.*

Conductor Marin Alsop is living proof that anything is possible—if you want it badly enough and you're willing to work hard to make it happen.

Born into a musical family, she demonstrated her own talent and ambition at a very young age; by the time she was eleven, Alsop had become an avid violinist. Maybe that's why her future just seemed to click into focus when she first glimpsed the legendary Leonard Bernstein on television as he conducted one of his famed *Young People's Concerts.*

To say she was inspired by the maestro would be an understatement: "I thought he was so cool. I was already getting some flak for moving around too much when I played my violin. Watching Bernstein, it was a relief to see that somebody could be so expressive and not only not get into trouble, but actually win prestige," she said.

"That's it," the young Alsop thought to herself. "That's what I want to do." Every year after, she would watch her hero in awe as he jumped and jived all over the stage. But her first real contact with the conductor she so admired didn't occur until almost two decades later.

In 1988, at the age of thirty-two, Alsop was awarded the pres-

1

tigious Leonard Bernstein Fellowship at the Tanglewood Music Festival. She was selected from among the nation's top young conductors to participate in his master conducting class—an experience she says "changed my life." After leading Roy Harris' Third Symphony in a performance described by *New York Newsday* critic Tim Page as both tender and brilliant, she earned an unexpected embrace from Bernstein.

"Things really took off for me after Tanglewood," Alsop said. "There was amazing chemistry between Bernstein and me. I was completely outside the orthodox view of what a conductor should be: I was a woman, young, American; I didn't have a conducting degree; I wasn't an assistant conductor somewhere.

"And here was Bernstein," she continued, "a conductor everyone loved to love and loved to hate. We really got along. It's a wonderful thing when your hero meets your expectations."

Alsop had the benefit of caring guidance all along. Her musical parents were a profound source of inspiration, as was Bernstein, whose namesake fellowship gave her the opportunity to work with masters such as Seiji Ozawa and Gustav Meier. Though she was awarded the fellowship two years running, the fact that the first time, 1988, also marked Bernstein's seventieth birthday celebration had ancillary effects: Some of the most influential eyes—and ears—of the music and media worlds were present at Tanglewood that year. And Alsop stood out among her contemporaries as the most obviously gifted conductor there.

Alsop's intimacy with music began long before she first watched Bernstein on TV. Her parents started her on piano lessons at the age of two. Although she played until she was six, Alsop hated every minute of it. "They kind of just threw me at the piano as soon as I popped out of the womb, but it just wasn't my instrument," she said jokingly.

"But when I was sent to summer camp," she recalled, "I began to learn the violin, which I fell in love with—the instrument and the sound. Pretty soon, I was practicing five hours a day, and my parents wisely just stood back and let me find my own way into music."

Granted, it would have been difficult for Alsop not to be touched by music somehow. Her father, Lamar, is a violinist and the former

Marin Alsop   Photo by Lisa Kohler

concertmaster of the New York City Ballet Orchestra. Her mother, Ruth, plays cello in the same ensemble. Both performed with the Radio City Music Hall Orchestra, Fred Waring and his Pennslyvanians, and the Buffalo Philharmonic before beginning their long careers with the New York City Ballet Orchestra.

Alsop realizes that her parents' careers—and the way they integrated their art into family life—made quite an impact on her own career choice. "When you're an only child, your parents tend to take you places," she said. "I heard a lot of important artists, and I must've seen *The Nutcracker* a thousand times."

With music in her blood, so to speak, Alsop attended the Juilliard preparatory school, knowing someday she would follow her parents' professional path. But then in the early 1970s, she decided to attend Yale.

"It was a very confusing time in my life," she explained. "I had already determined to be a musician, but Yale scattered my attention in other directions. Because I couldn't practice and get straight As and be perfect at everything I did, I wasn't very pleased with myself. So I left Yale and came back to New York."

Never one to look back, Alsop received a scholarship to study violin at Juilliard. Soon after, she established herself as a freelance violinist, playing with a number of orchestras—sometimes alongside her parents—while also pursuing commercials and recording dates with the likes of Billy Joel. She even founded an all-woman, fourteen-piece swing band, "String Fever," which still plays an expansive range of music—from disco to Bach—today.

By any measure, Marin Alsop had proved herself a professional success by the time she was in her early twenties. Yet she knew she had another calling. "I'd always wanted to conduct, but I was a little bit discouraged from doing so when I was a kid," she explained. "One reason was because of my age, which I knew I would outgrow. But the other reason was, 'Girls don't do that,' which I did find disheartening."

So she kept her biggest and dearest dream very close to her heart for a long time.

Finally wanting to change her status as a self-ascribed "closet conductor," Alsop applied to Juilliard's post-graduate conducting program. To her surprise, her application was rejected. "They sent me a form letter back saying that my academic credentials did not meet their standards," she explained, her voice taking on an incredulous tone. "Now I had been at Juilliard since I was eight, I studied at Yale, and then came and received my master's degree from Juilliard. I can't believe they read my application."

Alsop was not prepared to be stymied. "I'm the kind of person who, when I found I couldn't get my foot in the door, I went around looking for the back door," she said with a smile. "And when I couldn't find the back door, I'd just punch a hole through the wall."

Rebuffed by Juilliard, Alsop rebounded with a plan: she'd teach herself how to conduct. So with the help of friends in the music world, she began to practice on her own. "I would watch every conductor I played under, not only to follow his beat, but also to find out his secrets," she said. "If I liked his work a lot, I'd ask for a quick lesson. I worked with Carl Bamberger. Karl Richter gave me a lesson. Later I studied with Gustav Meier, Harold Faberman and others."

Alsop's determination is evidenced in the lengths she would go to for a lesson. Instead of simply admiring and emulating the work of Walter Hendl, for example, Alsop hunted for cheap air-fares to Buffalo so she could work with him over weekends during one of his conducting stints in Chataqua, New York.

Despite her efforts, Alsop's hard work was not immediately rewarded. Though she'd taught herself to conduct, Alsop was forced to continue earning her living by playing the violin. "I was making good money but growing very frustrated," she said. "I needed an outlet to conduct. So I decided to follow through on a daydream of mine, save my freelance money, and found my own orchestra."

The result was Concordia, which early publicity touted as "a chamber symphony with a touch of jazz." The orchestra played its debut concert at Manhattan's Symphony Space in December 1984. To this day, Alsop considers the creation of Concordia her most satisfying achievement.

"That one evening cost me $10,000—all I had—but it was worth it," she said. "I got to lead Mozart's 29th Symphony, Stravinsky's Dumbarton Oaks, the Bartok Divertimento, and some jazz works. It was a beginning."

She eventually found financial backers for Concordia, which now plays several concerts a year at Alice Tully Hall in New York City's Lincoln Center, and will celebrate its tenth anniversary next season. Under Alsop's leadership, the dynamic fifty-piece orchestra has commissioned and premiered thirty-two new works for chamber orchestra, all in the pursuit of breaking down barriers between jazz and classical music. Concordia's debut recording, *Blue Monday,* was released in May 1993.

The ensemble also attempts to increase the accessibility of its music through "It's Elementary," an educational outreach program designed to teach young children that music is joyful and creative. At an outing to a third-grade class in a New York City public school where a lack of funds has meant a defunct music department, Alsop credited the Concordia program to Bernstein's memory. "He loved teaching more than anything," she said. In working with young people, Alsop hopes to share not only her love of music, but a valuable lesson from her own life.

"It's never too early to pursue a career you feel a true calling for. Just do it," she said. "The key to success is perseverance, so just don't give up. It's that pure and simple."

True to her word, Alsop is pursing her calling with an intensity that is sure to break down the barriers that threaten her success. Already she has appeared with the Philadelphia Orchestra, the New York Philharmonic, the National Symphony, the Los Angeles Philharmonic, and the Boston Pops Orchestra among others. She also is the music director of the Eugene Symphony Orchestra, the Long Island Philharmonic, the Cabrillo Music Festival in California, and Oregon's Festival of American Music, as well as principal conductor of the Colorado Symphony Orchestra.

Alsop is widely recognized as one of her generation's leading conductors—and many musical colleagues, critics, and fans believe she could become the first woman conductor to ever enjoy a world-class career. Among the many professional accolades she's received, two of the more noteworthy are winning the Leopold Stokowski Conducting Competition sponsored by the American Symphony Orchestra and being the first woman to claim the Koussevitzky Conducting Prize at Tanglewood.

Just the same, success has not come easily to Alsop. "The challenge of securing opportunities in a male-dominated field has made me more determined and committed, but I have never altered my 'big picture' plan," she said. One reason Alsop's been so successful at staying on track is that she simply refuses to interpret rejections as gender-based. "You can really start to develop a little bit of a chip on your shoulder if you do this," she said. "So instead of thinking, 'I didn't get it because I'm a woman,' I tend to think, 'I didn't get it because I'm not good enough. I have to get better.' This way, every rejection becomes an inspiration to work harder."

Though she has never faced overt sexual discrimination, Alsop doesn't kid herself that barriers clearly do exist in the music world. For instance, she points to the invisibility of women conductors on the rosters of important American orchestras as one sign. But that hasn't stopped Alsop from setting her sights on conquering new horizons, namely Europe, knowing all the while that "there are strikes against me—my age, my sex, and my nationality." Indeed, her youth and gender may decrease the likelihood that any time soon Alsop will receive invitations from the Berlin or Vienna orchestras, which are both known to be staunchly conservative and male-dominated.

Alsop frowns on all the rigid hierarchies so prevalent in the classical music business and she aims to confront the conventional notion that only middle-aged, European men are worthy of conductorships. On a more optimistic note, she observed, "In America at least, I've found very little resistance to the idea of a woman conductor. It's still unusual enough that the orchestra might even get some publicity for engaging me."

Experience has taught Alsop that optimism and an ability to look at the positive side of things can mean the difference between success and failure. "If you have some perseverance, you can do anything," she said, recalling an instance when her own future looked so bleak. "My first review was an absolute slam—*The New York Times* killed me. I didn't get out of bed for ten days. But these things build character. I try not to take anything that happens too much to heart, positive or negative. It's all subject to change."

In a field subject to pretension, Alsop's up-tempo personality keeps her refreshingly down-to-earth. Performance after performance, she exudes a friendly, energetic warmth that prompts audiences and fellow musicians alike to connect with her. Her body language says it all: fluid and rhythmic, she strides about the stage with so much animation that each concert feels likes a personal and moving experience.

Although all eyes are often on her during a concert, Alsop

doesn't see herself as the star performer. "I don't think I'm a wunderkind," she said. "I would never presume that I'm going to tell the musicians anything they've never heard before. The worst thing a conductor can do is assume that he's teaching the players. You're engaged to lead a concert, not to teach school. Even when it's only a semiprofessional orchestra, you must treat the players with tremendous respect."

Her ability to do so has been applauded by colleagues. Said Lois Martin, Concordia's principal violist, "Marin is great to work with. She has a great ear, and she rehearses thoroughly and efficiently. She is a better conductor every time I work with her—and not just a little better but a lot." Kay Stern, Concordia's concertmaster for many years, agrees: "Marin is wonderfully communicative. She gets results immediately, yet keeps everybody feeling comfortable, eager to play their best. It always feels like a real team effort."

Alsop achieves this kind of rapport by following three golden rules: "I will be open, nonjudgmental, and I will never, *never* play favorites in the orchestra. Sure, I have friends among the players—but I won't cross that line when performing."

Unwilling to be seduced by the glamour of her position and her growing fame, Alsop takes a straightforward approach to her work. "The conductor is the messenger, the footbridge between the composer and the orchestra," she said. "You have to be entirely selfless and entirely self-indulgent at the same time. It's one of those jobs that if you do well, no one pays attention to you, and if you do poorly, everybody complains. What you do, really, is create a visual portrait of the score; the conductor must be able to demonstrate in space what the music should sound like."

That she loves her work is obvious, and it is from this love that Alsop derives her greatest sense of achievement. "Success means pursuing a career that inspires you—brings passion to your life and totally absorbs your energy," she said. "To be in love with what you do is success to me."

That she has been able to excel in her chosen field is something she attributes to her parents. "In dealing with so many people, you need an understanding of diplomacy, a good sense of humor, and real compassion." These characteristics, she said, were instilled in her by her parents. "They would stand behind me no matter what path I decided to take," she said, "as long as I had enthusiasm for it and it made me happy."

If there is one drawback to her career, it's that being a conductor doesn't allow for a traditional family life. With so many demands on her schedule, Alsop is more often on a plane or in an airport than in her Manhattan apartment. She manages to stay close to her parents because they frequently travel with her. "They plan their social calendar around my schedule," she said with obvious pride. "Mom said, 'Well, we're not having grand-children, so your career will be our grandchildren.'"

For all her success, Alsop isn't satisfied in some ways. "I need twenty-four more hours in the day, or even just four more. I need time to study and learn," she said. With so much achievement and acclaim behind her, Alsop is still looking—and listening—to what's ahead.

Del M. Anderson

∼You just have to be tough. Say,
'I want this,' and go after it.

If the students and faculty at San Jose City College didn't understand from the newspaper articles lauding her appointment that their new president, Del M. Anderson, would be a strong leader, they realized it her first week on the job. Anderson, who is an African American and the first woman to hold the college's top post, didn't hesitate to go head to head with her faculty over the nomination of a dean in the language arts department. After twice rejecting nominations from a process she considered unfair, Anderson took matters into her own hands.

Many new leaders would have chosen to avoid controversy so early on, and a woman new to a job formerly the province of men might have been particularly eager to shy away from conflict. But Anderson was a president with clear ideas on how things should be done, and she thought the nominating process was unduly restrictive: each time the department had sent her the name of only one candidate.

"In fifteen years as an administrator I have never seen that system used," she said. "It is customary to send three names, and then the president usually selects from those."

Anderson wanted selection procedures that were fair and equitable—even if she had to upset an established apple cart to get them. She investigated and found that the college's practices violated state regulations requiring affirmative action recruitment.

So despite objections by many faculty, she brought the matter to the attention of the college's board and opened the position to outside candidates.

"People will find that I am not into expediency," she told a reporter from the campus newspaper during the height of the controversy. "I'm very high on process and having things done consistently and fairly and out in the open."

While Anderson's determination to do things the right way, no matter the risk to her popularity, may have caught the campus off guard, the episode was characteristic of her bold approach to life.

Born in Vicksburg, Mississippi, in 1937, the third of four children, Anderson went to segregated public schools and became the first member of her family to graduate from high school. From an early age, she had no choice but to shoulder family responsibilities while her parents, both laborers, went to work.

Anderson recalled that her mother "would draw out a map of where you paid the gas bill and other bills. She had the money all divided up for me, and I would go pay the bills. My mother trusted me as a young child to handle adult responsibilities—and by doing this, she gave me great confidence at an early age."

Summers were time for a different kind of responsibility. There were no day- or sleep-away camps for Anderson; she spent school vacations on her great-grandmother's farm. "I did everything from cutting down trees to slaughtering animals and curing meats and canning foods," she recalled.

By age eleven she was working on Saturdays, running errands and cooking for an elderly white woman. The job gave Anderson more than pocket change. In her employer she found a mentor: someone who believed in her and taught her to believe in herself, someone who supported her ambitions and encouraged her to use her intelligence.

While Anderson fixed her employer's hair, they talked. "She would tell me that I had to do well in school because I was going to be a leader for my people," Anderson said. "She reinforced my confidence and my desire to go college."

But even as a young girl, Anderson knew that there was little opportunity for her in the segregated South. "My career choices were limited more by race than gender," she said. "As a white person I would have been exposed to more career options and choices. As a white male, every door would have been open to me for consideration. My career choices were significantly limited by being an African-American female."

If doors were to open for Del Anderson, she'd have to do the opening herself. At age seventeen, armed with her high school diploma and her determination, she enrolled in Alcorn College, a small, rural, all-black public college. It was there that Anderson experienced one of the more important episodes in her life when, at nineteen, she was expelled from the college as one of several students involved in civil rights demonstrations. After that, she moved to the San Francisco Bay area, where family helped her start over.

"Once I left Mississippi, I considered myself to be practically indestructible," she said.

Anderson began working her way through college, supporting herself with secretarial jobs. She also signed up for modeling school. "I felt I wanted to be more polished and more poised and make the best presentation of myself that I could," she recalled.

This goal ultimately opened a door to a new career. When Anderson was introduced to the director of the Ebony Fashion Fair, a show sponsored by *Ebony* magazine, she was hired on the spot. Anderson traveled across the country with the Fashion Fair, modeling haute couture fashions and posing for the cover of *Jet* magazine. The high point of her modeling career was a White House luncheon, complete with a welcome from President Kennedy.

Anderson said modeling "helped me a lot subsequently to be at ease in public situations, to feel comfortable with my body and in presenting myself." And while this stately college president still considers herself a "clothes horse" with a keen eye for fashion, modeling was never a career she considered seriously. After one season with the Fashion Fair, she left to return to college.

Although she still had a long way to go before graduation, Anderson was determined to stick with her studies. At the time, she recalled, "I was the full-time, sole support of myself." It took her ten years, but her hard work paid off in 1965 with a degree

Del M. Anderson

from San Diego State University. Two years later, she earned a graduate degree in social work from the same school.

"You just have to be tough," she observed. "Say, 'I want this,' and go after it."

Anderson's social work studies formed the foundation of her current career. "My training in social work really helped me in understanding people and their motivation and how to get the best out of them," she said.

Her alma mater also gave her the chance to fulfill her dream of becoming an educator. When San Diego State's School of Social Work asked some of its recent graduates to fill teaching positions and integrate the faculty, Anderson was the first graduate to whom the dean turned. She excelled at the work, no doubt because of her intelligence and drive, but mostly because, as she put it simply, "I love students."

Anderson gravitated toward the community college system where she could work closely with students and where, she said, "you're judged by your teaching ability as opposed to your research and publications."

Anderson was judged well, and her career progressed steadily. She moved on to become dean of guidance services at Grossmont College; then dean of students at Los Angeles Harbor College; and vice president of instruction at Skyline College. Among her accomplishments: developing a computer- ized transfer information system and a matriculation program that became the model for community colleges throughout the state of California.

Reflecting on her career, Anderson said, "I've either done or supervised just about everything you could have in a commu- nity college."

So it was no wonder that the firm conducting a nationwide search for a new president for San Jose City College came look- ing for Anderson. In 1991, she was chosen from a field of 67 applicants to head the culturally diverse, 13,000-student com- munity college.

"City College has got itself a winner," said Ronald Kong, chan- cellor of the San Jose/Evergreen Community College District, in announcing Anderson's appointment. "She really understands the scope of the job from an instructional standpoint as well as student services."

True to her determined style, Anderson set an ambitious agenda for her new job. She was concerned about modernizing campus facilities and attracting talented faculty. Most impor- tant, she wanted to recruit students straight out of high school and curb the college's dropout rate.

Anderson strives to be a president her students and faculty can see, touch, and talk to. Though she works ten- to fourteen-hour days and her desk is piled with work coming from district and state offices, Anderson still makes time to go to student and faculty events, and to visit classrooms where teachers are trying new approaches. "Your presence means a lot to people who are on the cutting edge of things," she said.

Anderson typically plays down any publicity that focuses attention on her as San Jose City College's first woman president. "I've been the first woman—and the first black person—so many times that I don't even think about it anymore," she said. "I'm a hard worker and I'm about business."

But she does recognize that she has special constituencies and makes it a point to undertake leadership development work with African Americans and women's groups. She takes pride in the fact that she was able to overcome the strictures of the segregated South, and feels a responsibility to help others surmount the obstacles they face.

"I think you have to be there for other people," she said. "It adds to the hours of my day, but I think you just have to do it."

When she steps back and looks at her life, Anderson said that even more than attaining the position of college president, she values "important contributions such as sending my sister and my niece to college and intervening in my niece's life in such a way that she is now an outstanding young woman when she was headed toward self-destruction. Working with my niece and other young people in trouble are the things I am most proud of and believe are the most important things I have done in my life."

Anderson tries to keep weekends for herself. She enjoys reading and relaxing with friends at jazz clubs. Divorced in 1982 after sixteen years of marriage, she now counts herself among the "happily single."

Like many women, Anderson wishes someone had encouraged her interest in science and had helped her pay more attention to her math studies. One can't help but think that the women at San Jose City College will get a different message about their abilities to succeed in these traditionally "male" subject areas.

Anderson believes that women leaders can make a difference in their institutions because, by and large, they manage people in a "less autocratic" fashion and are more willing to "seek partnerships." Asked to describe her own leadership at City College, Anderson said, "I'm trying to make it known to everyone that I like problems not swept under the rug, but talked through. A college does not have to be a place where there is a continuous struggle taking place. It can be a place where people can have differences of opinion and come to reasoned conclusions."

But even before she became a college president, during a stint in her career when she worked as a hospital administrator, Anderson experienced the difficult dynamics of being one of the few women in meetings attended mostly by men. "I would say something in a group, it would be an important point, and it would just land and no one would say anything," Anderson recalled. "Then later on, a man would pick up the same point and the men would say, 'Oh, that's a good idea. Let's do that.' It's very subtle discrimination and very debilitating, because if you speak up and say, 'Now, wait a minute. I said that,' it looks like you're on an ego trip."

Still, Anderson knows how to make it clear that she's a woman to be reckoned with. "Because I was once a professional model and 'beauty queen,' and I have an easygoing manner, people frequently misjudge my will and tough-mindedness," she said. "But I learned to simply tell people not to underestimate my determination and they learn quickly."

Despite a life that many would say was filled with hardship, Anderson says there's little she would have changed. What others view as problems, Anderson is determined to see as exciting challenges. "I have not encountered anything I would consider to be an obstacle," she said.

"As an African-American woman I always knew I would have to work—it was just a matter of what kind of work it was going to be. It has simply been a matter of setting one goal and accomplishing it and working with others to create opportunities for my next adventures."

Priscilla Beard

*∼Don't get discouraged because someone says 'no.'
Anyone can say no. Someone special will
eventually say 'yes.' And whenever or
wherever that happens, the possibilities—
and the power—are in your hands.*

Some people might argue that combining entrepreneurial ambitions with an active social conscience is a foolhardy proposition doomed to failure. But try telling that to Priscilla Beard, founder and president of Message!Check, and she'll prove you wrong. Less than a decade old, her Seattle-based company is making millions from Beard's idealistic brainstorm to create specialized checks that would support causes such as Greenpeace and the National Organization of Women.

Beard's knack for successfully marrying two seemingly opposing forces surfaced early in life. When she was five, Beard and fellow neighborhood children banded together to sell rocks and mounted butterflies—not to buy candy or toys, but to aid the Korean Relief Fund. Together, the children raised $100 for the charity and earned recognition in a local Vancouver, Washington, newspaper.

Beard found other ways to distinguish herself in her formative years. Already the budding activist, she started an entomology club because her school had no extracurricular activities for students interested in science. She also served as a class officer, consistently made the honor roll, and was voted "friendliest girl" in junior high.

While accounts of her happy, active childhood may bring to

mind scenes from television's popular family programs of the day, Beard had something most members of the baby boom generation did not: a working mom. Though it was unusual for the times, the experience had a positive impact on Beard.

Now forty-six and an entrepreneur herself, Beard can appreciate that her mother—a piano teacher who set aside time and space in their home to operate her business—was a pioneer of sorts. "She didn't need to do it for the money," Beard explained. "She just needed to do something on her own." In fulfilling her ambition to teach, Beard's mom also taught her children a valuable lesson: how to balance work and home life. "This issue is what people still struggle with today," Beard observed.

Looking at her own success, Beard is quick to credit her parents as her main source of inspiration. "They always encouraged us to be the best at whatever we chose to do, without limitations or fear of failure." For Beard, that meant caring about the environment—a love she acquired on annual family camping expeditions to Washington's Lewis River—and caring about people. In college, Beard's passions prompted her to protest the atrocities of the Vietnam War through active involvement in administrative shutdowns and boycotts.

Her vision for helping people—often in untraditional ways—didn't stop there. On her path to establishing her own business, Beard worked as a teacher for ten years. Though often frustrated by the rigidity of the public school system, she always took it upon herself to get the job done. A case in point: When her class of disabled boys was unable to grasp the essentials of grammar, Beard brought in a troupe of all-male dancers who taught adverbs through their movements. Learning was made easier when the students could actually visualize "quickly" or "gracefully," Beard said.

In the face of adversity, Beard's motto is "never give up." And there is ample evidence that she has employed this motto time and again in her own life.

For instance, she faced severe budget restrictions throughout her tenure as an educator. When the Washington state school district in which she worked could not persuade voters to pass the school levy—which meant funds for new books and programs never materialized—the determined Beard wrote a

Priscilla Beard

$25,000 grant proposal and looked to outside sources to provide her classroom with much needed supplies and activities. After two years, she even had enough money left over to support assemblies and other programs for the entire school.

Her ability to raise money led Beard to a new career: fundraising for the arts. In typical fashion, Beard threw herself into the endeavor, which she admits was particularly challenging in her home turf of metropolitan Seattle. "There are so few major corporations in the area that make funding for the arts a priority," she said. Beard is particularly interested in children's programming, which tends to pull in fewer resources because "children's groups are so fragmented and giving to children draws less fanfare."

Five years of trying to squeeze money out of big business left Beard yearning for more. Her ultimate desire was to provide a valuable service to consumers, while at the same time giving back to the community.

She realized this dream in 1985 by founding Message!Check. "I wanted to start a business that had a product that people used all the time—one that had repeat orders where a percentage of the business could go back to worthy causes," Beard said.

The idea for her company hit her one day as she was writing out a check. "This check is really ugly," she thought to herself. "Wouldn't it be great to have an image on here that represented an organization—so consumers could voice their support, and at the same time, raise money for its cause?"

She began researching the idea and then approached Mothers Against Drunk Driving and Greenpeace. Encouraged by their responses, she started investigating printers, a process she describes as "nightmarish."

"The check-printing industry wasn't exactly ready for change, and I wasn't sure I could get around all the complicated regulations involved," Beard explained. "In the beginning, I had no idea of the complexity of the industry. And of course it didn't help matters that it was entirely dominated by men."

Beard proposed her idea to several large check printers who told her that imprinting specialized messages on checks simply could not be done. But finally she met with a senior marketing executive who was willing to take a chance. "He hadn't seen any innovations in the industry—and he had been in it for forty years—so he took one look at my idea and said, 'I think we should give you a chance,'" Beard recalled.

From this simple—and some would say idealistic—beginning, Message!Check has grown into a $3 million business. Not bad for a company that forgoes traditional marketing techniques such as heavy advertising and promotion investment. In fact, the business has expanded primarily through the visual equivalent of "word of mouth." Each check is seen by at least ten people as it moves from the original check signer, to the check recipient, and then on through the banking system. At every point along the way, potential customers see the checks and take note.

"We get a lot of calls from men who want to carry our pro-choice check, even though they aren't members of NOW," Beard explained. "They just see the checks and want to support the cause."

But just any cause won't do where Message!Check is concerned. Beard's company avoids doing business with organizations that support ideas and goals she outright opposes. "Our basic philosophy is to serve groups that are working for a better world versus ones that might place limitations or negative labels on segments of society via their checks," she said.

"Ultimately, we create a partnership with our member organizations," Beard explained. "We deal a lot with their people, and customers often think they are calling the organization to order checks—when actually they're calling us. So from a practical standpoint, taking on an organization that supports ideas we cannot support doesn't make sense."

Like its founder, the company operates in a style that's straightforward and highly effective. First, Message!Check arranges an exclusive agreement with a participating organization, such as the National Audubon Society, to determine a message and design for the checks. In this example, the phrase "Protecting Habitats" is printed under the society's name and combined with a beautiful illustration of birds in a tree.

Once the slogan and design have been determined, Beard's company promotes the checks to the organization's membership, primarily through ads in the group's magazines and newsletters; occasionally Message!Check uses direct mail, but in general, this method has proven cost-prohibitive.

When members order their specially imprinted checks, Message!Check donates a percentage of net sales—not net profits, which is normally the case—back to the organization on a quarterly basis. "We take the upcharge the banks would normally be earning through their check printing operations, and we give this money back to our member organizations," Beard said. The contributions range from nine percent to twelve percent, depending on the size of the organization.

Tight cost controls and realistic pricing are the mechanisms that have allowed Message!Check to offer such high returns to participating organizations, Beard said. Her company pre-dates many of the similar "affinity" programs that are so popular today. In fact, several start-ups that attempted to recreate the success of Message!Check simply worked themselves out of business by pricing their checks too low. "Considerable costs are involved in printing checks," Beard explained. "Some of these new groups just looked at the size of some organizations and thought they could offer checks for $7 and still have a lot of money left over after contributing back to the organization."

Checks printed by Message!Check cost $14, a price that hasn't changed since the company's inception. The reason: "We've just gotten better at controlling our costs and staying ahead of technology," Beard said. In part, this has been achieved by forming a long-term relationship with a progressive check printing company.

Beard's former printer lacked up-to-date computer technology—which became a major problem when she realized that her customer base included "about four hundred David Smiths," she said. "What if David Smith calls up to find out about the status of his checks and we can't figure out which one he is?" Beard wondered.

Wanting to offer her customers the best possible service, Beard began to look for a new vendor. "Most of my costs come from actually printing the checks," she said, "so I had to find a company that could be as flexible and hard-working as we are."

She found what she was looking for in Minneapolis, at a company called Liberty Check Printers, which is operated by David Copham. That was the beginning of a beautiful partnership between two like-minded businesspeople who have since become personal friends as well.

As an employer, Beard strives to run a "humanistic organization," and her caring commitment to her staff comes through in a variety of ways. For instance, she provides her five employees with full health and dental coverage as well as some unusual perquisites. "I helped one of my employees put a down payment on a house, and the only mother in the group now has a home office to eliminate some of her commuting time, freeing her up to enjoy her eighteen-month-old baby," she said.

Operating a small company gives Beard the flexibility she needs to enhance the working environment for her employees whenever she chooses to—which is often. On any given day, the mood in the office is friendly and relaxed; popcorn and sweatpants are the norm. And Beard makes a concerted effort to keep things that way, no matter how hectic the pace.

That Beard is concerned about quality of life, both at work and home, is obvious. Message!Check is located on scenic Vashon Island, a ferry ride away from Seattle, in an old grocery store lovingly repaired by her husband, Jon, an artist and furniture craftsman she met when she hired him to redo the ceilings in her home. Their marriage is one of her most important achievements, Beard said. "I have a loving and happy partnership with a creative individual who supports my goals and strength."

Now in a position to expand her business substantially, Beard has decided to keep the company at its manageable size. "I just don't want to own a big, big business," she said. "I'm more concerned about having control over my time. I have other things to think about, other dreams to pursue."

Chief among them is the desire to somehow incorporate children into her life. Characteristically candid, Beard admits that one of her deepest regrets is not having children, so she and Jon are actively considering ways to surround themselves with the younger generation. Inviting exchange students for an extended stay or starting a summer arts program are two ideas the Beards have discussed.

Community involvement is another serious commitment for Beard. Last year, Message!Check adopted two families during the holidays, in an effort to spread seasonal cheer to those less fortunate. While Vashon Island is a small stretch of land—thirteen miles by eight miles—the 7,000 year-round residents represent all economic backgrounds. And Beard recognizes there are all too many families in need of help. This year, her company is considering adopting a family full time, and providing money for food and rent while the key breadwinner is out of work. "People who are out of work suffer a kind of double jeopardy," Beard observed. "How can they focus on finding jobs and improving their skills if they can't feed their families?"

It comes as no surprise that the mission of Beard's company is to "help organizations achieve positive social change." Although somewhat disappointed by corporate America's ability to get more involved at the community level, Beard cites The Body Shop and Ben & Jerry's as two companies that are leading the way to much needed change. "They are inspirational to businesses big and small," she said.

When it comes to inspiring others herself, Beard keeps the message simple. "Don't get discouraged because someone says 'no.' Anyone can say no. Someone special will eventually say 'yes.' And whenever or wherever that happens, the possibilities—and the power—are in your hands."

Elaine L. Chao

*⤳Americans share a unique spirit of voluntarism
that is part of our national tradition. United
Way represents this... and who we are as a
charitable and generous people.*

For Elaine L. Chao, honoring one's father and mother is more
than a Bible commandment or a quaint Asian custom. It is the
guiding principal of her life.

When Chao arrived in this country by boat from Taiwan at age
eight, she didn't speak a word of English. Her family was her
anchor in a strange new world. As she grew older, graduated from
Harvard Business School, rose through the banking profession
and the federal government, eventually becoming the highest-
ranking Asian-Pacific American ever appointed to the executive
branch, the love of her parents and five sisters saw her through.

"One of my overriding goals is to bring honor to my family,"
said Chao. Now forty, she's had a wide-ranging career that's
included stints as the director of the Peace Corps and deputy secretary of the U.S. Department of Transportation. "My parents
sacrificed a tremendous amount to come to this country and I
would never want to disappoint my loved ones."

That sense of honor has served Chao well, especially as she faced
the latest and largest challenge of her career: restoring respectabil-
ity and trust to a national organization rocked by scandal.

In November 1992, Chao became president and chief executive officer of United Way of America, an organization whose

charitable work is so well known and its humanitarian efforts so widespread that some regard it as a national institution. Earlier that year, United Way's president of twenty-two years had been forced to resign, amid revelations that he used charitable donations to pay for trips on the Concorde, condos in New York and Florida, and chauffeured limousines.

As a result, donations dropped for the first time since 1946. Local United Way chapters began withholding dues, while charities across the country were suffering from the continuing recession and a wave of corporate layoffs.

Chao couldn't have stepped in at a worse time. But for someone who seems to thrive on overcoming obstacles, the choice was compelling. "I didn't want to look back and think I was asked to undertake an incredibly worthwhile challenge and I declined—that I didn't step in when I could have and be part of the solution in rebuilding an institution that is so near and dear to the hearts of millions of Americans," she explained.

In 1961, Elaine, her mother, Ruth, and her younger sister, May, stepped off a boat from Taiwan in the port of Los Angeles. They were greeted by their father, James, who had immigrated three years earlier. It was their first sight of a country that, in coming years, would seem to offer limitless opportunities for the family.

Whenever Chao is asked about her success, she always mentions the struggles her parents went through to give her and her sisters a chance at a better life. "Theirs is actually a wonderful love story," she said. "They came from very different environments and backgrounds...during any other time, they would never have met."

James and Ruth Chao immigrated separately to Taiwan in 1949. They had met earlier on the mainland, but were separated because of the war. After arriving in Taiwan, James spent two years looking for the girl he knew he would marry. He finally located her in a high school and they wed a short time later.

In Taiwan, James Chao became the youngest sea captain in recent history and often was gone for long periods of time. His eldest daughter found ways to amuse herself. "One of my fondest memories of Taiwan was playing with the red clay of the earth, as we had no toys," Chao recalled.

Elaine L. Chao

When she was five, her father left for further study in America, hoping to find greater economic opportunity for his family. He sent for them three years later. The family settled in Queens, New York, where their apartment was furnished through a United Way-funded agency. The Chaos' first celebration in their new home was James Chao's graduation from St. John's University. The commencement speaker was Sargeant Shriver, then director of the newly formed Peace Corps. Young Elaine had no way of knowing then that she would one day head both organizations.

Soon the Chao family was living the American dream. James Chao established a successful shipping business and moved his family to Long Island and then to affluent Westchester County. James and Ruth stressed the importance of education and sent their daughters—they had six by this time—to the best schools. Elaine earned an undergraduate degree in economics from Mount Holyoke College in 1975 and an M.B.A. from Harvard Business School in 1979.

James and Ruth made it clear that anything was possible for their daughters—but they couldn't rely on others to open doors for them. James Chao taught his girls to be self-reliant and self-starters, and often took them with him on overseas business trips. At dinner, the family discussed current events.

Elaine Chao's career eventually would take her all the way to the nation's capital. But she never forgot how far she had come.

"The first few years were very tough," she recalled. "I didn't speak English. My father was working very hard. But despite the difficulties, we just knew we were going to be okay because we were together. We had tremendous confidence and optimism in the basic goodness of this country, that people are decent here, that we would be given a fair opportunity to demonstrate our abilities."

During her varied and successful career, Chao would prove time and again how far-reaching her abilities really were. After Harvard, she became an international banker at Citibank, specializing in transportation finance. In 1983, she won a yearlong fellowship at the White House, blazing a new path in government that has inspired many other Asian-Pacific Americans.

In 1986, then Secretary of Transportation Elizabeth Dole asked Chao to return to Washington from San Francisco, where she was a vice president for BankAmerica, to become deputy administrator in the U.S. Maritime Administration. There Chao's banking skills—and her expertise in maritime transportation—were put to good use.

Her duties included supervising government guaranteed loans made to U.S. ship operators and shipbuilders to help them compete in the international market. Many of those loans were in default when Chao arrived. She instituted broad administrative reforms and tighter standards. As a result, she rose quickly through the federal government ranks and soon was appointed chairman of the Federal Maritime Commission, the youngest and first Asian-Pacific American ever appointed to lead the agency. While she was chairman, the Commission embarked on one of the most aggressive and successful trade malpractice and enforcement programs in its history. Chao's success at the Commission led to her appointment to the number two spot in the Department of Transportation.

As deputy secretary of transportation, Chao was the highest-ranking Asian-Pacific American in the federal government at that time. She also was part of a DOT team that created and implemented policies in response to the bombing of Pan Am Flight 103, the Exxon Valdez oil spill, the San Francisco earthquake, and the Persian Gulf War.

Her efforts earned her the respect of her boss, Elizabeth Dole, now president of the American Red Cross. "I think she's a real role model," Dole said of Chao. "She's put in the hard work and dedication it takes for success."

Chic Dambaugh, executive director of the National Association of Returned Peace Corps Volunteers, met Chao in 1991 when George Bush named her director of the Peace Corps. "Basically, she wants to go as far as she can go with her life as fast as she can," Dambaugh said. "She is always on the move, always thinking, exceptionally bright and capable."

At the Peace Corps, Chao's tenure coincided with the breakup of the Soviet Union. She led the Peace Corps in its historic move of establishing the first program in the newly independent states.

Speaking at the National Press Club to announce the establishment of this historic program, she recalled a trip she had taken to the Baltic in early 1992 with then Vice President Dan Quayle. "The people were experiencing their first winter of democracy. They felt such hope because after forty years they finally achieved independence and democracy. But they also felt such despair because they were in need of so much and they thought the outside world had forgotten them. People wept in the wake of our delegation," she said. "They were looking to America for assistance. How could anyone refuse to help?"

In 1992 came another cry for help and once again, Chao could not refuse. United Way of America, an umbrella group financed by 2,100 local chapters across the country, was involved in the largest scandal in its 105-year history. Trust in the organization had been shattered because of reports that the past national president had used donations to support his own lavish lifestyle.

Raising money through workplace campaigns, the United Way funds volunteer agencies ranging from shelters for battered women to the Boy Scouts. Nearly every American has been touched in some way by the United Way. That's why the abuses hurt so much, and why there was so much at stake in restoring the organization's credibility, said Chao, who was sought out by the United Way's search committee; she became the unanimous choice of United Way of America's Board of Governors, which considered over six hundred candidates.

Accepting the position, Chao pledged to do "whatever is necessary to ensure such (abuses) will never happen again."

In her first few months on the job, she instituted unprecedented cost controls and accountability procedures. The cutbacks started with her own salary—at $195,000, it's less than half of what her predecessor made. And she began the hard work of restoring trust, visiting more than 35 local United Way communities and meeting with more than 6,500 volunteers and professionals in the first four months of her tenure.

In a very real way, her work has been like mending a rift in a family. "Trust and confidence once damaged will take a great deal of effort and time to heal," she said.

But she is confident that the organization will recover. "Americans share a unique sense of voluntarism. It is part of our national identity, our national tradition. United Way represents this unique sense of voluntarism and who we are as a charitable and generous people. United Way brings relief and comfort to millions of Americans every day through its funded agencies.

In February 1993, Chao married Mitch McConnell, a U.S.

senator from Kentucky, in a simple ceremony at the Capitol. Along with sending the Peace Corps into the former Soviet Union and becoming the highest-ranking Asian-Pacific American in the U.S. government, Chao now lists getting married and "acquiring a soul mate" as one of her most important accomplishments.

McDonnell, a fifty-one-year-old Republican, has compared his position on the high-profile Senate ethics committee to Chao's job at the United Way. "Elaine is busy cleaning up the United Way and I'm cleaning up the Senate," he jokes. "We're the mop-up crew."

Theirs is not a typical marriage. McConnell does most of the cooking; Chao is frequently on the road. He also doesn't mind letting her have the spotlight.

"It's fascinating to watch the reception she gets from Asian-American groups," McConnell said. "She is clearly the most prominent Asian American in the country. It's like a bunch of teenagers recognizing a celebrity. She symbolizes more than any other...what America means to immigrants."

Linda Chavez

*⌒Success is creating something original and
lasting—whether it is a company, a work of art,
an idea or analysis that influences others,
or a happy and productive family.*

Linda Chavez has a mind all her own and she's not afraid to
make her opinions public—even in the face of angry opposition.
In fact, her sometimes unpopular positions won Chavez the
attention of former President Ronald Reagan, who gave her the
highest-ranking post of any woman in the White House.

In 1985, Chavez was appointed director of the White House
Office of Public Liaison, a job that entailed promoting administration policy among members of Congress and the public at large.
While her tenure in the position lasted only ten months, Chavez
has stayed in the public eye ever since—largely because she sees
success as much more than a high-profile Washington post.

"Success is creating something original and lasting," she said,
"whether it is a company, a work of art, an idea or analysis that
influences others, or a happy and productive family." And while
controversy seems to follow her wherever she goes, she offers
only one explanation: "I'm driven by my sense of what's right."

Chavez's life in politics began when she moved to Washington,
D.C., in the mid-1970s and worked for such organizations as the
Democratic National Committee and the National Education
Association. But she grew skeptical of these organizations
because she felt they treated her as a "token Hispanic." For

instance, her experiences at the NEA convinced Chavez "they were specifically looking for a Hispanic woman. It was clear to me they expected me to be the Hispanic lobbyist, to be their link to the Chicano caucus inside the NEA. I balked at that."

Chavez then joined the staff of the American Federation of Teachers, where several years later she took over the editorship of its influential quarterly, *American Educator*. Through this publication, she began to question "traditional" minority policies such as affirmative action, comparable worth and pay equity, and bilingual education programs. It was the beginning of a philosophical journey that would eventually lead her to the Reagan White House and the political limelight.

Before then, she served in a number of political positions, from Congressional staffer to presidential appointee to the Office of Education in the Department of Health, Education, and Welfare. She even worked as a consultant for President Jimmy Carter's Office of Management and Budget Reorganization Project before her appointment as staff director of the Civil Rights Commission under President Reagan.

During this time, Chavez switched political allegiance from the Democratic Party to the Republican. While this move prompted critics to charge that her opinions seemed to conveniently change for political gain, Chavez maintained that her strong views represented a lifetime of thoughtful observation and learning.

Born in Albuquerque, New Mexico, in 1947, Chavez was not blessed with a blissful childhood. Her father, Rudy, had built a career as a small contractor, but was often out of work. Though he came from a prominent Mexican-American family that had prospered in the Southwest for more than three centuries, the family's good fortune ended when his father— Chavez's grandfather—was jailed for bootlegging during Prohibition.

The incident forced Rudy Chavez, who was only a teenager at the time, to drop out of school to help support his family. Aside from a short stint with the military during World War II that gave him a sense of fulfillment, he often felt bitter and was driven to drink. He died in 1978.

Chavez's mother, Velma, is an Anglo American of English and Irish ancestry. She came to Albuquerque to work in the post

Linda Chavez   Photo by Susan Noonan

office, and later held jobs in retail.

Chavez was one of four children, two of whom died before reaching adulthood. Reflecting on her less-than-ideal childhood, Chavez said, "A lot of people seeing who I am today assume that I come from at least a middle-class background, and I don't. I had it very tough growing up."

Life was so rough that the Chavezes had to share a bathroom with four other apartments when the family relocated to Denver.

"It never occurred to me that people had their own bathrooms," Chavez said. It was in Denver, at the age of nine, that Chavez first experienced discrimination. Called "dirty Mexican" and "chiquita," she was hurt to learn that some neighborhood parents forbade their children to play with her. Still, Chavez said, "I don't see myself as a great victim of discrimination. Blacks have experienced the most severe discrimination in our society."

Refusing to let cultural identity stand in her path is a lesson Chavez recieved from her father, who taught her to value her heritage without using it as an excuse. Her mother said, "Linda's dad would tell her, 'Screaming and yelling doesn't accomplish anything. You have to think about things, decide what's wrong and do something about it.'"

Her father also instilled in Chavez a love of literature, which helped shape the course of her studies once she finished twelve years of Catholic school and entered the University of Colorado as an English major.

"My favorite activity as a child was to accompany my father to the library," she said. "Although he had little formal education, my father was very well read and introduced me to literature early." Though she was a successful student, Chavez can't recall being encouraged to excel or further her education. "I made it on hard work," she observed.

During her first year in college, Chavez's dance teacher suggested she start working with disadvantaged black children. One day, she invited Chavez home to meet her son, Christopher Gersten. The two were married in 1967; both were nineteen. Two years later, the first of their three sons was born.

While some people consider early marriage and motherhood stumbling blocks for women's careers, Chavez has always been very purposeful about balancing the various demands on her time and energy. "My family is critically important to me and I have tried to choose jobs that allowed me to create my own schedule," she said. "Even while I worked in high-profile jobs in the Reagan administration, I managed to be home early, often bringing work home with me that I could do after the kids were in bed."

Despite the demands of a young family, Chavez was determined to explore the teaching profession by working with people hard-pressed to succeed—such as the group of Mexican-American students she tutored in a remedial program. It was during this time that some of her more conservative views began to take root. Specifically, she became disenchanted after learning that her students were urging the school's administration to lower minimum grade requirements.

The very idea defied everything Chavez holds dear: "I love this country and what it stands for, and the way in which it allows people like me to make it on their own initiative," she said. "I still have a sense that if you work hard enough, you'll make it, and I don't think it does a service to people when you say, 'Well you don't have to work very hard because we'll give you a preference.' Then I think everybody loses...but minorities lose most."

Chavez applies this hard line against low standards most ardently on herself. For example, she never wants to be hired to fill a racial or gender quota. "It destroys the sense of self," she said. "Nobody wants to be picked for a position because they fill somebody's category."

Chavez conducts her life according to her views. For instance, while she's opposed to affirmative action, she firmly believes in integration. That's why when she and her family moved from Denver to Washington, D.C., they settled in Shepherd Park, a predominantly black neighborhood. "If you really do believe in integration," she said, "then it's incumbent on you to live your life that way."

The move to Washington was prompted by a series of experiences Chavez had when applying to and attending graduate school. Wanting to earn a Ph.D. in English literature, she applied for a minority grant. The Ford Foundation flew her to the East Coast for interviews with top-notch schools and put her up in a fancy hotel. Still overwhelmed from her first airplane ride, she put on her best dress and prepared herself to impress.

Yet nothing could have prepared her for the treatment she would receive once she got to her meeting. "I went in there, and there were these two Anglo men and a Puerto Rican woman, and they asked me to talk about myself a little bit, and I did," she recalled. "The next thing I knew, one of the men said to me, 'You speak English so well, Miss Chavez.'"

"And I was stunned," she continued. "I mean, here I am applying for a Ph.D. in English literature, I've got a 3.85 grade average in English—and they're telling me I speak English well. It was really unbelievable, and it went downhill from there. I call it noblesse oblige, and I don't like it. I don't like being patronized."

So Chavez chose the University of California at Los Angeles and at the same time, her husband began to work on an AFL-CIO voter registration project. All the while, the young couple struggled to find the money and time to manage their family, educations, and careers. "We got scholarships, loans, and we worked," Chavez said matter-of-factly.

But 1970 proved to be a turbulent time for race relations in Los Angeles. After fierce riots broke out among Mexican Americans in the city's east side, Chavez, the only Hispanic Ph.D. student in the UCLA English department, was pressured to teach a class on Chicano writing—despite her vehement objections that there was not enough Hispanic literature available at the time to cover a whole course.

What started out as a negative experience only got worse. Chavez was immediately disappointed that her students were more interested in talking about their own experiences than in reading and learning. "They sort of expected that this was the course they could take to come and 'rap,' in the jargon of the day," she said. "They *lived* Chicano literature, they didn't want to read about it."

When Chavez insisted that real classwork take place, some students protested by turning their backs to her as she lectured. "It was a disaster," she said. And when Chavez finally failed some of the students for not finishing the course's reading list, they retaliated by vandalizing her home and car, and threatening her family.

That experience only reinforced Chavez's view against affirmative action and other programs based on quotas. "I saw professors who I thought were manipulating these kids, radicalizing them and not doing them any good in terms of education," she explained. "The kids were doing badly in school, and rather than being told, 'Look, you've got to work not twice as hard but three times as hard as these middle-class kids from the suburbs,' they were being told, 'Go demand that you be allowed to stay in school with a lower than 2.0 grade-point-average.'"

Discouraged by the lack of standards that she felt open admissions programs perpetuated, Chavez left the university without receiving her Ph.D. Giving up her plans to teach, she moved to Washington with her husband, who had accepted a position with the AFL-CIO's Committee on Political Education.

While Chavez's entry into the political world may have gone unnoticed, she had begun to stir things up by the time she reached the Civil Rights Commission in 1983. Once there, she issued memos recommending the reversal of many traditional civil rights measures, including racial quotas. One such infamous memo read, "Racial preferences merely constitute another form of unjustified discrimination and create a new class of victims."

She also hired consultants and temporary employees whose views were closer to her own—which fostered criticism that she was turning an impartial agency into an instrument of the Reagan administration. But the way Chavez saw it, she was simply correcting the liberal bias of years past and was well within her rights to take action.

"I have had more difficulty with what I consider discriminatory and prejudiced behavior from liberals who thought they were doing me a favor than I have ever experienced from bigots," she said. "Maybe it shaped some of my attitudes on the whole affirmative action and quota business."

When she finally reached the White House, Chavez found her position somewhat wanting. "I learned how little policy actually emanates from the White House—whether by design or accident," she explained. "My chief reason for wanting to leave the Civil Rights Commission to join the White House staff was to be able to have a greater role in influencing administration policy on a broad array of issues. What I discovered was that the White House was more involved in the process than policy."

In her next move, Chavez ran for a Maryland senatorial seat in 1986. She won the primaries but faced a tough general election against Democratic Representative Barbara Mikulski in a state where two-thirds of the voting public was registered with that party.

Chavez ran on a "family values" platform and was accused of

mudslinging when the campaign became heated. Despite her efforts, she lost by more than twenty percent. But the experience was not a total loss.

"Ironically, what was probably the biggest defeat in my career turned into a tremendous opportunity to do what I most enjoy—writing and speaking," she said. "The publicity associated with my government and political career opened doors that might otherwise not have been opened in the publishing and lecture field."

Chavez then accepted a post as the president of U.S. English, a private nonprofit organization that lobbies to make English the official national language. Once again, Chavez demonstrated her determination to do what's right—even if it means taking a contrary stance.

"I think it's ironic that you have government intervening to keep kids functioning in their native language," she explained. "What sounds like a humane thing in the short run, can in the long run, turn out to be devastating. By creating a group of people who live in ethnic enclaves, you can stop the assimilation process and create second-class citizenships."

While Chavez still believes in the organization's mission, she left U.S. English because she felt its founder, John Tanton, was anti-Hispanic and anti-Catholic. Not surprisingly, Chavez's critics have wondered how she could have been duped by what some people consider to be a racist organization.

Chavez offers no apologies. "I do go against the grain," she acknowledged. "I do things that are not always popular. There's a tenacity there. I guess I've always thought of myself as different and sometimes I've gotten more attention for myself that I wanted."

Instead of hiding after her career misstep, Chavez joined the Manhattan Institute of Policy, a conservative think tank in Washington, as a John M. Olin fellow. In this role, she currently serves as director of the Center for the New American Community, which studies "the common heritage threatened by multiculturalism."

Her most notable accomplishment in recent years is writing *Out of the Barrio: Toward a New Politics of Hispanic Assimilation*, which was published by Basic Books in 1991. The idea for the book, which discusses affirmative action and Hispanic involvement in all levels of politics, rose out of a difference of opinion between Chavez and Arnold Torres, a former executive director of the League of the United Latin American Citizens.

"His was a view of Hispanics as this unassimilated group of poor and disadvantaged people who were not going to make it in society unless there was a massive infusion of government help," Chavez explained. "Yet I saw lots of opportunity. I saw Hispanics rapidly moving into the middle class. I saw my generation, and particularly the generation after me, making huge strides—and yet I didn't see that reflected in the rhetoric."

Because no one was espousing similar views, Chavez turned her ideas into a book, once again refusing to dilute her opinions. She does have some insight, however, into why her perspective may not be so popular.

"I think that to the organized Hispanic movement, what I say is not in their best interest. If you were an organization trying to get support from the private and public sector to help Hispanics who are poor and disadvantaged permanently and discriminated against, my coming along and saying, 'Wait a second, we are really doing okay, we're moving into the middle class and discrimination has not been nearly as severe as it has been for blacks'—that isn't a view you want out there."

Subtlety may not be her strong suit, but formulating definitive opinions certainly is. And while Chavez is clear about what she thinks, her perspective is never one-sided. That's why she can comfortably say she's all for immigration, even as she insists that all immigrants should learn English when they reach American soil. That's why she's in favor of special programs to increase the skills of people who come from economically disadvantaged backgrounds, but warns against too many entitlements and preferences. That's why she is often criticized by both Hispanics and liberals for opinions that still surprise, confuse, and anger.

"I don't presume that skin color always determines how you're going to think about a subject," she said. "I'm proud of my heritage," she continued, "but I see myself as what I am. It doesn't mean I have to endorse the whole agenda. Nobody owns me."

Elizabeth Dole

*∽I've always been interested in making a positive
difference in the lives of others. For me, the most
rewarding times in my government service
career were not spent in smoke-filled rooms
exchanging political gossip. Rather, they were
in classrooms, listening to at-risk youth and teen
mothers who were turning their lives around;
in fields, meeting with migrant workers who
needed a voice; and in far-flung corners of
the world where people needed help.*

Mention the name Dole in Washington, D.C., and some people
think of the powerful Senate minority leader, Bob Dole of
Kansas. But others are just as apt to think of Elizabeth Dole, his
equally influential wife.

Bob and Elizabeth Dole were practicing power-sharing long
before Bill and Hillary Clinton made it the subject of headlines
and talk show debates. Bob Dole is a former presidential candidate and the ranking Republican in Washington since George
Bush left town. Elizabeth Dole is a two-time Cabinet member
and current president of the American Red Cross. When
Congress is debating a tax bill, it's Bob Dole's face Americans see
on the evening news. But when floods hit the Midwest or hurri-
canes strike the coast, Elizabeth Dole is on the front lines, coordinating disaster relief.

And while the hard-edged senator is certain to head a list of

Republicans running for the presidency in 1996, his wife wins the popularity polls hands down. A former debutante with the good manners of the sorority house and the political instincts of the back room, Elizabeth Dole attracts fans of both sexes and political persuasions. *Esquire* magazine lauded her as one of the "Women We Love," and a 1988 Gallup poll named her one of the world's ten most admired women.

"Whenever Bob Dole's name comes up, people start talking about Elizabeth Dole," said Peter Hart, a Washington public opinion analyst. "Americans like her. One of the most frequent comments is, 'What a great couple.' He's had kind of a tough image over the years. She softens him."

But make no mistake, if there's one thing Elizabeth Hanford Dole is not, it's a cream puff. Sure, she's been criticized for leaving high-profile positions to help her husband strive for higher office. But she also has debated him on *Good Morning America*. She's been mentioned as a possible candidate for president and her name has also popped up on the shortlist of vice-presidential nominees.

Around Washington, the Doles are known for their Nick-and-Nora-style repartee. When Bob declared that Dole would not be a candidate for president in 1984, Elizabeth jumped to her feet: "Speak for yourself, sweetheart," she came back. And when he was asked if being married to a powerful woman made him feel emasculated, she quipped, "Hold it, cupcake. I'll take this one."

At fifty-seven, Elizabeth Dole possesses a record of accomplishments that's impressive by any measure. But for a woman who came of age in the fifties in a small town in the South—a region of the country where, as a character in *Fried Green Tomatoes* once observed, an assertive female is a "contradiction in terms"—her record is downright remarkable.

Dole grew up with all the advantages an upper-middle-class life could afford. She was born in an historic North Carolina town in a brick-and-stucco house with a spiral staircase and magnolia trees in the yard. "Salisbury is still the kind of place where people on the street tip their hat in welcome, and where conversations start with a friendly 'Hey.' You don't need a holiday as an excuse to fly the flag. And families mean a lot," she

Elizabeth Dole

wrote in *Unlimited Partners,* the Doles' 1988 autobiography.

Religion was as much a part of life as was a reverence for the ancestors buried in the old cemetery down the road. "In a world where so little seems permanent, we draw strengths from external truths, expressed in customs handed on like fine family silver from one generation to the next," she wrote. "...Washington is full of excitement and professional challenges. But Salisbury is home. It is my Rock of Gibraltar."

John Hanford, Elizabeth's father, was like most Southerners of his day, a registered Democrat (although he later changed his affiliation to vote for Dwight Eisenhower). Dole recalls that she was twelve years old before she learned that there were two political parties. She showed signs of her own political ambition early on—when she was elected president of the third-grade bird club.

Her mother, Mary Cathey Hanford, was a gifted musician who devoted herself to Elizabeth and son John, and to local causes ranging from historic preservation to establishing a home for victims of Alzheimer's disease. Though Mary Hanford had set aside her own career aspirations to focus on raising a family, she encouraged her daughter to test her wings.

After graduating from Duke University—where she was elected student government president and crowned May Queen—Elizabeth got a job at the Harvard Law School library, studied for a summer at Oxford, worked for a North Carolina senator on Capitol Hill, rode Lyndon Johnson's campaign train through the South, and led tours through the United Nations.

Dole's mother was concerned when her daughter announced in 1962 that she was enrolling as one of only two dozen women at Harvard Law School. But she supported her daughter's decision just the same. Now ninety-two, Mary Hanford remains Elizabeth Dole's best friend and most trusted advisor. They talk on the phone almost every day.

"Mother has been my own personal 'cabinet,' offering constant support and shrewd advice," Dole said. "She cuts to the heart of world problems with the same common sense she applies to a neighbor's problems."

In setting her sights on law school and a career in public service, Dole was charting a course that women of her mother's generation could scarcely imagine. The going wasn't easy. On her first day at Harvard, a male student asked her why she was there. "Don't you realize that there are men who would give their right arm to be in this law school, men who would use their legal education?" he said. One law professor refused to acknowledge his female students except for the one day a year when he required them to read an original poem before the rest of the class.

Dole eventually would put her legal education to good use by helping to level the playing field. In 1982, Ronald Reagan named her to head the White House Coordinating Council on Women. The council was charged with bolstering opportunities for women in the Reagan administration and the country at large. As the first female secretary of transportation, from 1983 to 1987, Dole increased female and minority representation at the U.S. Department of Transportation. And as secretary of labor from 1988 to 1990, she initiated a program to help crack the "glass ceiling" by withholding federal contracts from employers that blocked women and minorities from moving up the corporate ladder.

When Dole resigned as transportation secretary in 1987 to help her husband campaign for the White House, some women felt she had betrayed them. It wasn't the first time Elizabeth Dole had put her career on hold for her husband's. She took a leave of absence from her job at the Federal Trade Commission in 1976 after Gerald Ford picked Bob as his running mate. She resigned from the FTC in 1979 when he launched his first presidential campaign.

Dole defends her choices: "How could I sit out on one of the greatest experiences of my husband's life? I made that choice to take time out to support him, not because I had to, but because I *wanted* to. I think that is what women have been fighting for—the right to make career decisions we think are right for us. Taking that step was important to my personal fulfillment."

If the Clintons are Washington's newest power couple, the Doles are the city's most perennial. They met in 1972, but it took several months for him to ask her out. Bob's marriage of twenty-four years had just ended, and he was concerned about the difference in their ages: He was forty-nine, she was thirty-six. But he eventually overcame those fears.

"We had so many mutual interests and friends, it was amazing how much we had in common," Elizabeth Dole said. "I remember long conversations before we actually went out together—forty-five-minute conversations on the phone. There was just so much to talk about."

They were married in December 1975. By all outward appearances, the balance of power in their relationship seems relatively equal. She warms up his image as a no-nonsense Republican; he gives her added political clout. During the 1988 presidential convention, when both Doles were mentioned as possible vice-presidential nominees, a prominent newspaper columnist asked Bob how he felt about a Bush-Dole ticket. "I'm not sure," he answered. "To tell you the truth, I don't believe I'd really be interested." To which the columnist replied, "Good—because I wasn't thinking of you."

In the Dole's autobiography Bob observed, "Our two careers enrich our marriage and make the time we have together all the more meaningful. We speak the same language. We share the same passion for public service."

These days, Elizabeth Dole's schedule is especially busy. In 1990, she became the first woman since Clara Barton to serve as president of the American Red Cross. Immediately she faced growing concerns about the threat of AIDS to the nation's blood supply. In response, Dole completely overhauled the way the Red Cross collects, processes, tests, and distributes blood. When Hurricane Andrew devastated southern Florida in the summer of 1992 and floods ravaged the Midwest the following spring, the Red Cross responded more quickly and efficiently because of improvements Dole had made in the organization's disaster relief services.

Some people were surprised that Elizabeth, a true Washington insider, would walk away from a twenty-five-year career in government and trade a prestigious Cabinet post for the Red Cross. In nearly two years as secretary of labor, she had forged closer ties with organized labor, emphasized worker safety, and cracked down on child labor law violations. She helped negotiate a settlement between striking coal miners and the Pittstown Coal Company in southwest Virginia in 1989, although she was criticized for not intervening in other labor disputes, such as the Eastern Airlines and Greyhound Bus strikes.

But the Red Cross position offered her more independence and higher visibility, and Dole reasoned that the career move probably wouldn't hurt her if she later decided to seek elected office.

But most importantly, her friends say, Dole took the job because she wanted to help people in crisis. She even turned down her first year's salary of $200,000, saying, "The best way I can let volunteers know of their importance is to be one of them."

"I've always been interested in making a difference, a positive difference, in the lives of others," Dole said. "For me, the most rewarding times in my government service career were not spent in smoke-filled rooms exchanging political gossip. Rather, they were in classrooms, listening to at-risk youth and teen mothers who were turning their lives around; in fields, meeting with migrant workers who needed a voice; and in far-flung corners of the world where people needed help. The opportunity to devote myself to these causes on a full-time basis is what led me to the Red Cross."

Lately, Dole has been striving to strike a balance in her own life. Even as a child, she was such a perfectionist that she cried all the way home when her second-grade teacher sent her to fetch a forgotten book. On Sunday afternoons when she would gather with her cousins to listen to Bible stories, her Grandmother Cathey taught them that there was no goal in life more worthy of pursuit than serving the Lord. But Dole writes that as she grew older, "the Holy Grail of public service became very nearly all-consuming....Though I was blessed with a beautiful marriage and a challenging career, my life was close to spiritual starvation."

Dole found that sustenance again in a church near Dupont Circle, where every Monday night, she and others meet for fellowship and prayer. And once again, she is setting aside Sundays for church, family, and friends—and most importantly, for herself.

"Spiritual growth is a lifetime process," she said. "I'm a long way from where I want to be." But she recognizes more than ever that the reward lies not at the end of the road but all along the way. "My grandmother has never exerted more influence than she does today, when I am reminded that what we do on our own matters little—what counts is what God chooses to do through us. Life is more than a few years spent on self-indulgence or career advancement. It's a privilege, a responsibility, and a stewardship to be met according to His calling."

Rita Dove

*⁓My greatest obstacle has been myself—
the nagging insecurities, the fear that I
would be laughed at or misunderstood if I
were truly honest in my writing. Of course,
I consider successful only those stories and
poems where I overcome this fear. However,
there has been a lot of wasted energy beating
down these interior devils.*

Though writing has always been her passion, Rita Dove never dreamed she'd earn her living from it. Nor did she expect to win the Pulitzer Prize at the age of thirty-five, or be named the nation's seventh poet laureate at the age of forty—two distinctions typically awarded much later in life, if at all.

Now forty-one, Dove has not only earned these accolades, she's achieved something far more valuable. For beyond the professional awards and public acclaim is the personal satisfaction of knowing she's achieved her own definition of success, which has nothing to do with "prizes, a huge salary, or expensive cars," Dove said. "To me, the sure sign that you are on the road to success is if you are never bored—finding a job that is interesting in which you are challenged and genuinely excited by the discoveries made in that job—is the greatest success story of all."

Born to Ray and Elvira Dove in Akron, Ohio, Dove had a Midwestern childhood complete with all the trimmings: three siblings—one brother and two sisters—two loving parents, a big house with rose bushes and fresh-cut lawn, her fair share of scraped knees and jump rope, and most of all, trips to the library. "I have always been passionate about books," she said. "From the time I began to read, as a child, I loved to feel their heft in my hand and the warm spot caused by their intimate weight in my lap; I loved the crisp whisper of a page turning, the musky odor of old paper, and the sharp inky whiff of new pages."

This love of reading and books compelled the painfully shy Dove to write, a natural gift that may never have been fully realized if her eleventh grade English teacher, Miss Oechner, had not taken her and a fellow student out of school one day to attend a book signing. There Dove met her first real live writer—a poet named John Ciardi. "At that moment," she said, "I realized it was possible to write down a poem or story in the intimate sphere of one's own room and then share it with the world."

Equally important, this experience helped Dove appreciate that writing could amount to more than a pleasurable pastime. "Although I wrote poems and stories as a child," she explained, "I did not really expect to become a writer. Before then, I had never met a writer and had no reason to think of writing as an adult occupation. The possibility was beyond my imagination."

This obvious absence of role models clearly contributed to Dove's initial ambivalence about pursuing her natural talent. "I wish that I had been introduced to more living writers— either by meeting them in person or by reading their works in textbooks—when I was younger," she said. "I believe I would have made up my mind to become a writer at the age of twelve if I had just known that it was possible."

Dove was so skeptical about building a career as writer that when she graduated from high school, she headed for Miami University in Oxford, Ohio, intent on studying law. But college exposed her to a world of wider possibilities, and so she returned to Akron one Thanksgiving to announce her plan to become a poet.

She still remembers her father's reaction: He swallowed once and then told her, "Well, I've never understood poetry, so don't be upset if I don't read it." Dove understood her father was having a hard time connecting with her lifelong passion and new-

Rita Dove   Photo by Fred Viebahn

found profession. But she appreciated his honesty and simply trusted that she would always have the support of her parents, both of whom she cites as strong influences in her life.

Her father, in fact, had preceded her in breaking down racial barriers—he was the first black research chemist to be hired by a major tire manufacturer. "I knew he had done something remarkable," Dove said of her dad. "He was a real role model."

Dove's parents gave her many lessons that she still holds dear. "They taught me the value of education, the joy of doing my best even if no one else was there to see it, and the renewable and infinite pleasure of reading."

Just the same, Ray and Elvira were less than thrilled when their daughter decided to become a writer, an endeavor they considered risky at best. "The relief when I got my first job teaching was so palpable that there must have been some concern," Dove recalled.

But any reason to worry has long since been erased, for Dove has enjoyed success in two competitive arenas: academia and publishing. As a student, she was named a Presidential Scholar and earned a Fullbright/Hays Fellowship. In addition to her bachelor of arts degree from Miami University, she studied at the Universität Tübingen in West Germany, and earned a master of fine arts degree from the University of Iowa, which is widely known for its writing programs.

More recently, as a teacher, Dove's assignments have taken her to Arizona State University and then to the University of Virginia, where she currently teaches creative writing as the Commonwealth Professor of English. On the literary front, she has been awarded a Guggenheim Memorial Fellowship and two National Endowment for the Arts Creative Writing Fellowships.

Her published works include four books of poems: *The Yellow House on the Corner; Museum; Thomas and Beulah,* for which she won the Pulitzer Prize in Poetry in 1987; and most recently, *Grace Notes.* She also has written a collection of short stories, *Fifth Sunday,* and her first novel, *Through the Ivory Gate.*

Poetry, however, remains Dove's first and truest love. "Poetry is language at its most distilled and powerful," she said. "It's like a bouillon cube: You carry it around and then it nourishes you when you need it."

Dove needs such nourishment most when she's writing prose, which she believes requires different but related skills. "That I practice writing often helped a lot," she said in describing the process of writing *Through the Ivory Gate*. "But I also had a lot to learn—like chronology. Novels encompass a different sense of time, so I had to keep color-coded notebooks to recall when certain things happened."

Years of poetry writing helped Dove craft her novel in much the same way playing one instrument may help a musician learn another, even if the two are as different as a piano and a saxophone. This kind of creative osmosis is familiar to Dove, who plays the cello—a skill she believes helped develop her ear for the music of poetry and the pleasure derived from simply hearing words.

As the nation's poet laureate, Dove dreams of helping young people appreciate the possibility of becoming a writer, or at the very least, thoroughly enjoying the art. But she's concerned that, as she puts it, young people today have a hard time looking beyond the trappings of "sun-drenched celebrities," and seeing "value in the shadows" of an intellectual endeavor such as poetry.

While poetry currently is enjoying a slight surge in popularity, Dove regrets that it doesn't compare with the magnetic draw of entertainment media. "This is a country that operates on stardom," she said. "Given the choice between watching television and reading a book, it is a difficult battle. You have to find ways to show people the pleasure of reading, and that it is something continual and deepening—not a quick bite."

The poet laureate's primary responsibility is to promote poetry, a task Dove's predecessors have found vague, frustrating, and under-resourced. "It'll probably ruin my life," she said of her new position, revealing that she is aware of the job's reputation as a largely ceremonial post whose responsibilities undoubtedly will leave her little time to devote to her own writing.

"But it's an incredible honor and I'd be crazy not to accept it," she said with an eagerness that has James Billington, the Librarian of Congress who appointed her, hoping Dove will help revitalize both the job and the art. "Having had a number of poet laureates who have accumulated multiple distinctions from lengthy and distinguished careers," he said, "we will be pleased to have an outstanding representative of a new and richly variegated generation of poets."

Indeed, the eyes of the poetry world are on Dove as never before. As David Lehman, editor of *The Best American Poetry* observed, "She'll have a great opportunity to either be as frustrated with the office and its lack of real responsibility and real purpose as the previous laureates, or with her intelligence and vitality, to make the position one that might expand the audience for poetry—which we all fervently hope for."

No one is hoping harder than Dove, whose goal is to reduce the perceived inaccessibility of poetry. "It is perplexing that poetry seems to exist in a parallel universe outside daily life in America," she said. Her task, she believes, is to eliminate the notion that poetry is a purely academic activity—something to be tested on, not simply enjoyed.

"Just the word 'poetry' increases people's anxiety level," Dove said. "They imagine us all off in an ivory tower somewhere, trying to imagine phrases and stanzas they couldn't possibly understand." That's why she's determined to spread the word that poetry can be an everyday art form, "something with a more obvious connection to our lives." To help prove her point, Dove is even entertaining such unheard of notions as poetry videos, similar to the popular music videos seen on MTV.

But then Dove is not your typical poet laureate. For one, she is the youngest. She is also the first black, a distinction that doesn't make much difference to her personally but which she can appreciate in a larger context.

"It is significant in terms of the message it sends about the diversity of our culture and our literature, which is just vibrant now," Dove said. "Even though there are still subtle barriers out there, on the whole, it's a wonderful time to be writing. We as a country have grown up enough to realize all ethnic variations are human beings. We don't all have to be out there with something to prove. That's something which should be a cause for rejoicing, rather than fear or anguish. Our differences are not threatening."

Yet Dove is adamant about not being categorized by race or culture. "I would never say that I'm not a black poet—but I object to being labeled," she explained. "Labeling says, 'This is your category,' implying that you can't step out of those bounds.

Being black tinges the way one sees the world, but not all of the time. I don't want to be put in categories that will limit me."

Limits—those set by others, but more importantly, those set by herself—are something Dove has raged a fierce battle against all her life. "My greatest obstacle has been myself—the nagging insecurities, the fear that I would be laughed at or misunderstood if I were truly honest in my writing," she candidly acknowledges. "Of course, I consider successful only those stories and poems where I overcome this fear. However, there has been a lot of wasted energy beating down these interior devils."

Interior devils aside, Dove has always had a quiet confidence in her abilities. "I think belief in myself has been the most important personal quality that has contributed to my success," she said. "Despite nagging feelings of insecurity, I have always had a fairly basic belief that, if I tried my best and were truly honest about my feelings, I would come out alright."

That she has been honest about her feelings is evidenced in her writing, which critics have praised for its concise style and its skillful weaving of autobiographical and historical elements. Many of Dove's stories and poems feature family members, from her maternal grandparents whose lives are loosely chronicled in *Thomas and Beulah,* to her parents and siblings, to Fred Viebahn, the German writer she has been married to since 1979, and their ten-year-old daughter Aviva. The Dove-Viebahn family now resides in Charlottesville, Virginia—close enough for Dove's frequent commutes to Washington, D.C., where she attends to her new responsibilities as poet laureate.

Though Dove has been reluctant to categorize her writing by race or culture, she readily acknowledges the influence of gender. "I'm a woman and a black and I write out of that," she said. "I think perhaps the woman experience is more important. Being a woman has made me more sensitive to the social interaction among people, since women are traditionally raised to attend to the needs—both physical and psychological—of their families."

True to this belief, many of her poems reveal the subtle power of family ties and the quiet moments that connect and define human relationships. Regardless of the perspective from which her poems are written—male or female, young or old, black or white—much of Dove's success stems from her ability to capture human emotion in simple words and everyday images that are surprisingly poignant. Her poem "Daystar" from *Thomas and Beulah,* is just one of many examples.

> She wanted a little room for thinking:
> but she saw diapers steaming on the line,
> a doll slumped behind the door.
>
> So she lugged a chair behind the garage
> to sit out the children's naps.
>
> Sometimes there were things to watch—
> the pinched armor of a vanished cricket,
> a floating maple leaf. Other days
> she stared until she was assured
> when she closed her eyes
> she'd see only her own vivid blood.
>
> She had an hour, at best, before Liza appeared
> pouting from the top of the stairs.
> And just *what* was mother doing
> out back with the field mice? Why,
>
> building a palace. Later
> that night when Thomas rolled over and
> lurched into her, she would open her eyes
> and think of the place that was hers
> for an hour—where
> she was nothing,
> pure nothing, in the middle of the day.

Through poems such as this one, Dove sends a strong message to every audience that will pay heed: "You can write from your own experience—the human experience—and it can be just as vibrant and relevant to a farmer in Iowa as it is to someone in Nepal."

Marsha Evans

∽I've seen what happens when you're confronta-tional with the system: You're basically excom-municated. When you work inside the system to change things, you often have more success.

When Marsha Evans joined the Navy in 1968, women weren't allowed to serve on ships or fly jets. Those jobs were reserved for male sailors and pilots. A quarter of a century later, women not only are serving on Navy support ships, they're commanding them. They can fly combat missions, lead battalions, and soon will be sailing on battle ships as well. Some of this progress is due to the pioneering efforts of Rear Adm. Marsha "Marty" Evans.

The forty-six-year-old Evans may have spent her entire Navy career on dry land, but she has helped turn the tide for other women, making it possible for them to have the opportunities she could only dream of. She was the first woman in U.S. history to command a naval station and only the fifth to reach the rank of rear admiral. Now the third highest-ranking woman in the Navy, Evans is married to a former jet pilot who doesn't seem to mind that she outranks him.

Throughout her twenty-five-year career, Evans has worked within a predominately male system to help create an atmos-phere in which people can be rewarded for their accomplish-ments, regardless of their gender.

"I've seen what happens when you're confrontational with the system: You're basically excommunicated," she said. "When you work inside the system to change things, you often have more success."

Evans' success has earned her a place in the spotlight. And occasionally on the hot seat. In the spring of 1993, she had just been named rear admiral when news broke of the infamous Tailhook scandal. The Defense Department had charged one-hundred-and-forty Navy and Marine Corps officers with sexual assault and misconduct resulting from the 1991 Las Vegas convention. Women attending the convention (including twenty-four female officers) said they were subjected to a human gauntlet in which drunken aviators grabbed them and tore their clothes. The men wore T-shirts and buttons with slogans such as "Women are Property" and "Not in My Squadron."

Evans was as sickened by the scandal as anyone. But she wasn't necessarily surprised. She too had been harassed by male colleagues early in her career, although never on the scale of Tailhook. But rather than be discouraged by Tailhook, Evans saw it as way to accelerate change.

She went on national television to discuss the incident and what the Navy was prepared to do about it. Even more importantly, she stressed how much still needed to be done, and publicly challenged a long-standing federal law that prevents women from serving in combat. Women had just served bravely and ably in Panama and the Persian Gulf, she pointed out, saying that although the military was making progress at removing barriers, women still were barred from many prestigious combat assignments considered crucial to career advancement.

"There is more than just a de facto glass ceiling," Evans said. "There's been a concrete reinforcement in the form of federal law. It is, in fact, the last remaining legally sanctioned gender discrimination in this country."

In some ways, it's surprising that Marty Evans chose a career in the Navy at all. Her father, Walter Johnson, was an enlisted sailor who was away at sea sometimes for eleven months out of the year. Her mother, Anne, was left to care for five children. When asked to describe her childhood, Evans remembers the weight of responsibility she felt from a very early age.

When she was five, her mother contracted polio. With her father

Marsha Evans

gone, Marty, the oldest, was expected to take care of her brothers and sisters and help out around the house. Although her mother recovered fully, the experience obviously left a strong impression.

"The Navy in those days was the kind of organization that didn't spend a lot of time worrying about families," Evans recalled. "We grew up knowing my dad was happy in his career. But we didn't talk much about the Navy. I'm not sure my mother was very happy about it. She was raising these kids on her own."

Evans said her family was never a "typical Navy family." They didn't live near the base. Her mother, who was an artist, didn't participate in the usual wives' functions. "We didn't even go down to the ship when it came home," Evans recalled.

But like most military families, they moved often—five times before Marty's senior year in high school. When she was seven, her father was transferred to an air station in North Africa for four years and took his family along. "It was such an adventure," she said, vividly recalling the excitement of arriving in Casablanca and seeing Arab women in their long flowing robes. From that experience, she learned to appreciate different cultures and developed an interest in working abroad.

Evans excelled in school, despite frequent interruptions in her education, and graduated from high school at age sixteen. (She jokes that it's because, at 5 feet 11 inches, she was the tallest person in the class.) At Occidental College in Los Angeles, she majored in political science and international relations. She was planning to pursue a graduate degree in East Asian studies when she noticed a photograph of a female military officer in the evening paper.

It was the summer of 1968. Students across the country, including many of Evans' friends, were demonstrating against the Vietnam War. But suddenly she saw the military as a way to temporarily escape the academic grind and to satisfy her thirst for adventure. At the same time, she said, "It occurred to me that citizens had a responsibility to serve" their country. And knowing that her father had loved his Navy job "subconsciously, at least, played a role in my decision," she explained.

Evans had to settle for being a "dry land sailor," however, since it would be another six years before women were allowed to serve on Navy ships, and then only on hospital ships. Yet she was able to satisfy her wanderlust. After finishing her initial two-year stint, she decided to stay in the Navy. For the next two years, she was stationed in Japan and traveled throughout Asia on an admiral's staff. Later, she served in London as the Middle East policy officer during the fall of the Shah of Iran.

As she rose rapidly through the ranks, Evans also was breaking down barriers. In 1973, she became the first female surface assignments officer in the Bureau of Naval Personnel. At the same time, she served as senior Navy social aide to presidents Richard Nixon and Gerald Ford. Her career also gained visibility when she received a White House Fellowship. In 1990, Evans assumed command of the naval station at Treasure Island, San Francisco, becoming the first woman to take charge of a U.S. naval station.

At the U.S. Naval Academy, where she served as a battalion officer and later as chief of staff, she met young female midshipmen who also were trying to break new ground. She advised their crew team, and on the bus to and from sporting events, they shared their frustrations with her. Evans realized that although these women were exceptionally talented, "they were accorded a sort of second-class status" because of their limited opportunities. And they were harassed by their male peers.

That experience strengthened Evans' resolve to work for change "within the system." No longer could she be silent while other women were prevented from reaching their full potential. "I guess at that point I decided you have to stand up and be counted and make a difference," she said.

In the aftermath of Tailhook, Evans was named executive director of a newly established Standing Committee on Military and Civilian Women in the Department of the Navy. The committee was more than just a face-saving gesture—members recommended sweeping changes in the naval service. The bottom line: Sexual harassment would not be tolerated. But the committee went further. It recommended that, for the first time in history, women be allowed to serve on all combat ships, planes, and submarines.

Many of the committee's recommendations already have been enacted. In April 1993, Defense Secretary Les Aspin lifted the ban on women flying combat missions. And Congress has repealed the law that prohibits women from serving on warships. Because of cramped living quarters, submarines may remain closed to women for the immediate future. But Evans is confident even that barrier eventually will be removed.

"My desire would be a genderless Navy," she said, "one where men and women are assigned jobs on the basis of ability and skills and potential, and where we don't have women's jobs and men's jobs."

She understands that many people in this country continue to be uncomfortable with the idea of women in combat. But, Evans asks, "In an all-volunteer military, where you want the best people to serve, can you afford to categorically exclude fifty percent of the people—when they can do the range of jobs? I think it's almost a moral decision."

Evans perhaps has risked being labeled a troublemaker for expressing these views. But she said she has not suffered for her opinions. In fact, she has gotten more opportunities because of them. It also didn't hurt to have a husband who always stood behind her.

Lt. Comdr. Gerry Evans, a retired jet pilot, obviously isn't intimidated by his wife's success. In fact, when she was the commanding officer at Treasure Island, he assumed the duties of a military spouse, organizing volunteer services and serving as honorary president of the officers' and enlisted wives' clubs. "Fortunately, I have a husband who has absolutely no ego problems," Marty said.

The Evanses live in an Alexandria, Virginia, neighborhood that borders a Civil War battlefield. When Marty isn't traveling around the country in her new role as head of Navy recruiting, she often can be found tending her roses or getting together with a few close friends. Gerry, now fifty-two, has traded his flight gear for golf clubs. Together, they enjoy playing tennis and skiing in Utah and Colorado. Also, Marty tries to work out at least four days a week. "I'm a believer in a balanced life. You have to take care of yourself or you won't be ready for the big stresses," she said.

The Evanses have no children, a choice that was influenced by their military careers. "The military is not the kind of career you can be part-time in," Marty said. "Many of my women officer friends have children and have been successful....I guess I'm not the Super Woman."

Some people might disagree. "With Marty, the issue has always been competence, competence, competence," said her sister, Cristine Watson. "I don't think she ever considered there was a male-female issue. She's an exceptional person—bright, motivated, hard-working—and was born with a nose to climb to the top."

Rear Adm. Thomas C. Lynch, who worked with Evans when she

was chief of staff at the Naval Academy, predicts that she will be the first woman three-star admiral. "I have tremendous respect for her," he said.

But for now, at least, Evans seems happy with her present job. As the first woman to head Navy recruiting—for both women and men—Evans will undoubtedly play a major role in changing the complexion of a military career.

As part of her job, Evans often travels the country, meeting young people who are just making the decision to join the military. It brings back memories of her own experience twenty-five years ago when she walked into a California recruiting office. Even though Vietnam demonstrators were picketing outside the door, she believed then that she'd made the right choice. And she still does.

"It's wonderful," she said of meeting the new recruits, especially young women, who are embarking on military careers. "You realize these people have such opportunities ahead of them. They can make something out of them or not...But we know the opportunities are there."

Helen Fisher

⁓Successful people have a plan for where they want to be a year from now, where they want to be five years from now, where they want to be ten years from now. Things happen to people who plan about it and dream about it and prepare themselves for it.

In the years when Helen Fisher's career was beginning to take shape, she often lay awake at night, planning what she would say if she were invited to give the commencement speech at Harvard.

"This was a fun game," she said.

But it was more than a game. While she was envisioning herself on a dais, addressing students and faculty at the most prestigious university in the United States, Fisher, now an anthropologist at the American Museum of Natural History, was preparing herself for success.

"I was assuming I would be well known in my field," she said. "I was incorporating into my being some expectations about who I am."

Planning for success, Fisher maintains, is as important to achieving it as hard work, talent, and drive. "Successful people have a plan for where they want to be a year from now, where they want to be five years from now, where they want to be ten years from now," she said. "Things happen to people who plan about it and dream about it and prepare themselves for it."

Fisher knows what she's talking about. Her planning and

dreaming—and her provocative theories about the biological nature of love, marriage, and divorce—have enabled this academically trained anthropologist to build a career that is both successful and off the beaten track.

While most of her colleagues publish their theories in professional journals, Fisher has written articles for *The New York Times, Penthouse,* and other mainstream publications. She is the author of two books, both of which became popular Book-of-the-Month Club selections.

Instead of teaching at a university, Fisher consults for businesses and lectures at colleges and professional meetings across the country. She served as the "house anthropologist" for NBC's *Today* show, and regularly appears on television and radio talk shows to discuss romance and male-female relationships.

Fisher was born in New York City in 1945 and grew up in Connecticut. She and her identical twin sister were the youngest of four siblings. Her mother, Helen, a sculptor and flower arranger who was active in environmental causes, showed Fisher that women have a place outside the home.

"She worked doing her own things," Fisher said. "My mother looked with great contempt at anyone who didn't make a useful contribution to society."

Fisher's father, Bud, an executive in New York, also groomed her for success. He made sure she knew how to catch a ball and told her, "Be useful as well as ornamental."

Fisher understood her parents' message. "I grew up thinking I could be anything," she said.

By her own admission, Fisher was "sort of a wild teenager." She came of age at a time when social strictures were loosening, and she took full advantage of the freedom. "I was a child of the sixties," she said. "Everything was available to me—sex, drugs, and rock 'n' roll."

While Fisher believes that young people should enjoy life and develop strong friendships, she regrets her own excesses. "In adult life, I'm having to go back and read the classic books and acquire a lot that may have been around me as a teenager, but I missed it." The partying she did as a teenager was a "stunting experience," Fisher said.

Still, she managed to earn good grades in college, and in 1968, she received a bachelor's degree from New York University. She planned a career in social work, which meant earning a master's degree. But as she was sitting on the steps in front of the university's school of social work, filling out the application, Fisher came to the realization that her interests really lay in another direction. "So I got off the steps," she recalled, "threw out the application, and went to the anthropology department and asked about graduate schools."

Fisher dates her interest in anthropology back to her earliest memories. She recalls comparing herself to her twin sister: "I remember standing in front of the mirror and comparing bodies, comparing hair, comparing everything," she said. "Long before I ever knew some of our behavior came from biology and some from learning, I was absolutely, intuitively comparing how much of my behavior was biological and how much learned."

As a child, Fisher loved popular science, and she was fascinated by other people's lives. "My great fun was to sit in the bushes outside of the neighbor's house and watch them eat dinner," she recalled. "It was a given; I was a born anthropologist."

A post-college job on a Navajo reservation where she worked on a project sponsored by the American Museum of Natural History convinced Fisher that she had an interest in anthropology, and she went off to the University of Colorado for graduate work. There, studying for her M.A. exam, she changed her party-all-week, cram-the-night-before study habits. "I realized I had to do this in a more organized fashion," she said. "It was graduate school that taught me how to think and work."

When it came time to choose a topic for her Ph.D. dissertation, Fisher realized that few people had written on sexuality. "The subject interested me as it does all young people," she said, "but it also interested me intellectually." She chose to write her dissertation on the evolution of female sexuality—a decision that led to her life's work.

"That was an incredibly important turning point," she said. "If I get remembered for anything, it will be for my contribution to the understanding of sexuality."

Fisher put herself through graduate school, working as a

Helen Fisher

teaching assistant. She prided herself on her ability to support herself and enjoyed her independence. "I've always supported myself," she said. "I look at women who gripe about supporting themselves with astonishment."

She maintained her independence even though when she

moved to New York City to complete her dissertation, she was living "hand to mouth," eating canned food discounted by the supermarket because the labels had been removed. "I got to know by the size of the can whether it was dog food," she recalled with a smile. To her way of thinking, one managed for oneself, so Fisher just "didn't think to ask" her parents for money.

In the mid-1970s, Fisher found her first job. Through a boyfriend, she got an interview at a publishing company and was hired to work on a coffee-table book about the American West. "I loved going to work from nine to five," she said. "I was so proud of myself to get a paycheck every two weeks."

At the same time, she continued to work on her dissertation at night. "I've always worked around the clock," she said. Fisher received her Ph.D. in 1975, but stayed on at the publishing company because she was learning so much. As chief researcher for a book on American Indians, she said, "I got the equivalent of an M.A. in American Indian ethnology."

While at the publishing company, she had an opportunity to go on radio, and she sharpened her writing skills. But she also had an upsetting experience on the job, with a boss who sexually harassed her and others. "Nobody could be left alone with him," Fisher said.

She complained, but the company took no action. Then when she was up for promotion, her boss declined to recommend her. Even now, the memory rankles. "It's funny how I'm still angry with him," she said.

Fisher left the job when she wasn't promoted. Sometimes, though, disappointment in one area can lead to opportunity in another, and Fisher's painful experience at the publishing company put her career on a new track.

"I might still be there," she said, "and my Ph.D. would have gone by the wayside. I wouldn't be what I am today. I guess the lesson is that bad things can happen that move you in a new direction, and if you've got the ambition and spirit to move forward, almost nothing is going to stop you."

Fisher moved forward by turning her Ph.D. dissertation into a book, *The Sex Contract: The Evolution of Human Behavior,* published in 1982. The book, which discussed the evolution of pair bonding, sold well and was published in five countries. For the first time, Fisher had made her views known to a wide audience.

"I strongly believe that science should be useful," she said, "and I believe that it should be useful not only to other scientists but to the public."

Writing the book showed Fisher she could make the contribution to society that her mother had taught her was so important— by developing ideas that would have relevance to people's day-to-day lives. Equally important, the book gave her the visibility she needed to get on the college lecture circuit, where she could talk to students about her ideas. She also began writing magazine articles, and in 1985, she was invited to appear on the *Today* show.

Wanting to make an effective presentation, Fisher approached her first television appearance in the same way she had managed her career. "I was really prepared," she said. "Life is preparation."

Her work paid off. The show's producers were impressed and offered Fisher a contract to do an eighteen-part series on anthropology.

She had found her niche. With topics like "Is Monogamy Natural?" and "Courtship: The Universal Pick-Up," Fisher showed a fascinated audience what anthropology could teach about our romantic behavior today.

Around that same time, Fisher also began developing ideas for her next book. Spurred by her lecture agent, who told her that Americans were interested in divorce, Fisher examined divorce data for sixty-two countries, then compared figures on human bonding with patterns of mating and "divorcing" in birds and animals. Out of her research came *Anatomy of Love: The Natural History of Monogamy, Adultery, and Divorce*—and some thought-provoking theories on the innate nature of human love, marriage, and divorce.

Fisher found that all over the world, divorces tend to peak about four years after marriage. She figured out the reason for what she called "the four-year-itch": it was the length of infancy in primitive society, the time a child required the care of two parents. It made sense, in a hunting-and-gathering culture, to raise a child with one partner, then move on to the next. It was a way for the man to spread his seed and for the woman to secure a better provider for her children. And the "divorce" was easy to accomplish in these societies because men and women had equally powerful economic roles.

Marriage for life became important, Fisher theorized, only with the advent of an agricultural society. Women became dependent on men; it was men who had the strength to wield the plow. And, Fisher pointed out in an article about her in *Glamour,* "when a farm marriage failed you couldn't just divide the land and move half of it someplace else."

Men and women are apt to divorce when both are economically independent. In the primitive hunting-and-gathering societies, women provided a good portion of the family's food. They could support themselves, just as women today can. Now that men and women have more economic equality, we are returning to the mating patterns of our forebears. Thus, Fisher said, there is nothing new about divorce.

Anatomy of Love, which came out in 1992, was published in sixteen countries worldwide and was chosen as a "Notable Book of 1992," by *The New York Times.* The book's widespread popularity is no doubt due in large part to the author's decision not to create an academic text. Fisher's clear prose makes her ideas accessible, and her subject matter is so compelling that the book is as readable as a good novel. Perhaps most important, the book provided a context for understanding our lives today. Fisher accomplished what she'd set out to do: make science useful.

Though Fisher's work is based on rigorous research, she sometimes is criticized by fellow anthropologists for "popularizing" her work. "I will never understand," she said. "Germaine Greer said, 'Why is it that academics feel that in order to be believable they have to be grim?' It's true, and I'm trying to buck that."

Fisher wants her work to be both useful and entertaining because, she said, "Entertainment is a critical part of learning."

Many of her colleagues agree. In 1985, Fisher received the American Anthropological Association's "Distinguished Service Award." The award reads in part: "In the tradition of Margaret Mead, you are bringing the findings and insights of anthropology to the American public and the readers of the world."

Today Fisher is the veteran of hundreds of radio and television appearances. When she is not at the museum or in her home office, working on new ideas, she's out lecturing or consulting with businesses. "I'm just as likely to call you from an airport in Miami as from my office," she said.

Fisher thrives on the freedom, the variety, and the action her go-it-alone career provides. But when she set out to become a non-academic academic, she could find no role models. She asked two of her graduate school professors for advice, but "they both looked blank," she recalled.

Without a guide or a map, Fisher had to pave her own career path. She followed her interests and abilities: she loved anthropology, she was interested in people, and she'd always been a good public speaker. "It came together for me," she said "which I think is what happens. You have all these strands of interests as a child, and they come together as a braid."

Fisher has needed plenty of pluck and determination to make a go of it as a freelance academic, for her life is not without stress. "There's no tenure in my business," she said. "As they say in show business, I'm only as good as my last performance."

While being a woman worked to her detriment at the publishing company, Fisher has found her gender helpful in the work she has done since. "Men in high places often have a great deal of respect for a woman who works hard and is also a woman," she said. "I've haven't tried to be a man."

And she thinks that as a female she is a more credible spokesperson for her theories. "I am a woman who talks about the evolution of divorce and adultery," she said, "and I do not think a man could have talked about it."

But Fisher, who is a founding member of the National Organization of Men, does not consider herself "politically correct." She toes no party line. "I make a great effort to be honest and say what science has to say as opposed to what people want to hear," she said.

Indeed, those who prefer to minimize gender differences might not like Fisher's theories about the sexes. Men and women are equal, she argues, but different. Genuine gender differences in the brain today evolved from the division of labor between the sexes eons ago. Women, the nurturers, developed superior verbal skills while men, who stalked the prey, developed mathematical and visual-spatial skills.

Fisher believes nature intended the differences to work to our advantage. In an article in *U.S. News and World Report* she said, "Nature not only intended men and women to put their bodies together; we're meant to put our heads together as well."

The article pictured a bright future: "There's every reason to believe the sexes will enjoy the kind of equality that is a function of our birthright." And Fisher believes her views are in sync with those of most women. "I think a great number of American women enjoy being women, like men, and simply want to get on with having a good profession."

Fisher, who was married briefly while she was in graduate school, acknowledges that she has never made the kind of plans for her personal life that she did for her career. "There's a great many women who, when you ask them what they want to be, say, 'I want a house. I want two children,'" she said. "But I had no plans."

Still, she's had an "exceedingly happy personal life," she said. "I've had the boyfriends I wanted and I've loved living in New York City."

Now Fisher is entering a new phase of her life. "I'm beginning to make personal plans, to create hopes and dreams," she said. She's rented a country house and wants a larger apartment. "And I'm finally ready to build a committed personal relationship. I haven't had the time."

Undoubtedly, Fisher will find a way to balance her new personal pursuits with the ambitious professional agenda she's set for the coming years. "To my horror, I've thought of my next book," she said. She is also at work on a four-part television series for Turner Broadcasting and plans more television projects. And she wants to continue her work on the lecture circuit.

True to her own prescription for success, Fisher is not resting on her laurels, basking in the recognition she's earned for her work. She is looking ahead, planning her next steps, dreaming new dreams. "I feel I'm just beginning," she said.

Whoopi Goldberg

*⁓I believe I'm here for a reason. And I think
a little bit of the reason is to throw little
torches out to the next step to lead
people through the dark.*

Raunchy, four-letter words frequently color her conversations, yet she can hold her own on serious topics ranging from AIDS to apartheid. Some call her difficult and unyielding, but only because she cares about the quality of her work—and the quality of her life. She also cares about the lives of others, from neighbors down the block to society's less fortunate who are forced to make their homes on the street. She's Whoopi Goldberg, one of today's highest-paid actresses—or actor, as she prefers to be called—and she has a story to share that's better than any Hollywood fabrication.

She was born Caryn Johnson and grew up in a New York City housing project, where she lived with her mother and younger brother. By her teens, she was heavily involved in drugs and eventually dropped out of school. "I just wasn't cut out for it," she said of her decision to abandon her education. At the time, she didn't realize she suffered from dyslexia, a learning disability that often left her feeling "retarded" next to fellow class-mates. Goldberg even attributes some of her earliest desires to act as part of that girlhood struggle to find some common ground with her peers.

"I was kind of a weird kid," she recalled. "All I wanted to do was have some way to communicate with people and be friends with people."

This is not to say that her early years were dismal. Urban adventures and cultural experiences brightened many a day because her mother, a nurse and Head Start teacher, was determined her children would have a better life. So she encouraged them to take advantage of opportunities outside their inner-city world—children's ballets, museums, even simple outings to the park.

That encouragement led Goldberg, at the tender age of eight, to the Hudson Guild and the children's theater program which first sparked her interest in acting. But before those young ambitions could take shape, Goldberg was drawn off track. Struggling to kick her narcotics habit, she married her drug counselor at nineteen and gave birth to her daughter, Alexandrea Martin. But the marriage soon fell apart and Goldberg found herself without a means of support for herself and her child.

Hoping to start a new life, she moved to California in 1974, first to San Diego and then to the San Francisco area. For the next seven years she lived on welfare and has never fully recovered from the emotional scars of that "degrading" experience. "Welfare was a way to catch my breath, which is what it's supposed to be," Goldberg said. "It's supposed to give you the ability to sort of settle in and figure out which direction you're going in, and to go. And then get off."

Goldberg feels her experience with welfare demonstrates the system's tendency to wear down individual dignity. Though she often sought employment—from roles in local theater productions to stints as a bricklayer and cosmetician in a mortuary—her caseworkers were intrusive, rude, and accusatory. They often showed up on her doorstep unannounced to spot check her cupboards and otherwise evaluate how she spent the money. Wanting to set a good example for her daughter, Goldberg was careful to report even the pitiful $25 checks she received for her occasional performances, knowing all too well the amount would be deducted from her next check.

One of her happiest memories from that period in life was the moment she realized she was earning enough money to go off welfare. "When they sent me my last check, I sent it back," she

Whoopi Goldberg

said proudly. "I kept my Medi-CAL card and had it framed just to remind me."

All the while Goldberg had been perfecting her craft, first as one of the founding members of the San Diego Repertory Theater and then later with various improvisational troupes. It was during this time that Caryn Johnson became Whoopi Goldberg. "It all started as a joke—Whoopi Cushion," she explained. Then came the French version, Whoopi Cushon. But when her mother told her that no one would ever take her seriously with that name, the actress, who was more than serious about her work, dug into her family history and picked Goldberg as her new surname.

It's not that she was struggling to find herself, for Goldberg, who considers herself a character actress, had identity matters well under control. In fact, she used her own experiences, and that of people she knew, to develop an entire entourage of solo characterizations that eventually paved her road to stardom.

In her act, she would wrap a yellow shirt around her head to portray a nine-year-old black girl who yearns to replace her kinky hair with blond locks because she believes only blondes can appear on *The Love Boat*. In the next moment, Goldberg would transform herself into a junkie with a Ph.D. in literature who hangs out in the unemployment line all day, or a thirteen-year-old surfer girl who gives herself a coat hanger abortion.

Collectively, these characterizations eventually became *The Spook Show*, a one-hour presentation that premiered in Berkeley and then played across the United States and in Europe. By early 1984, Goldberg's critically acclaimed show had reached Off-Broadway—and the attention of prominent director and producer Mike Nichols, who first described her as "one part Elaine May, one part Groucho, one part Ruth Draper, one part Richard Pryor, and five parts never seen before."

Nichols offered her the opportunity to bring her act— renamed *Whoopi Goldberg*—to Broadway's Lyceum Theater. Again, her characterizations received rave reviews from critics, fans, and the likes of director Steven Spielberg, who was so taken by Goldberg that he hired the relatively unknown actress to play the lead role in his upcoming movie adaptation of Alice Walker's novel, *The Color Purple*. Goldberg received an Oscar nomination for her portrayal of Celie, the poor, abused southern black woman who finds her own unconventional brand of love and wisdom.

Sometimes questioned for her choice of roles in such movies as *Burglar*, *Fatal Beauty*, and *Jumpin' Jack Flash*, Goldberg is quick to point out Hollywood's tendency to typecast actors and the relatively slim pickings available for talented actresses, especially if they're black. For example, she has repeatedly asked studios to cast her opposite such respected actors as Dustin Hoffman. The typical response, according to Goldberg: "Well, you can only do a comedy. You can't do a love scene because nobody's ready (for an interracial love story)."

But ever ready to test convention, Goldberg in 1993 starred in the romantic comedy *Made in America* opposite actor Ted Danson, with whom the tabloids reported she was also carrying on an off-screen romance.

Other important roles for Goldberg have included *Ghost*, which won her an Academy Award for Best Supporting Actress and reversed her post-*Color Purple* career slump, and *Sarafina!*, which cast her as an inspirational educator in apartheid-torn Soweto, South Africa. But *Sister Act*, the surprise Disney hit that featured Goldberg as a Mafia informant hiding out in a convent, is the film credited with fully reinstating her star status.

Now considered one of the most powerful women in Hollywood, Goldberg is serious about the responsibility that comes with her increasing visibility. "I now have a voice that is heard above the din," she said. "I feel like I have to do something. Because I believe at some point I'm going to find myself in need of the services that I sent out letters about or go and appear for. And I want some dignity involved. I don't want to be talked down to anymore, I don't want to be dealt with like a non-entity. And I don't want other people to have to feel like that."

As a testament to her commitment, Goldberg regularly co-hosts *Comic Relief*, televised to raise awareness for the homeless, with Robin Williams and Billy Crystal. AIDS and racial issues are other important concerns on Goldberg's agenda because they have touched her own life.

"Living in San Francisco and Berkeley for as long as I did, we knew about AIDS before the rest of the nation knew about it," she said, "and friends were dropping like flies, and we didn't know why, and we didn't know what it was, and we couldn't make them comfortable, and we couldn't get them any help." With the amount of information about the fatal disease available today, Goldberg wonders why so many are reluctant to help.

Though similarly frustrated by racial tensions that have broken out in Los Angeles and elsewhere, Goldberg boils her thoughts down to simple truths. "I figure, you look at me and you see I'm black," she said. "I don't have to say it. That's the way I was raised, I just am. But what I am is a humanist before anything—before I'm a Jew, before I'm black, before I'm a woman. And my beliefs are for the human race—they don't exclude anyone."

Aside from acting in movies and acting on her strongly held beliefs, Goldberg has made time for a variety of other projects, including her role as Guinan, the psychic bartender in *Star Trek: The Next Generation,* and a voice role in the cartoon series *Captain Planet and the Planeteers.* She has even hosted her own syndicated talk show, *The Whoopi Goldberg Show,* which aired during the 1992–93 season.

Though praised by the critics, the show, which features Goldberg talking with one guest each weeknight and two on Saturday—without the help of a backup band, studio audience, special announcer, or gimmicks—did not draw audiences away from the likes of David Letterman, Jay Leno, and Arsenio Hall. While Goldberg herself acknowledges that the program may not have boosted her career, she enjoyed the opportunity to find out what was on the minds of people like white supremacist Thomas Metzger, Senator Dianne Feinstein, and Al Gore when he was still running for vice president.

Goldberg's latest efforts include a foray into the advertising world, first in print through a popular Gap advertisement that featured four generations of her family, and more recently a role as the voice-over for commercials produced by Avon Products, Inc. Goldberg is careful about her association with the advertising community and candidly acknowledges that she does them for her own reasons.

The Gap ad, for example, began to run in magazines about the time her daughter, who was fifteen then, gave birth to granddaughter Amarah Skye. Goldberg figured the tabloids would have a field day with the celebrity's-child-gone-awry story and preempted the shoddy coverage by being very forthcoming with the news.

"I told my daughter 'we'd go through this together,'" she said.

Although an emotionally trying episode in her life, Goldberg views it as just another reminder that even celebrities, flush with fame and fortune, are not immune to pain. The unexpected pregnancy was a positive learning experience for her and her daughter, Goldberg said, and she feels blessed to have a new addition to her family.

She is equally contemplative about other aspects of her private life, which she admits has never been easy. Her brief second marriage to a Dutch cinematographer ended in 1988, leaving Goldberg somewhat skeptical about the prospects of ever remarrying. "Relationships are difficult for me because there are buttons, big and easy to push, that can send me into a tailspin," she said. "But less so now that I've gotten older, and because I actually know that regardless of whether those people like me or not, I am an okay person."

To those who know Goldberg personally, she's more than okay. Fellow actor Mathew Modine, for example, offers this insight into the actress: "When she says, 'You know,' it's not because she doesn't. It's not a colloquialism. She is addressing your intelligence, your imagination, your compassion. She is the kind of person who can tell anybody to wake up and smell the root cellar from which they came. And then wink."

This ability to laugh at others and herself has earned Goldberg the respect of the public, as well as her peers. Funny, smart, compassionate, and real, she believes in simple human dignity and lives her life accordingly. "I believe I'm here for a reason," she said. "And I think a little bit of the reason is to throw little torches out to the next step to lead people through the dark."

Cathy Guisewite

Different comic strips have different functions. Mine is—especially for women—to let them feel they are not alone.

Cathy the cartoon character is about to face a new day.

"My hair will work today," she tells herself from under the covers. "Something in my closet will look great...My makeup will come out exactly the way it did the one time it looked perfect."

About to jump out of bed, her affirmations continue: "My thighs will have shrunk in the night...I won't have to root through the dishwasher for a semi-clean coffee mug...I will be able to get ready in twenty minutes instead of the full hour and a half it always takes..."

Cathy Guisewite the comic strip writer invented Cathy, her alter ego, by making light of life as a single, thirtyish, career woman waiting for Mr. Right. Her escapades mirror Guisewite's life—but not exactly.

For instance, it took three years for the trauma of a high school reunion to filter into the *Cathy* comic strip. "But if I meet someone, she might meet someone," Guisewite said of her alter ego. "And if I'm traveling a lot, I tend to send Cathy on a business trip."

Once Guisewite left a boyfriend in the middle of an argument because she wanted to jot down the details of their debate. But she swears she never incorporates last week's date into the comic strip—at least not the way it actually happened. Most of the situations and characters she depicts are composites—part reality, part artistic license.

Along with a mother who drives her crazy and a problem boss, Cathy of the comics is known to overeat and overshop—a bit like Guisewite, but not exactly.

"I think my job is to offer a couple minutes of relief during the day," said Guisewite, who has been blending angst with humor since 1976 when *Cathy* first appeared in newspapers.

"Different comic strips have different functions," she explained. "Mine is—especially for women—to let them feel they are not alone." Guisewite wants readers thinking: "I'm not the only woman who balances my checkbook by switching banks and starting all over. I'm not the only woman who buys $50 of fresh fruit and vegetables at the grocery store, and then stops at McDonald's for a Big Mac on the way home."

Cathy's mom is no better. She's the type who diets with her daughter one minute, then rushes over with a pie because Cathy is depressed. Over the years, the strip has featured an assortment of characters who people Cathy's life, chief among them her even-tempered dad and her best friend, Andrea, an ardent feminist who plays counterpoint to Cathy, a junior executive who irons shirts for chauvinistic boyfriends.

Guisewite draws the two friends from aspects of herself: Andrea is her conscience; Cathy is pure emotion. Like most women, Guisewite struggles to find some middle ground between these two forces.

On top of these neurotic conflicts, Cathy's eternal optimism makes her the most endearing character in the comics since *Peanuts*. It's why things like having only 14 cents in her checking account a week before payday never get her down. Cathy comes across so human because her creator delves into the four basic guilt groups: food, love, mother, and career.

"*Cathy* is really my point of view on the world, and it's the only point of view I've got," said Guisewite, who claims she writes about things she's truly thinking, going through, or having anxiety attacks over—not just because these issues are funny, but because they ring most true with her readers.

At first Guisewite was reluctant to name the comic strip character after herself, so she bought a book of baby names for inspiration. But nothing seemed to quite fit. Maybe it was because the character resembled her a little physically, explained Guisewite, who shares Cathy's long straight hair, large expressive eyes, and ready smile.

"She had to be Cathy, to be, well, me," said Guisewite. "She's so close to how I think. Using the same name can be a little embarrassing at times, but it helps me to keep her true to life."

But how did Cathy jump from her creator's imagination to the pages of more than one thousand daily newspapers? Guisewite had a big boost from a lady who knows talent when she sees it—even if it is her own daughter's. After all, what are mothers for?

When Guisewite, now in her forties, was first on her own, working in advertising as a writer for television commercials, her career was flourishing, but her love life floundered. "I would try to meet men and nothing would happen," Guisewite recalled. "Or I'd meet men I just didn't want to go out with at all."

Frustrated with this state of affairs, Guisewite would spend evenings at home, pouring her feelings into a diary. The practice was a throwback to childhood, when Guisewite's mother had told her to write feelings down, rather than sharing them with people.

"One night, instead of just writing about it, I drew a stick figure of what I looked like sitting there writing these depressing things and eating everything in the kitchen," said Guisewite, who was fifty pounds overweight at the time.

Just to let her mother know she was coping with life in her usual way, Guisewite sent home the drawing with a clever caption. Soon she was making a habit of sorting out the day's events by creating comics to send to her mom. One series of sketches, which later became an early comic strip, depicted her anxiously eating everything in sight while waiting for the telephone to ring; she packed away three bagels, two bowls of fudge ripple ice cream, thirty-seven Oreos, and a Twinkie.

"So what?" Guisewite had Cathy say. "He'll never call me again." When the phone rings, she adds: "At least not after he sees me tonight."

Anne Guisewite thought the feelings her daughter captured in caricature were universal—and suggested that she try to market

Cathy Guisewite

them. Cathy Guisewite was less than enthusiastic: "I was humiliated by that concept," she said. "It was very personal stuff and me at my worst."

But Anne wasn't about to let a little embarrassment hold her

Cathy back, so she took it on herself to go to the library and research comic strip syndicates. Then she composed a list of markets she thought would be receptive to her daughter's work.

Faced with the prospect of having her work mailed off with a letter from her mother, Guisewite assembled eighteen samples. "Just to get her off my back, I finally sent my drawings to the name on the top of her list," she recalled.

Never mind that Guisewite's drawings were rudimentary or that she was content as a vice president at an ad agency. Once again, her mother butted in—or helped out, as the case may be. "Mom bought me a how-to-draw-cartoons book that helped me get started," Guisewite said. "Mom has always believed that her children can do anything; lack of training is just a detail to be overcome."

When Universal Press Syndicate received Guisewite's samples, they signed her up right away. It didn't matter that her work wasn't in the right form, because she offered something they had been looking for: a comic strip dealing with what it's like to be a young, single, working woman. But until *Cathy* showed up, they hadn't found anything with the ring of honesty that Guisewite offered.

Such instant success was a fluke. "Cartoonists generally work for years developing strips," Guisewite explained. "Mine was a very bizarre and lucky situation."

Even after all these years, Guisewite marvels at her good fortune and feels honored to have a chunk of the limited space that's available in newspapers today. "There are thousands of people fighting for the same space," said Guisewite. "And I feel a real obligation...a weekly pressure to live up to the standards people expect."

Although the strip is often only four panels with a punchy ending, Guisewite typically spends many hours writing it. "I throw out a lot, and I rework it a lot," she said, explaining that unlike most comic strips, *Cathy* is more word-oriented than art-oriented.

Despite her continuing success, Guisewite admits she's never completely sure that what she's created is good, and true to her character, she often obsesses on what would make it better. "I feel that ability to torture myself is one of the qualities that makes it possible for me to write this strip," said Guisewite, laughing. "It's what people identify with. It's part of the package."

The pressure to be perfect, a theme that frequently pops up between the cartoon Cathy and her mother, is rooted in real-life experiences. Anne Guisewite has never been a cookie-baking, apron-clad mom—the kind that Guisewite longed for and therefore presents in the comic strip.

Guisewite remembers that her mother was always on the move, taking her three daughters to art museums and foreign films. "I hated everything she dragged us to," said Guisewite, the middle child. But these cultural excursions weren't the half of it; Anne also encouraged her girls to make greeting cards and illustrate miniature books as gifts. On their completion, she would declare the work worthy of publication.

In fact, she saved Guisewite's childhood drawings and even sent her first story, written at age six, to a magazine. The rejection slip is now one of the cartoonist's favorite keepsakes. "Most mothers tape their children's work to the refrigerator door," said Guisewite. "Mine would send them off the Museum of Modern Art."

Ever the proud and determined mom, Anne Guisewite didn't give up, even as her girls were growing up. When Guisewite was at the University of Michigan, where she received a degree in English, she exhibited a flair for humor by writing *A College Girl's Mother's Guide to Survival*. It was a Mother's Day gift to Anne, who proceeded to mail it to the American Greetings Corporation. Although the company was initially enthusiastic, they never published the work.

These days Guisewite is a slim size five, having long since lost the weight that perpetually plagues the comic strip Cathy. Still, Guisewite can abuse food with the best of them and she often weaves this eternal female conflict into *Cathy* illustrations, which by now have developed a life of their own.

Guisewite has published collections of past comic strips in book form, composing titles that are pure Cathy: *Two Pies, One Fork; Sorry I'm Late, My Hair Won't Start; Thin Thighs in Thirty Years; It Must Be Love, My Face Is Breaking Out; Revelations From a 45-Pound Purse;* and *What Do You Mean, I Still Don't Have Equal Rights??!!*—to name just a few.

Cathy's first television special aired on CBS in May 1987, with

Guisewite's father supplying the voice of the character's dad. The show won an Emmy Award for the best prime-time animated program. A second TV special, *Cathy's Last Resort,* aired in November 1988.

Guisewite now produces a diverse line of novelty products for Cathy lovers—everything from daily planners, to aprons, to sweatshirts, to wall hangings, all featuring the comic strip character with captions such as "Love is Non-Fattening."

Yet the course of Guisewite's love life is still unclear. By necessity, her relationships with men are subordinate to her career, although she attracts financially secure types who are busy with their own lives. "I require less from a man in the sense that I'm not waiting around at 5:30, wondering what to do with the evening," said Guisewite, claiming that if she gets an idea, she much prefers working on it to going on a date.

Which doesn't make her mom too happy. Anne Guisewite still would like to see her daughter married—she wants grandchildren. "Mom sends me conflicting messages," said Guisewite. "If she calls on a Saturday night and I'm working, she'll say, 'Oh, Cathy, you're young! You should be going out!' But if she calls and I have a date, she'll say, 'What about your wonderful career?'"

As one would expect, this cartoonist isn't about to let good material like that go to waste, because it's these inconsistencies and ironies that inspire some of the most funny, touching episodes in *Cathy.* For example, Cathy's mother once operated a dating service, hoping to find her daughter a mate—but things backfired when the computer paired Cathy with a married man.

For her part, Anne Guisewite has continued to be the supportive mom by being good-natured about seeing herself portrayed saving twist ties and tinfoil. And she accepts that anything she does may end up exaggerated in newspapers across the country.

"We're open about the mother-daughter trauma that exists between us," said Guisewite. "It's a real combination of love and devotion and just total anxiety."

Even though her stock-in-trade is angst, confusion, and obsession, Guisewite has actually gotten her life under control. Everything from her appearance to her studio is ultra neat—not at all like the Cathy who must root through the dishwasher in search of a semi-clean coffee cup.

So now, one wonders, where does Guisewite get the inspiration for Cathy's craziness? She often listens to depressing music, visits malls, flips through women's magazines, and yes, sometimes in desperation, she'll even resort to calling her mother.

With an income that's in the six-figure range, Guisewite has all but forgotten her early reservations about trying to make it as a cartoonist. It's a great career, she said, because it's a wonderful way of expressing yourself. But she also cautions anyone trying to break into the profession not to copy existing comics, because the syndicates always seek new voices.

Asked to name her professional role models, Guisewite cites Charles Schulz as a key influence. "I feel that *Peanuts* really paved the way on the comic pages for a strip like mine," she said. "It was the first strip that dealt with real human feelings, real insecurities, and frustrations in the comic pages." Guisewite said the thing she admires most about Schulz is that he's still excited to go to work every morning.

As for her own work habits, Guisewite admits to being a passionate workaholic, and says she drives herself so that she'll have time to work harder. "They say success is the end of hope," she mused, "and it sort of is."

Guisewite's efforts have paid off in more ways than money. In 1982, she received the Outstanding Communicator of the Year Award from Los Angeles Advertising Women, and she was included in a San Mateo, California, museum exhibit as one of "ten influential twentieth-century cartoon artists." In a *World Almanac and Book of Facts* poll by editors at daily newspapers across the country, Guisewite was selected as one of "America's Twenty-Five Most Influential Women" in 1984 and in 1986.

Writing *Cathy* has taught Guisewite one of the great lessons of life: "Anything is possible if you listen to your mother."

Bernadine Healy

∼I've never felt like one of the boys. It doesn't matter to me that the club is angry with me, because I've never been a member.

The sickest patient that doctor Bernadine Healy ever tried to heal was the National Institutes of Health. When she was named NIH director in 1991, the $10 billion agency, which ranks as the world's largest biomedical organization, was desperately needing a strong dose of leadership.

Accepting a job that nobody seemed to want—the post had been empty for nearly two years—Healy, the first female director in the agency's 104-year history, joked that "things were so bad they couldn't find a man to take the job." By the time this forty-six-year-old cardiologist stepped to the helm, much of the authority the post entailed had been encroached on by the directors of NIH's individual institutes. Comprised of sixteen institutes, each with unique goals and needs, and housing some four thousand scientists, the NIH is charged with shaping the nation's research agenda and ensuring that America maintains global domination in medical science.

Healy's predecessor had been forced to resign during the Bush administration, partly for not opposing abortion. But from day one, Healy made it clear she would not bow to such pressures. Nor was there any doubt she would have her hands full between the formidable politics in Washington, uncompetitive government salaries for researchers, and the iron hand of

87

America's medical establishment.

During her first year on the job, a time when many incoming directors redecorate their offices and survey the political climate, the tenacious Healy plunged boldly into one fire storm after another.

Recognizing that women had been categorically excluded at the NIH—from research studies and from senior staff positions—Healy chose as one of her first acts to announce a $600 million, 14-year study of the effects of lifestyle changes and hormone therapy on older women's health problems, chiefly ovarian cancer, osteoporosis, and heart disease. (Although heart disease afflicts both sexes, the NIH had never studied female subjects.) Healy also reversed another historic imbalance by appointing women to top-level posts at the NIH.

That was only the beginning of a controversial two-year reign some criticized as tyrannical and others praised as pivotal. For her part, Healy seemed to take the critiques in stride. "You can't be NIH director if you want to be loved," she once said. Time and again, she proved she wasn't about to back down, even when her course of action clearly made her unpopular.

For example, realizing that government scientists had helped discover the AIDS-fighting drug AZT, Healy gave a nonexclusive patent to a generic-pharmaceutical company, in an effort to force down the drug's price. The move prompted a court battle with Burroughs Wellcome, the company that originally monopolized the AZT market.

In another instance, Healy's decision to support a new NIH practice of seeking patents on pieces of genes ignited a bitter battle with James D. Watson, the Nobel laureate who co-discovered DNA and was the head of the NIH's human genome project, which aims to map all of the estimated fifty thousand to one hundred thousand genes in the human body. The debate ended with the geneticist resigning.

Healy also pushed for surveying teen sex behavior and researching the use of fetal tissue, but was overruled on both. In another move, she stirred up the NIH's parent organization, the Health and Human Services Department, as well as the scientific community by proposing a grandiose strategic plan for all biomedical research.

"I do not believe in kneeling at the altar of consensus," she said after angering bureaucrats below her by investigating how the NIH handled several volatile misconduct cases and by taking action to ease out two top male NIH officials.

"I've never felt like one of the boys," she said. "It doesn't matter to me that the club is angry with me, because I've never been a member."

Healy's breakneck pace and head-strong style prompted disgruntled colleagues to nickname her "She Who Must Be Obeyed." While critics debated her methods, no one could argue that the NIH, which had floundered after so many months without a permanent head, demanded the kind of dedication and determination Healy brought to the job.

"Dr. Healy has pluses and minuses, but her pluses far outweigh her minuses," said a top official at the Health and Human Services Department.

Others speculated that Healy's detractors resented having a woman running the once male bastion. As one NIH scientist put it, "She acts swiftly and decisively, and some people get intimidated by that because she's a woman. When you get a guy who acts that way, it's leadership."

If the constant analysis of her every move bothered Healy, she never let on. "When you make decisions, you get more than criticized," she once said. "You become cannon fodder." Still, Healy never weakened in her resolve to "make this place better."

Her vision for the NIH was unabashedly expansionist: "The single most gaping failure of NIH today is that it has not become a truly visible public and policy priority." Historically the director's job had attracted anonymous, ivory-tower types—not a go-getter like Healy with her openly ambitious agenda.

But then, it's hard to imagine Healy taking any other approach. A cardiologist who's renowned for her research into the pathology of heart attacks, Healy credits her ambition and aspirations to a father who taught her that women deserve every opportunity open to men.

Bernadine Patricia Healy was the second of four daughters born to second-generation Irish Americans. She grew up in Long Island City, a middle-class section of Queens, New York, where

Bernadine Healy

her parents ran a perfume oil factory from their basement.

Even as a child, Healy knew she wanted to help people when she grew up, and saw herself as either a nun or a doctor. But her father dissuaded her from the convent, pointing out that she was too independent for that. "You can't be a nun," he told her, "you'd always be taking orders from a priest."

Healy fondly remembers her father—a man who never went to school beyond the third grade—as a progressive renegade of sorts. "The prevailing notion then was that you shouldn't over-educate a woman," Healy explained, "because her major role was to be a good Catholic mother, and if you get her too educated, she might have other ideas."

Her father broke church tradition by sending his daughters to Hunter College High School, an elite public school in New York City. "It was a school for girl eggheads, and our notion of an after-school activity was the philosophy club," Healy recalled. After graduating first in her class, Healy attended Vassar on a scholarship. Majoring in chemistry and minoring in philosophy, she graduated summa cum laude three years later. Never dating until college, Healy attributes her inner security to the experience of spending her early years at all-girl schools.

At Harvard University Medical School, Healy was among ten women in a class of one hundred and twenty; she graduated cum laude in 1970. It was at Harvard that she first encountered sexism when some teachers made obscene jokes and fellow students chided her for depriving a man of the coveted opportunity to attend the prestigious school.

Such comments didn't get Healy down. "After my years in women's schools, I just thought it was silly," she explained. Little did the sheltered Healy realize that the attitudes she was associating with her Harvard colleagues actually pervaded society. Nor could she imagine these attitudes would resurface with particular virulence as she built her career.

Healy completed her internship and residency at Johns Hopkins University in 1972, then spent two years as a fellow in pathology at NIH's National Heart, Lung, and Blood Institute. Returning to Johns Hopkins, she became a fellow in the cardiovascular division of the School of Medicine, where she was a professor. As director of the Coronary Care Unit from 1977 to 1984 and the school's first female assistant dean of postdoctoral programs, Healy juggled teaching, cardiovascular research, writing, and treating patients. Equally important, she established a reputation as a highly creative professional capable of forging new directions in research.

She was also known as an energetic joiner—the type who volunteered for thankless hours on the dean's committee. "I guess I tended to see those administrative issues, often seen as dreary work burdens, in terms of their broader policy implications," she explained. Besides demonstrating management skills, she began to develop her own ideas about how doctors could benefit patients, both through treatment and through instituting effective policies.

Healy's well-intentioned tactics eventually made her the target of students who spoofed her in an obscene comedy revue staged by an all-male club. She was not amused. "It would be one thing if a men's club got together and wrote degrading, pornographic things about each other," Healy said. "But when they started…to bring women faculty into it, I thought it was offensive."

In typical fashion, she moved swiftly, calling a meeting of the club's officers. "I went around the table and questioned their integrity, their sensitivity, their character," she said later. "I made every one of them answer how they would have felt if the skit was about their sister, their mother, or their wife."

Healy left Johns Hopkins in 1984 when President Reagan appointed her deputy director of the White House Office of Science and Technology Policy. The following year, the Cleveland Clinic Foundation hired her to head its research institute—which doubled in size during the five years Healy ran it. Her job entailed directing the research efforts of nine departments, among them cardiology, immunology, and cancer.

While at the foundation, Healy and some of her colleagues voluntarily agreed not to invest in or serve as paid consultants for companies whose drugs they were testing. The move was prompted after an article in the *New England Journal of Medicine* mentioned Healy and others as stockholders in a company that produces a clot-dissolving drug she had researched while at Johns Hopkins.

Healy met the controversy head-on. She defended herself by explaining that although she had helped design the study, she'd left Johns Hopkins by the time patients began taking part in the research. "We want to eliminate even the perception or hint that what scientists are doing is for personal gain, instead of for the betterment of patients," Healy said at the time.

Healy's belief that patients come first has been a guiding force during her career. For instance, in 1988, after becoming president of the American Heart Association, she initiated an innovative study of heart disease that ultimately contradicted the common notion that women's complaints about chest pains were emotional or inconsequential. "The problem is to convince both the lay and medical sectors that coronary heart disease is also a woman's disease—not a man's disease in disguise," Healy said.

Similarly, when she took over at NIH, Healy was determined to address practices that had allowed research studies to occur chaotically, and sometimes in secret. She wanted the process out in the open by getting scientists more involved. When some scientists raised concerns that tighter controls would inhibit research, Healy argued that scientific advances couldn't flourish under free-for-all conditions. "Priorities have always been set for research," she said. "The NIH does not exist to do science for science's sake—but to do science in service of the public, to improve the health of 250 million Americans."

Healy still has her eye on those millions of Americans, but her focus has changed somewhat. Since leaving the NIH in June 1993, she has become one of the major Republican voices in the health care reform debate. Healy is an advocate of universal and portable health insurance coverage, as well as malpractice and small market insurance reforms designed to lower health costs. She has criticized the Clinton health care reform plan, which she's said "will lead to health care rationing, a huge new federal bureaucracy, job-killing payroll taxes, and a loss of patient privacy."

In September 1993, Healy, a life-long Republican, announced her candidacy for the U.S. Senate from Ohio. She cites health care reform, crime control, reducing taxes and federal spending, and reforming the way Congress works as her top issues in the race.

Although Healy has a reputation for being an intimidating, even combative opponent, she has many fans who describe her as warm and personable. A female cardiologist who studied under her at Johns Hopkins said of Healy, "She's a strong figure, and there were always people around who found her threatening. But she was a supportive, encouraging mentor." Likewise, Dr. Edward Schuster, an admiring Connecticut cardiologist who also studied under Healy, said, "Many people who worked with Bernadine would jump off a bridge for her, including me—and I was a chauvinistic pig when I met her."

An ardent feminist, Healy learned to work Washington society with finesse. Not long after she started at the NIH, Healy was introduced to General Colin Powell, then Chairman of the Joint Chiefs of Staff. "He smiled," she recalled, "shook my hand strongly and said, 'Welcome to the NFL!' I had to laugh because for years I used an analogy of brain power versus muscle power."

As Healy's medical career climbed, she had often remarked that women could compete just as well as men when it came to being doctors—but not football players. So the meaning of Powell's jesting remark was not lost on Healy, who knew her new job would pit her against the male medical establishment, not to mention Washington's back stabbers and deal makers. She realized, "Now that I'm here and it's brawn and muscle, I guess I have to compete with greater wit and brainpower."

She did just that, prompting the press on more than one occasion to take note of her humor. For instance, one night at a black-tie White House dinner of Washington power brokers and reporters, Healy exchanged clever one-liners with TV talk show host John McLaughlin as they negotiated the terms of an appearance on his show. "You're lace-curtain Irish," McLaughlin told her, clearly charmed by this feisty blond who carries herself with elegance and poise.

Despite enormous achievements, Healy's ambitious career exacts a toll. During her NIH tenure, for example, she divided her time between Washington and Ohio. Staying in a house on NIH grounds during the work week, she'd grab a plane on Friday nights, heading home to an affluent suburb of Cleveland to be with her husband and two school-age daughters. Bartlett Ann Bulkley is from Healy's marriage to surgeon George Bulkley, whom she divorced in 1981, and Marie McGrath Loop is the daughter of her present husband, cardiologist Floyd

Loop, chairman of the Cleveland Clinic Foundation—and one of Healy's strongest supporters.

"The one thing she has is true grit," Loop said. "You don't see that a lot in Washington. Lots of people are going along to get along. But she is not that way at all."

Determined to protect her family's privacy, Healy is pointedly guarded about her personal life. But there are occasional clues, such as the photo she kept in her office of the girls nestling up to their mom the day of Healy's NIH inauguration.

So how does this dynamic doctor manage her demanding lifestyle? "I have very good help," she said, laughing. "The children bring you back to reality. When the chicken burns, that's the most important thing in the world right then."

Charlayne Hunter-Gault

*~Their rocks, their bricks, their spit never touched
me, because in my head I was an African queen.*

Never mind that her high school guidance counselor advised her
to become a teacher. Never mind that while growing up, her professional role model wasn't a real person but a comic strip character, the feisty newswoman Brenda Starr. Most of all, never
mind that the University of Georgia, which had been educating
the state's white children almost since the Revolutionary War,
only allowed blacks to clean its classrooms—not learn in them.

In 1959, none of that mattered to Charlayne Hunter-Gault.
What did matter to the bright, determined young black woman
as she finished her senior year with honors at Atlanta's Henry
McNeal Turner High School was her future. Hunter-Gault, who
was editor of her school's newspaper, *The Green Light,* knew she
wanted to be a newswoman like her comic strip hero—and the
University of Georgia was the only college in the state with a
journalism school. So, along with high school friend and fellow
black student Hamilton Holmes, Hunter-Gault did what was
unthinkable for most people in the segregated heart of Dixie:
She applied for—and eventually won—admission to the
University of Georgia.

Such boldness earned Hunter-Gault a permanent place in U.S.
civil rights history as the first black woman to attend the
University of Georgia. But more important than gaining civil
rights fame, Hunter-Gault had earned the opportunity to pur-

sue and fulfill her professional dreams.

In the thirty-plus years since she challenged the university's bigotry and broke its racial barrier, Hunter-Gault has crafted an award-winning career in print and broadcast journalism. Admired equally by peers and the people she covers, Hunter-Gault has developed an impressive reputation for incisive and compassionate reporting on major issues of our time. Whether she's assessing the quality of health care for the poor in the United States, dissecting the effects of apartheid on blacks and whites in South Africa, or detailing the impact of famine and war in Somalia, Hunter-Gault is known for first-rate reporting that adds depth, candor, and perspective to the media's more common journalistic fare.

A striking woman with a charmingly disarming style, Hunter-Gault has demonstrated throughout her career the same tenacious spirit that propelled her as a teenager with a dream—and the courage—to challenge the racist practices of a Southern white institution.

"It was just the spirit and the atmosphere of the times that you broke barriers," Hunter-Gault now says modestly of her integration battle. "I did not set out with a global aim. There was something to be done—and it turned out to have monumental consequences, but it was my effort to secure for myself the type of education I needed."

At the time, many people in the state of Georgia didn't care about the educational needs of a black girl. The Civil Rights Movement was still in its infancy in 1959. The Rev. Dr. Martin Luther King's Southern Christian Leadership Conference organization was only two years old, and the University of Georgia wasn't about to voluntarily break racist Southern tradition and accept any black student, regardless of talent or intellect.

Backed by a prominent group of Atlanta civil rights activists, Hunter-Gault and Holmes turned to the federal courts to ensure they got the education they wanted and deserved, asking that the government require the University of Georgia to enroll them. The ensuing court battle lasted two years, during which Hunter-Gault attended Wayne State University in Detroit, Michigan.

She and Holmes eventually won their case. A federal judge

Charlayne Hunter-Gault

ordered the University of Georgia to integrate, and in January 1961, the former high school classmates became the first blacks in history to walk the university's halls as students. Recalling that moment, Hunter-Gault said: "At the time, I wasn't happy with the celebrity that followed because I felt that, but for the color of my skin, getting accepted to college was a fairly routine exercise."

College proved anything but routine for Hunter-Gault. During her second night on campus, a group of openly hostile students gathered outside her dormitory, chanting, "Two, four, six, eight, we don't want to integrate" and "Nigger go home." When demonstrators began throwing rocks, police resorted to tear gas to disperse the crowd.

"I stayed in my room, unpacking my clothes, being calm, thinking to myself, 'So this is what it feels like to be in the middle of a riot,'" Hunter-Gault recalled. "As I was unpacking, a brick flew through the window, splattering glass all over my new college clothes."

In the wake of the riots, the university suspended Hunter-Gault and Holmes, who was living off campus, supposedly for their own safety. But their lawyers intervened and they were readmitted the next day. Two years later, in 1963, Hunter-Gault received her bachelor's degree in journalism.

Hunter-Gault credits her family with giving her the strength, poise, and confidence to earn her education on her own terms. "My whole family was really remarkable," she said. "They were all smart people."

The oldest of three children, Hunter-Gault was born in 1942 in Due West, South Carolina. Her father, Charles S. H. Hunter Jr., was a Methodist chaplain in the U.S. Army, so he was often posted on long tours of duty abroad.

In 1954, the family moved to Atlanta where her mother, Althea Hunter, took a job as a secretary in a real estate firm. With a father who was rarely home, Hunter-Gault and her two younger brothers were reared largely by her mother and a grandmother who strongly influenced her.

Hunter-Gault remembers her grandmother as an energetic, inquisitive woman who, despite a formal education that ended in the third grade, never stopped learning. She was a voracious reader who loved to travel, and she often took her granddaughter along.

"She used to read three newspapers a day," Hunter-Gault recalled. "She was innately curious about the world. She was intrepid and strong. But she was also very gentle, and I think I owe a lot of my character to her."

Hunter-Gault's mother is an equally avid reader (she still devours four or five books a week). And Hunter-Gault remembers her father as a brilliant intellect. "He was an important part of my life and development because he set standards for me that were very high. And I was aware of what his expectations were," she said. "It never occurred to me to try to diminish those expectations."

During her fight to get into—and graduate from—the University of Georgia, Hunter-Gault's upbringing helped her retain the resolve to achieve her goal. "My mind was set on doing this, and it never occurred to me to leave," she said. "Their rocks, their bricks, their spit never touched me, because in my head I was an African queen."

As she fought for her right to the best education Georgia had to offer an aspiring journalist, Hunter-Gault received a real-life education few young reporters ever have a chance at. Being a central character in a major civil rights news story gave Hunter-Gault a unique vantage point from which to witness the best and worst sides of the news media. That experience formed a lasting impression on her own journalistic style.

"I saw how different journalists worked and how I was treated as a story," she said. "There were journalists who were sensitive and I wanted to be like them. On the other hand, there was one reporter who pulled a mob together so that he could film them—he'd missed the real riot."

As a student journalist, Hunter-Gault worked weekends for the *Atlanta Inquirer,* a newspaper founded by college students from around the state who were frustrated by the failure of Atlanta's existing newspapers, black and white, to adequately cover the growing Civil Rights Movement. She had tried briefly to work for the University of Georgia's student newspaper, but the editors "didn't know what to do" with her, she recalled.

While at the university, Hunter-Gault also got married shortly before graduation—in secret to fellow white student Walter Stovall. After graduation, they moved to New York City and soon had a daughter, Susan, who's now an aspiring singer.

"The reason we got married was the reason most people get married: they are in love with each other," Hunter-Gault said. "We felt that we had to be very special if it could flourish under those stressful conditions, and in point of fact, it was very special."

Several years later, though, Hunter-Gault and Stovall divorced amicably. (She remarried in 1971 to Ronald Gault, a black Chicagoan who specializes in public finance. They have a teenage son, Chuma, and live in New York.)

"Socially, politically we were very much in sync," she said of her young marriage to Stovall. "But Walter wasn't in much of a hurry, and I was. I was out to prove to the world that I should be famous and not because I was black."

Hunter-Gault began her road to professional fame at *The New Yorker*, one of the country's most prestigious magazines. Shortly after graduating from college, she was hired by the magazine as a secretary, with the understanding that she would eventually be offered writing assignments. A year later Hunter-Gault was promoted to staff writer, making her the first black to write for the magazine's "Talk of the Town" column; she also occasionally contributed short stories.

Hunter-Gault left *The New Yorker* in 1967 after winning a Russell Sage Fellowship to study social science at Washington University in St. Louis, Missouri. While there, she edited articles for *Trans-Action* magazine, which eventually sent her to Washington, D.C., to cover the "Poor People's Campaign." A few months later, Hunter-Gault joined the staff of an NBC affiliate television station in Washington as an investigative reporter and anchorwoman for the local evening newscast.

Her career was progressing at a rapid pace. In the following year, 1968, Hunter-Gault joined the metropolitan staff of *The New York Times*, creating the post of Harlem bureau chief and specializing in covering the urban black community. She quickly earned a reputation as a careful reporter with an eye for detail and a keen understanding of the aspirations and frustrations of inner-city blacks. As an urban reporter for the *Times*, Hunter-Gault capitalized on an impressive array of contacts among black leaders that she had gained because of her involvement in the Civil Rights Movement. Those contacts added depth and authority to her reporting.

Arthur Gelb, then the metropolitan desk editor, said Hunter-Gault gave readers "a sense of being on the scene and explaining a complex story during a tense period" in the late 1960s and early 1970s.

Hunter-Gault shared *The New York Times* Publishers Award in 1970 with Joseph Lelyveld for an unusually vivid and disturbing account of the life and death of a twelve-year-old heroin addict. She subsequently won two additional Publishers Awards: in 1974 for "writing under deadline pressure" about Mayor Abraham Beame's nomination of Paul Gibson Jr. as New York City's first black deputy mayor; and in 1976 for "outstanding performance on a beat," particularly for her front-page stories on black crime and the renaming of Harlem's Muslim Mosque for Malcolm X. She also received the National Urban Coalition Award for Distinguished Urban Reporting and, for a piece on teenage unemployment, the Lincoln University Unity Award.

Characteristic of her courage and persistence, Hunter-Gault single-handedly took on the editorial board of the *Times* in the 1970s for insisting that reporters refer to African Americans as "Negroes" rather than "blacks," the term preferred by most civil rights activists. Hunter-Gault wrote an eleven-page memo to the editors protesting that all of her references to blacks were changed to Negroes. In the memo, she assailed the assumptions that her white bosses made about blacks and black news coverage. Openly challenging the newspaper's editorial policies was a daring move. But in response to her eloquent and forceful argument, the *Times* changed its policy.

"Now it seems almost silly," she said of the infamous memo. "But it was one of those defining moments in the history of black journalism in major white institutions."

In 1978, Hunter-Gault left the *Times* to return to broadcast journalism as the third correspondent and swing anchor on public television's *The MacNeil/Lehrer NewsHour.* Hunter-Gault saw the move as a "chance to expand to a broader range of interests."

MacNeil/Lehrer offers a format and approach to news that caters to Hunter-Gault's strengths. The highly regarded national news program delves beneath the day's headlines, exploring events in depth through live interviews with prominent figures and extended on-the-scene reporting and analysis. In 1983, when the show expanded to its current hour-long format, Hunter-Gault was named national correspondent, the position she holds today.

Since joining *MacNeil/Lehrer,* Hunter-Gault also has had a chance to produce award-winning documentaries on public television. Most recently, she was selected as the host for a new public television series called "Rights and Wrongs: Human Rights Television."

In 1986, she received the George Foster Peabody Award, a highlight of her career, for her acclaimed documentary about life in South Africa, "Apartheid's People." The Peabody Awards are broadcast journalism's equivalent to the Pulitzer Prize; but more important to Hunter-Gault, the Peabody Awards are bestowed by her alma mater, the University of Georgia.

"'Apartheid's People' was a high point," Hunter-Gault said, "because it was at once so personal and it was not personal. I like to think that I brought to that the same qualities that I bring to all my stories. I bring all of my instincts and experiences and sensibilities to every story that I do—if not in an objective way—at least in a fair way. But that one was different in the sense that it put me back into a point in time where I was very personally involved. It took me back to the South of the Civil Rights years. Parts of it were like déjà vu.

"I was fair," she said of her coverage, which emphasized apartheid's brutality, "but I was passionate because I saw. And that's what journalism is all about—getting out there and seeing it with your own eyes and being able to tell other people or show other people what you saw. That's all. That's the best you can do."

Another high point of Hunter-Gault's life and career came in June 1988, when she returned to her alma mater as the first black to deliver the University of Georgia's commencement address.

"I think that things came full circle for me when I went back and made the graduation speech," she said. "That was twenty-five years and I had gradually been working up to my final reconciliation with it. I think that may have been the closure of it, but it had taken years.

"I mean, I had gone back to do a documentary on race relations on the campus, and I had gone back and had done a magazine article. And I had been invited back to be on the advisory board of the journalism school. All those were small steps toward reconciliation, but it hadn't happened until I walked across that big, old football stadium that June, with the entire eyes of the campus and all of the ghosts of the past looking on. I knew that we had really reached a significant milestone in the reconciliation between the Georgia we entered and the Georgia I wanted it to be. I mean, it's still not there yet, but there's enough there now that I feel my efforts can bear fruit in a more concrete way than in the past."

With the historic commencement address bringing her full circle, Hunter-Gault has since recounted her life in her recently published memoir, *In My Place.* The book has been described as "a remarkably generous, fair-minded account of overcoming some of the biggest, and most intractable, obstacles ever deployed by Southern racists."

Hunter-Gault maintains that her experiences as a Southern black woman, obstacles and all, have helped fuel her successes as a nationally acclaimed journalist.

"I think being Southern helped me survive in this profession," she said. "Being black and a woman and being in the Civil Rights Movement helped me survive, too. All of those things helped me to forge my armor, because I think you do need a suit of armor, particularly if you're black, if you're a woman, if you're in this kind of business."

Mae Jemison

⌁Never limit yourself because of others' limited imagination; never limit others because of your own limited imagination.

On September 12, 1992, shortly after takeoff of the space shuttle *Endeavor,* Mae Jemison watched her hometown of Chicago pass beneath her. "I went to the window, looked down and, literally, we passed right over it."

One hundred and twenty-seven orbits of the Earth later, Jemison returned to her hometown a hero. Speaking at Morgan Park High School, where she graduated in 1973, the nation's first black woman astronaut told hundreds of students at a homecoming rally to follow their stars—even when others want to hold them back.

"Sometimes people want to tell you to act or to be a certain way," Jemison cautioned. "Never limit yourself because of others' limited imagination; never limit others because of your own limited imagination."

She recalled how people tried to discourage her from pursuing her dream of becoming a scientist and someday soaring into outer space. "Some people say I don't look like an astronaut," she said in a later interview. "But that's okay—'cause I am....all peoples of the world have astronomers, physicists, and explorers."

As a young woman growing up on the South Side of Chicago, Mae Carol Jemison didn't set out to become the first black female astronaut. But neither did she let herself become discouraged by the fact that, at the time, all the nation's astronauts were white and male. She remembers as a child, "looking at the stars, wondering what was up there, knowing I'd go up there someday, though I didn't know how." Later, as she watched telecasts of the Gemini and Apollo space flights, she knew one day she would be aboard. "Very clearly, I was sure I wanted to go into space," she said, "even if there had never been any astronauts, period."

But "being an astronaut isn't something you can plan for," she explained; the chances of being selected are far too slim, because there's no special field to go into to become an astronaut. So Jemison did the only thing she could—she held onto her dream and with both feet planted firmly on the ground, began preparing herself for a career in science and medicine. While some may have questioned the wisdom of such choices for a young black woman growing up in the sixties, Jemison's family was always there to encourage her. Her father, Charlie, was a roofer and carpenter by trade, who in later years worked as a maintenance supervisor at United Charities of Chicago. Her mother, Dorothy, was an elementary school teacher. Jemison also has two older siblings: Ada Jemison Bullock, a child psychiatrist, and Charles Jemison, a Chicago real estate broker.

Born October 17, 1956, in Decatur, Alabama, Jemison was three when her family moved to Chicago. As Jemison grew older, she proved to be an energetic, inquisitive student. But she once confessed, "I didn't get straight As in school like my sister because I was a little rowdy." She did study outside class, however, pursuing her interests in such subjects as anthropology, archaeology, and particularly astronomy.

As early as kindergarten, Jemison knew she wanted to be a scientist. But when she mentioned this to her teacher, the woman summarily dismissed young Jemison's unorthodox ambitions by asking, "Don't you mean a nurse?" But Jemison was undeterred, thanks in large part to parents who encouraged her curiosity. As a result, she said, "I ended up being constantly aware of the world around me."

Jemison didn't spend all her time as a youth in the science lab or gazing at the heavens through a telescope, though. With a trim, athletic build and dazzling smile, Mae Jemison could hardly be stereotyped as the class nerd. In high school, she was a member of the pompon squad and she has nurtured a lifelong passion for dance. In fact, one of the items she carried with her on the *Endeavor* mission was a poster of Alvin Ailey, the African-American dance theater group.

The strong-willed Jemison resists any suggestion that her seemingly polar passions are incompatible. "There is science in dance and art in science," she said.

At Stanford University, Jemison took advantage of a National Achievement Scholarship to pursue her wide-ranging interests. She majored in chemical engineering as well as African and Afro-American studies; played intramural football; was head of the Black Student Union; and produced, directed, and choreographed dance and theater productions. After graduating in 1977, she enrolled at Cornell University Medical College in New York City. She explains her choice of a medical career with typical matter-of-factness: "I could have gone into dance, which I love, or I could have gone to medical school. I chose medical school."

The choice proved a wise one. Her medical studies gave Jemison an opportunity to travel the world in a way she might never have as a dancer. She spent time in Cuba and Kenya, and worked in a Cambodian refugee camp in Thailand. "I learned more about medicine there than I could have in a comparable time somewhere else," she said. After earning her medical degree, she spent two and a half years as a Peace Corps medical officer in the West African countries of Sierra Leone and Liberia.

When Jemison returned to the United States in 1985, she took a job as a general practitioner with a health maintenance organization in Los Angeles. But she had not abandoned her dream of traveling among the stars. She began taking evening courses in engineering at the University of California at Los Angeles. And in October of that year, she applied for admission to the NASA space program.

The nation's astronaut training program traditionally has been an exclusive club. For many years, membership was open only to white male military jet pilots who seemed to have "the right stuff." But in the late 1970s, NASA began seeking civilian scientists, especially women and minorities, for its emerging

Mae Jemison

shuttle program. The basic requirements: a degree in math, engineering, or biological or physical science, plus three years of related work. A doctorate or a medical degree counts toward the three years experience.

Jemison fit the bill perfectly. But she would have to wait almost two years to prove it after the January 1986 explosion of the space shuttle *Challenger* temporarily grounded the shuttle program.

While Jemison was saddened by the tragedy, she wasn't dissuaded from her goal. When NASA reopened the selection process the following October, she was one of two thousand applicants.

Jemison made it through the first round of grueling physical and medical exams. On June 4, 1987, her childhood dream at last came within reach. Jemison was sitting at her desk, waiting for her next patient, when the phone rang. It was Houston. She had been selected as one of fifteen astronaut candidates.

"I was very happy," she recalled. "I still had to go see patients... so I had to hold it in a little bit. I didn't jump up and down and do a dance, but, yes, I was very excited."

She had reason to celebrate. As the first African-American woman ever given the chance to become an astronaut, Jemison was opening a door for others. But she is quick to credit the white female and black male astronauts whose contributions had helped clear the path, including Guion Bluford, the first black man in space.

Houston television anchor Linda Lorelle, Jemison's friend and former Stanford roommate, said it never was part of Jemison's plan to be the first black woman to explore outer space. "She just wanted to do it. If somebody else had come before her, that would have been fine and she would have loved that."

But before Jemison could strap herself into a space shuttle, she had one more hurdle to pass. For one year, she and the other astronaut candidates were put through a series of tests to familiarize them with the shuttle and to determine if they could withstand the rigors of space flight. Once again, she passed with flying colors. In August 1988, Mae Carol Jemison officially became an astronaut. Her title: mission specialist.

With her background in biomedical engineering, she was tapped to work on a joint mission between the United States and Japan. Dubbed STS-47 Spacelab J, the mission involved dozens of experiments in life sciences and materials processing. The most highly publicized experiment was designed to determine how organisms would develop in space without gravity. During the *Endeavor* shuttle flight, Jemison would fertilize frog eggs and monitor the embryos. "Because frogs, like other life forms, take so much of their basic knowledge from their environment, we were curious if they would turn out to be...well, normal frogs," she said. "When we got back to Earth, the tadpoles were right on track, and they have turned into frogs."

NASA also was anxious to know more about the effects of space flight on humans. Jemison would experiment with auto-genic feedback, a technique that allows one to control the auto-nomic functions like pulse and sweating. This was a way to possibly control "motion sickness," Jemison said.

And she would investigate the loss of calcium. "In space, humans lose calcium from the bones, and this loss starts imme-diately," she explained. "Some people ask 'should women, who are more prone to osteoporosis on Earth, be careful or limited in space travel?' I would counter that black people tend to have heavier bone skeletons than whites. But we don't have a lot of data on women. The longest a woman has been up is ten days. Does this mean that we should be wary about sending women up for long periods? Or that we should send only black people? The real issue is how to keep people healthy while they're in space."

In addition to carrying the first black woman into space, the September 12, 1992, *Endeavor* flight became noteworthy for two other "firsts": NASA's first husband-wife team of Mark Lee and Jan Davis; and Japan's first astronaut, chemist Mamoru Mohri.

When the moment Jemison had waited for nearly all her life arrived, a million thoughts raced through her mind as she and the six other crew members prepared for takeoff at Kennedy Space Center in Florida. But mostly, she recalled, "I had this big smile on my face. I was so excited. This is what I had wanted for a very long time....It was the realization of many, many dreams of many people."

Jemison was in space for eight days—officially, one hundred and ninety hours—that would forever change the way she viewed the world. The first thing she saw when she looked out the shuttle window after takeoff was the familiar skyline of Chicago, her hometown. But later, she would recognize the African nation of Somalia and realize that while she was experi-encing a once-in-a-lifetime trip, people on Earth still were fight-ing ancient battles and dying of starvation.

When Jemison returned to Earth, she was in constant demand

as one of NASA's most sought-after speakers. She had numerous requests from professional societies, schools, museums, and filmmakers to talk about her experiences as the nation's first black woman astronaut. Normally astronauts limit their public appearances to two per month. But Jemison "always had a lot of requests and she never was able to work them all off," said Barbara Schwartz, a spokeswoman at the Johnson Space Center.

Jemison didn't mind sharing her message, but she was uncomfortable with her new celebrity status and reluctant to be touted as a role model. "The thing that I've done throughout my life is to do the best job that I can and to be me," she said. "And that's really all I can do. In terms of being a role model…what I'd like to be is someone who said, 'No, don't try to necessarily be like me or live your life or grow up to be an astronaut or a physician—unless that's what you want to do. I believe you should do things you want to do, regardless of whether anyone's been there before.'"

Having accomplished her goal of flying in space, Jemison resigned from the astronaut corps in March 1993. She continues to live in suburban Houston, where she enjoys gardening, listening to the music of Etta James, and spending time with Sneeze, the cat she adopted in West Africa. Although she says she would "go to Mars at the drop of a hat," Jemison has put space travel behind her for now and is moving on to the next phase of her life. Specifically, she's established the Jemison Group, a company that researches, develops, and markets advanced technologies. She has also taught a course at Dartmouth College on space-age technology and its relationship to developing countries.

As a scientist and former Peace Corps physician, Jemison is especially interested in the potential use of satellite and telecommunications technology to improve health care in Third World countries. And as a black woman who once was told that soaring among the stars was beyond her reach, Jemison is spreading the word that space exploration is "the birthright of everyone who is on this planet."

"The fact is that space and its resources belong to all of us, not to any one group," she said. "So we all have to be there from the beginning, helping to determine what happens to these resources. We all must have a say in how space is used."

Julie Krone

∽I guess I don't think it's a big deal that I'm a woman competing against men....Whether you're a girl or a boy or a Martian, you still have to go out and prove yourself again every day.

Jockey Julie Krone has a mom who loves to tell the story about the first time her daughter rode a horse. Picture this: Mom Judi is trying to sell a palomino to an interested buyer. Wanting to demonstrate the horse's gentleness, she picks up her two-year-old daughter, Julie, and plops her on the palomino's back. The horse proceeds to canter away with the baby on board. Then, to everyone's surprise, little Julie simply reaches down, tugs on the reins, and the palomino obeys, promptly trotting right back.

On reflection, no one—least of all her mom—is surprised that even as a toddler, Julie Krone seemed to know instinctively what to do on a moving horse. Maybe it was because her mother had ridden throughout her pregnancy; even in the womb, little Julie had felt the rhythm of horses. Years later, she would observe, "I was always going to be a jockey—and a *great* one, too."

Now at age thirty, Julie Krone is indeed the most successful female jockey in the history of horse racing. In fact, no other woman rider even comes close.

Since she began riding professionally at age sixteen, Krone has won more than 2,000 races and earned more than $52 million in purses for her horse owners. In 1993, she fulfilled a life-long dream by winning the Belmont Stakes, one of the jewels in racing's prestigious Triple Crown. But as far as Krone is concerned, it's a minor historical footnote that she happened to be the first woman to win one of the Big Three.

"I guess I don't think it's a big deal that I'm a woman competing against men. Who cares about that?" said Krone, who consistently ranks among the top ten jockeys in the nation—male or female. What matters most to Julie Krone is not breaking down gender barriers but simply beating everyone else over the finish line. "Whether you're a girl or a boy or a Martian," she said, "you still have to go out and prove yourself again every day."

It's what she does best. At age fifteen, Krone convinced her mom to fake her I.D. so she could get a summer job at Churchill Downs as a "hot-walker," someone who walks the horses after the races to cool them down. The following year, she climbed a fence at Tampa Bay Downs in Florida, and fast-talked a trainer into trying her out on one of his mounts.

She kept talking—and winning—her way to success while everyone else was still saying that girl riders were a joke. She's been thrown down, stomped on, and sideswiped by other jockeys. But somehow Krone never fails to get up, dust herself off, and get back on the horse. Even a devastating fall in the summer of 1993, in which she was trampled by several horses and left badly injured, didn't dampen her spirits for long. After a few weeks in the hospital, Krone was flying around in her wheelchair, whipping her crop like she was riding a filly into the stretch.

"She's got more energy than anyone I've ever met," said her longtime agent, Larry "Snake" Cooper. "She loves what she's doing and she never quits."

At 4 feet 10½ inches and 100 pounds, Krone has always felt like she had a lot to prove. Back home in Eau Claire, Michigan, kids made fun of her Munchkin body and Mickey Mouse voice. But what young Krone lacked in size, she made up for in pure spunk. By age three, she was making half-mile solo trips on her horse. By thirteen, she had taught herself to stand on the back of a galloping horse, wearing nothing but a deerskin, and do a split onto the steed's back just as it ducked into the barn. She rode with the reins in her mouth and jumped fences like John Wayne in *True Grit*. She harnessed up her Great Dane and went sled-

Julie Krone   Photo by Michael J. Marten

ding in the snow. She even surfed off the bumper of a moving school bus.

"I was a wild kid," Krone admitted. "I got bit, I got stepped on, I got kicked in the head. I got dumped five miles from home; the pony ran back and I had to walk."

Her parents weren't much on enforcing discipline, but they were big on encouraging dreams. Don Krone was a college photography teacher who might disappear for hours into his darkroom. Judi Krone was a former Michigan state equestrian champion who spent most of her time dreaming about horses, when she wasn't breeding them, or showing them, or teaching other people's kids to ride them. So it's no wonder that daughter Julie was infected with the desire to race thoroughbreds from a very young age. She would even tie reins to her bedpost, saddle an old trunk, and use a fly swatter to pretend she was Willie Shoemaker riding in the Kentucky Derby.

The Krones didn't believe in setting limits for their children; they wanted them to be free to follow their dreams. "Every day was a missile launch," Don Krone said of the constant chaos that reigned on their ten-acre farm. "Yes, there was always that element of possible disaster, but it was just like a missile—if it *goes*, god, there's going to be that moment of glory."

When Julie was fifteen, whatever slim force of gravity held the family together disappeared with her parent's divorce, and Julie's world began to spin out of orbit. Don Krone moved out and her older brother, Donnie, went with him. Judi Krone got a job tending bar late at night. Julie's grades began to drop. She got caught writing worthless checks on an account she'd opened with winnings from half-mile fairground races. At one point, she almost left home to join the circus, after impressing the owner with her Annie Oakley-style stunts. But she changed her mind at the last minute.

Instead, Julie dropped out of high school in the middle of her senior year to try her luck at the track. After her summer at Churchill Downs, she gathered an envelope full of pictures and some local press clippings and headed for Florida, where her grandparents lived. She got as far as the entrance to Tampa Bay Downs.

When the race track's security guards refused to let her in, she walked down the fence a ways and shimmied over. Once inside, she was mistaken for a lost little girl by a nice lady who took her to see trainer Jerry Pace. That was the only break the spunky Krone needed.

She was so determined to ride that Pace agreed to try her out on one of his horses. During a practice session, she took the horse to the wrong starting position. "How am I supposed to put you on your first winner when you don't know where the poles are?" he said, laughing.

"I was thinking then that I probably had a lot to learn, and he wouldn't put me on the horse," Krone recalled. "But he did." Five weeks later, she won her first race on a gelding named Lord Farckle.

Krone wound up in the money in nearly half of her next forty-eight races. Her riding was good enough to impress ex-jockey Julie Snellings, whose career had ended after she was paralyzed in a riding accident in 1977. Snellings gave her riding tips and introduced her to Chick Lang, who would become Krone's first agent. Lang took her to Baltimore so that she could ride at Pimlico, home of the Preakness Stakes.

Within a few years, Krone was living her dream and making enough money to put fairgrounds racing behind her forever. But the "wild kid" still was looking for bigger thrills and trying harder than ever to prove that she was tough enough to make it in a macho profession. Out of frustration, Krone occasionally used her fists to make the point. Most folks wrote it off as self defense. "The guys try to intimidate women jockeys, but Julie let them know that she's not going to tolerate foolishness," said track steward Richard Lawrenson after one particularly nasty fight.

"I didn't know how to act," Krone now admits. "I didn't have anyone to copy. I thought if I showed any feelings, they would be taken for weakness."

Krone's suspension in 1981 for possession of marijuana wasn't so easy to ignore. After being caught with the drug in her car at Bowie Race Course in Maryland, she was suspended from racing for two months and ordered to submit to drug testing for a year. It was a devastating blow to her self-esteem and a damaging setack for her career. Krone experienced a second setback several months later when she was thrown from her horse during a race and broke her back.

But when she returned to the racing circuit, her luck seemed to have left her completely. After eighty races without a win, she was close to giving up. "One day on the backstretch, I yelled, 'I quit! I quit! I quit! I can't stand it!'" Krone recalled.

Instead of quitting, though, she dug deeper and found something of the fearless little girl who rode like the wind with the reins between her teeth. Krone began to cultivate what she called her "apple pie image" and worked harder than ever to win the confidence of trainers. Slowly, they started taking notice. In late 1981, Kentucky Derby-winner Bud Delp took her on as an apprentice jockey. She won one hundred races for him before moving on to Atlantic City, where she led the standings for the next two years.

The more Krone won, the harder she pushed. Up before dawn, she'd "breeze"—or work out—horses from 6:30 A.M. to 10 A.M., then race all afternoon. At night, she'd drive to another track and ride until midnight. She kept up this pace six days a week, twelve months a year, without vacations.

Krone's iron-willed dedication took a toll on her personal life. The first man she ever fell in love with, an assistant trainer, asked her to choose between him and eighteen races a day. He hit the trail.

But the owners for whom Krone was winning as much as $1 million were in awe of the way she could sit ever so lightly on a horse and then bend it to her will with a gentle word or a few strokes of the whip. They said she could communicate with horses and make them relax. "She thinks like a horse," said owner Peter Shannon Jr.

Not all her fellow jockeys were as impressed. Krone got into some well-publicized scraps, the wildest with Panamanian jockey Miguel Rujano in 1986. Rujano, who claimed Krone had fouled him during the race, slashed her across the face at the finish line. During the post-race photo session, Krone noticed her ear was bleeding. "Excuse me, I have to go hit someone," she said casually, then strode over to the scales where Rujano was weighing in and punched him in the nose. As the story goes, Rujano then threw Krone into the jockey's swimming pool and held her head under water for a few seconds. She escaped and decked him with a pool chair. Both were fined $100 and Rujano was suspended for five days.

Krone was equally gutsy about asking experienced jockeys for advice, but then she might take what she'd learned and turn the tables on them. Trainer John Forbes recalled the day Krone trapped Laffit Pincay and Pat Day behind a couple of slower horses and refused to let them out. "There they were, two of the greatest riders in the sport, screaming at her to let them the hell out, and she wouldn't budge," Forbes said. "'What kind of racing is that?' Day screams at her after the race. '*Race* riding, Pat,' she says to him. 'I *used* you.' She became a diabolical rider."

By the time she was twenty-three, Krone's record was speaking for itself. She won $2.3 million for horse owners in 1986, the highest winnings recorded by a woman that year. (The jockey keeps about ten percent.)

Two years later, in 1988, Krone changed horse-racing history on two counts. First, she passed Patricia Cooksey to become the leading woman rider of all time, a distinction she has maintained ever since and for which she has no close competition. (Women have only been racing thoroughbreds professionally since 1968. Even today, they make up only about a quarter of all jockeys.) Also that same year, Krone raced head-to-head against her idol, Willie Shoemaker, the most successful jockey in history, and beat him. He gave her his goggles as a token of respect.

In the meantime, Krone continued to rack up firsts: first woman to capture a riding championship at a major track; first woman to compete in the prestigious Breeders' Cup. In fact, young Julie Krone broke so much new ground that it no longer was meaningful to talk about her in terms of gender—something she strongly discouraged whenever writers brought it up in interviews or press conferences. "She is an athlete who must be compared not to other female riders, but in the context of her performance against men," Paul Moran wrote in *New York Newsday*.

Angel Cordero Jr. gave her perhaps his highest compliment when he said simply, "She don't ride like no girl rider."

But for Krone, there was at least one milestone left to cross. She had not yet won one of the Triple Crown races—the Kentucky Derby, the Preakness, or the Belmont Stakes. In June 1993, she crossed that threshold as well when she rode to victory at Belmont Park.

Two months later, however, she would be lying on an operating table as surgeons painstakingly fused two metal plates and fourteen screws to the shattered fragments of her right ankle. The accident happened on the final day of the season at Saratoga.

Krone needed four wins—the exact number of races she was scheduled to ride that day—to tie jockey Mike Smith for the track title. In the first race, a rookie jockey steered his horse into Krone's path, tripping her mount and tossing her onto the dirt in front of two dozen galloping hooves. In the resulting pileup, Krone was trampled by at least two horses.

As she lay in the hospital recovering from her injuries, which included a crushed ankle, a severely lacerated elbow, and a bruised heart, Krone wondered if her career was over. The doctors predicted it would be at least six months before she could ride again competitively. For someone who had been racing ahead at full speed her whole life, six months seemed an eternity.

"When something you do, something you live for, is yanked away and you're in the dark, you reach for God, religion, family....," she said. As she contemplated getting on a horse again, Krone said, "for the first time, I thought, this is dangerous and kinda scary."

But whenever those dark thoughts lingered, Krone said she would look at a photograph of Colonial Affair, the 13-to-1 long shot that had carried her to victory at Belmont, "and I'd get so much more energy." At a hospital press conference, she showed reporters a sign someone had made for her that read, "Our greatest glory is not in never falling, but rising each time." And with a twirl of her wheelchair and a crack of her whip, she predicted she'd be riding again soon, stronger than ever.

After all, it was what she was born for.

Amy Langer

〜Don't be afraid to ask and act. Find smart
people and let them be your mentors.
Don't think you have to settle—and
certainly not because you're a woman.

By the time she turned thirty, Amy Langer was pulling down a six-figure income as a senior vice president at a prestigious Wall Street firm. From all outward appearances, she was a young professional who had it made: promotions, a powerful position, and a private office in the posh headquarters of Shearson Lehman Brothers. But Langer, a self-professed workaholic, was paying a price for her fast-track style: she had no time to spend her phenomenal income and her marriage was falling apart.

Still, she might have kept pushing ahead if cancer hadn't stopped her in her tracks. "There's nothing like a life-threatening disease to make you really look at your life and see what you're doing, what you want to be doing, and where you're going," she said.

Although it's been almost a decade since she had the mammogram that revealed she had breast cancer, Langer can still describe the experience in vivid detail. "It's quite unusual to have a mammogram at thirty," she explained, "but because my mom had died of cancer and because my gynecologist said, 'Gee, you know you have very lumpy breasts—you ought to get a mammogram just to be sure,' I decided to get tested. But in my mind, it was a routine thing—like you'd go to the dentist."

It took Langer two months to get around to the mammogram. At the time, she was involved in a major stock underwriting, so she lugged along a briefcase full of files: "I remember I had papers spread all over the waiting room, underlining things with my marker." Engrossed in her work, Langer was caught off guard when the nurse appeared in the doorway, crooking a finger to summon her back into the doctor's office. "When they said I had early breast cancer," Langer said, "I suddenly had that feeling when you know your world is turning upside down."

With the same determination she'd applied to her career, Langer began researching the disease. "Being an informed patient is often a matter of life or death in breast cancer because unfortunately, many doctors don't know all the options and don't have an approach that's conducive to women taking charge of their treatment," she explained. Langer found out about the newest treatments and was insistent about receiving breast-conserving surgery at a time when it was still considered investigational. (In 1993, she celebrated nine years of being cancer-free.)

When she got out of the hospital, Langer wasted no time in returning to her high-profile job and resuming her hectic pace. But as she sat alone in her office, often late into the evenings, an ice pack hugged to her chest as the doctor had ordered to ease the swelling from her surgery, Langer came to terms with the hard truth that she no longer had the heart for Wall Street—the business seemed more cutthroat and her colleagues more chauvinistic than she had remembered.

"I decided I had to do something else, but I wasn't sure what," she recalled. This much Langer did know: "Whatever I did, I would make time to volunteer in the area of breast cancer, because I felt I had been very lucky."

Langer quit her job and opened a private consulting practice in 1987. That same year, after reading an article in *Vogue* magazine about a fledgling group called the National Alliance of Breast Cancer Organizations, she called and volunteered her expertise as a businesswoman. But she was told the organization was new and just getting organized—and wasn't sure how to use someone with Langer's background. "Fine, I'll be over there tomorrow," said Langer, who laughs at the memory.

Amy Langer

Sure enough, she found an administrative tangle and began untying knots. Because the organization had only forty members, she said, "One of the first things I did was call each of them up. I asked them who they were, why they joined, and what they felt NABCO needed to be."

Moving swiftly, Langer created membership files and mailing

lists, contributed to the newsletter, and initiated programs. "Little by little, I really got very seduced by the whole business," she said, "because I felt that there was a real chance to make a difference, to help other people, and to join what was at that time a fairly quiet consumer voice." Langer became so devoted to NABCO that she ultimately curtailed her consulting business. In 1988, she was put on the NABCO payroll and two years later, Langer was named the group's executive director.

In the decade since she confronted breast cancer, Langer has turned her life around and transformed NABCO from a well-intentioned but struggling group into a premier nonprofit organization that's widely recognized as a leading authority on breast cancer. "I really had a vision for the organization and the energy to accomplish it," she said. "And I've never not been able to do anything I've set my mind to."

Simply put, NABCO serves as a clearinghouse for anyone—women, medical professionals, organizations—in need of information about breast cancer but uncertain about where to turn. NABCO routinely receives five hundred calls a month, many of them from women who've recently been diagnosed and are wondering about everything from whether they should get second opinions to the benefits of joining a support group.

"We can usually help them," said Langer. "And if we can't, then we tell them what the next step is."

Under her leadership, NABCO has expanded to include a network of three hundred professional and medical organizations, and individual memberships now number more than one thousand, which means NABCO represents a significant constituency.

Langer couldn't be happier. "It's a wonderful position to be in—you can sort of go everywhere and do everything within breast cancer."

In addition to her NABCO activities, Langer co-founded the National Breast Cancer Coalition, a grassroots organization inspired by the AIDS movement and designed to change public policy. While both organizations share common threads, NABCO is an educational effort and professional network, whereas the Breast Cancer Coalition is an advocacy group that aims to get thousands of women directly involved in the fight against breast cancer.

It is battle that has engaged Langer so wholeheartedly that at times her eyes turn teary as she talks about the devastating impact of this disease. In the early days of NABCO, news of the group traveled mostly by word of mouth, but now Langer is interviewed almost weekly by both the medical press and mainstream media. Whenever and wherever an opportunity arises to share the breast cancer message, she tirelessly fields questions, offering facts tempered by compassion—because she knows that often the only answers available just don't go far enough to satisfy people who may be fighting for their lives.

Breast cancer is diagnosed in 182,000 American women every year, and it kills 46,000. It's the most common form of cancer in women and it's on the rise. But why is one of those questions "nobody knows the answer to," Langer said. "Unlike many other cancers, we don't know what causes it, so we can't prevent it." Even more alarming are statistics which refute the common notion that breast cancer is a post-menopausal problem. "Not any more," Langer continued, "twenty-five percent of cases occur in women under fifty."

Nationwide there are literally thousands of organizations dealing with breast cancer, from hospitals to mammography centers to support groups to cancer agencies. That's why, Langer said, "The founders of NABCO felt it was important to have one umbrella resource to keep them all in touch with one another and apprised of developments in the field." Taking a comprehensive approach has made NABCO unique in an already crowded field. "If you call the National Cancer Institute, and it's a day when a new treatment for colon cancer has been announced, or if you call the American Cancer Society, and they're in the middle of National Smoke Out Day, you may not be able to get your questions answered," Langer said. "Or you may not get a person who's knowledgeable about breast cancer."

NABCO has built a reputation as an expert and reliable source. For instance, Langer said, "We're often invited as speakers at medical meetings. We have good close relationships with a number of government agencies and we participate in activities ranging from the National Cancer Institute to the Food and Drug Administration to the Centers for Disease Control."

NABCO is funded through membership dues as well as grants from corporations, foundations, and the government. Sadly, memorial donations also come in, Langer said. And in the tradition of nonprofit organizations, NABCO periodically throws benefits. "We had the first 'Celebrate Life' luncheon last year," said Langer, describing how NABCO honored President Clinton's mother, Virginia Kelly, who battled breast cancer for many years until it took her life in late 1993.

But unlike most nonprofit groups, NABCO is not saddled with a reputation for being sluggish and unprofessional, thanks to Langer's drive. "One thing that's very different here from most nonprofits is the pace at which we run," she said. "I'm not great at doing a little bit of something and then going home. I like to really pack my days and work at one hundred miles an hour...well maybe I'd prefer eighty."

Equally important, she has infused NABCO with principles she learned at Harvard Business School. "I didn't see any reason to run this organization differently than a business, with strategic planning, marketing, and packaging of services," said Langer, who earned a master's degree in business administration from Harvard after graduating cum laude with a bachelor's degree from Yale.

Though Langer may be using many of the same skills that made her a whiz at Shearson Lehman, in most other respects, NABCO is a world away from Wall Street. She works out of cramped quarters that she shares with a female staff of seven—not nearly enough people for the job at hand. And because resources are limited, Langer wears many hats, often doing what's needed most at the moment, even typing and filing.

Her job routinely involves managing finances, writing proposals, organizing projects, and reading tons of mail, but her days are typically unpredictable. "Anything can happen when the phone rings—it can be the White House calling," said Langer, who's on a number of federal boards. Between unexpected opportunities and the occasional crisis, she said, "My life has to very scheduled—I even plan my trips to the ladies' room."

Even with her seemingly runaway responsibilities, Langer is

enthusiastic when she contemplates NABCO's future. "In our growth so far—and we've just finished our adolescence—we've jumped at every opportunity. We wanted to be everywhere, and help as many people as we could." Along the way, NABCO's mission changed for the better, Langer said, "but we have not kept our priorities quite as sharp as we need to. We don't say 'no' often enough yet."

She hopes to extend NABCO's reach by collaborating with corporations on special projects. One such project took shape in 1993 when NABCO teamed up with Avon Products, Inc., in an effort to raise monies for breast cancer awareness by selling specially designed pins. The Avon pins, which resembled pink ribbons and were accompanied by educational literature, were sold primarily through the company's sales representatives, who number almost a half million in the United States.

"We're very proud to be associated with Avon," said Langer. "The magnitude of the dollars is going to be greater than anything that anyone has *ever* seen from the private sector for breast cancer." Avon's Breast Cancer Awareness Crusade is slated to span several years, with proceeds being donated to community programs—which is a critical point from Langer's perspective since NABCO was originally conceived as a professional network, not a group that would help women directly. "We don't have an 800 number, so the women who call us are often the women who can afford to. We are increasingly aware of who we are not talking to."

Thanks to the Avon association, now when NABCO receives requests such as how to provide screening for women at local prisons or how to bring breast-care education to high schools, Langer can offer financial support. "It's like Santa Claus, you know," she said with a smile. "It's so exciting. We are just beside ourselves about this opportunity to help."

Seeing the person Langer is today, it's hard to picture her as a Wall Street powerhouse. Perhaps that's because her values have taken a 180-degree turn. By her own account, in those days all she thought about was: "How much money am I making? How much are my colleagues making? What is my title? What are their titles? Will I get a promotion?"

But illness made her reconsider what's important. Now

Langer values herself, her organization, and her feelings about what she is accomplishing. Her definition of success has been pared down to a single question: "Am I making a difference?"

"I'm a believer in fate," she said, explaining that her Wall Street years provided a comfortable nest egg and the luxury to do something more meaningful, something closer to the person she really is. It enabled her take a job at one tenth of her former salary—a job that freed her from the constant pressure of competing in male environments. "It's a great relief to work with women, to come to work without makeup, if you want to," said Langer, who has abandoned her dress-for-success wardrobe for comfortably casual blouses, slacks, and flats.

Though some people are skeptical of the dynamics in an all-female office, Langer said, "I've never found it to be catty." As NABCO's executive director, she's clearly the boss, but she does not boss the staff around. "We're all colleagues—good women working with other women," she said. "It's a lovely feeling."

About the only thing that hasn't changed in Langer's life are the crazy hours she keeps. Like many professional women, she performs a daily balancing act between the demands of her career and family. Langer met her second husband, Charles, through a friend in 1986, when she had given up on remarrying. Sharing a common background, the couple longed for a baby, but knew there would be some risks involved. For one, Langer was in her mid-thirties, and although there was no solid research on the outcome of pregnancy after breast cancer, the medical establishment took the position that it was a dangerous idea. The main concern: pregnancy increases a woman's production of estrogen and estrogen fuels the growth of breast cancer.

But after thinking about it for a long while, Langer decided to conceive, with her doctor's approval. "Here I was a very public person in breast cancer, walking around with a belly," said Langer. Despite the perceived risk, she said most people responded positively, seeing her pregnancy as a "life-renewing experience." (Ironically, early in Langer's pregnancy, the National Cancer Institute published the first report stating there are no negative effects on women who wait a couple years after successful breast cancer treatment to conceive.)

"A baby adds the most incredible joy and complication to your life, but it's all worth it," said Langer, who beams as she shares a photo of her son, Henry. "I have a great baby—he's adorable, funny, and intelligent—but he doesn't see enough of me."

So what if Henry can't adjust to his mom's career as he grows older? Langer pauses to contemplate the question, then pointing her index finger at Henry's picture, she said jokingly, "You're fired, baby." But the truth be known, she and her husband haven't ruled out having another child.

"I've worked more hours than most sixty-year-olds have," Langer said. "The balance has got to shift to my family." Typical of most working moms, Langer laments that spare time is nonexistent, and that hobbies like reading and cooking are out of the question. But her biggest regret is that she doesn't see family and friends as much as she'd like. And her husband is quick to point out that while Langer works long hours ensuring other women's health, she tends to neglect her own. "I have cut myself out of the deal," Langer acknowledged. "I need to look at that and fix it."

Just the same, she does an admirable job of juggling a life many would envy. How does she do it? "I have great help," said Langer, who confides that Henry adores his baby sitter. "The two of them are a major item."

Her other salvation: a sense of humor on the job. "You have to laugh, or you'd be shattered. It's important to lighten up when things are sad, or else it would be too depressing here to function," she said, adding that her profession is more uplifting than people think, because so much is happening in breast cancer.

As much as she loves her work, Langer believes every career has a life cycle and that one day she'll leave NABCO—though she will continue to be involved in breast cancer, perhaps by planning marches or mailing campaigns, or working on government committees. Whatever she does next, Langer will undoubtedly take a businesslike approach, for you might say it was bred into her.

Growing up an only child in Orlando, Florida, Langer felt her parents showered her with attention, opportunities, and resources. But back then, Orlando was an anti-Semitic community and Langer attended a public school where she was one of only a handful of Jewish kids. Painfully shy, Langer preferred the company of books. "From age six to eleven, I read twenty books a week," she said. Carrying a cardboard box to the library, she'd methodically borrow books by theme, and especially loved biographies, mysteries, and female authors. She was also fascinated with the world of offices and business.

"The person who made me into a business child was my grandfather," said Langer, explaining how he had come from Poland, opened a factory, and after making significant money, invested it wisely. When she was eight, Langer's grandfather taught her how to write checks and balance a checkbook. On her own, she pretended to be the secretary of a business tycoon: "I would actually envision myself behind a desk and even called myself Miss Collins—but you have to bear in mind this was the fifties, when it was unthinkable for a woman to be the boss."

Although opportunities have improved, Langer believes seasoned role models are still rare. Asked what advice she'd offer to tomorrow's working women, she said, "Just be really confident that you can do what you want. No one can stop you. Don't be afraid to ask and act. Find smart people and let them be your mentors. Don't think you have to settle—and certainly not because you're a woman."

Langer is particularly concerned that some teens today seem angry rather than optimistic about their futures. "It's not cool to be hostile," she said. "It doesn't work."

Who would know that better than Langer, for in spite of a bad break when she was young and everything seemed to going her way, she's upbeat in every respect.

"I've been very lucky," she said. Lucky because a doctor discovered her cancer early and she survived it; lucky because she found love and had a baby. Today she has her health, a happy family life, and a fulfilling career.

"I'd take this life again," Langer said. "If it weren't for breast cancer, what would I be today? A multimillionaire, highly neurotic banker."

Siri Marshall

*⌒The important thing for girls as they grow up
is to think that anything is open to them.
And to try....The important thing is thinking
you can do it.*

If you had asked ten-year-old Siri Marshall "what do you want to be when you grow up?" chances are she probably would have said wife and mother. Today she is happily both—and more. At forty-five, Marshall is a senior vice president and the top lawyer at Avon Products, Inc., which makes her one of only three women in the country to hold the position of general counsel at a Fortune 500 company. While Marshall has achieved a level of success many would find enviable, it's all the more amazing considering she didn't even think seriously about a career until her senior year in college.

"It was very hard growing up when I did—when you didn't see women in leadership roles," said Marshall, who was raised in New England suburbs during the fifties and sixties. Marshall's mother, who had been a nurse, was a stay-at-home mom.

"We were a typical *Leave It To Beaver* household," Marshall said. "I didn't know any women who worked...other than teachers in my school. And frankly, I had absolutely no expectation that I would work either."

Now with the same ease she might cross a living room, Marshall manages a high-profile career that routinely has her mingling with top-level executives and negotiating high-pressure situations, not to mention the ever present threat of litigation. Her multifaceted responsibilities include acting as an advisor to senior management and the board of directors to ensure that Avon complies with the law on matters ranging from how products are manufactured, to environmental issues, to treatment of employees, to the use of the company's trademark. "If we are going to buy or sell a company, for example, I advise them on the best way to do that," said Marshall, who also promotes a program alerting Avon employees to the dangers of corporate espionage.

"It's a great job," she said. "I really love to come to work. Not that every day is wonderful, but I'm very absorbed with my job."

Everything about Marshall exudes a quiet confidence. Her office is decorated in beige, accented by oriental paintings and carpets. Her desktop is loaded but methodically organized, with paperwork carefully stacked in neat piles. Likewise, she projects an image that's fashionable in a classic, understated style that conveys her competence. Marshall sometimes dresses in soft colors because she believes accentuating her femininity can be helpful in a job where she is often required to take a firm legal stand in potentially explosive discussions.

She typically spends ten-hour days at the office, and very often takes work home on evenings and weekends when she feels a need to tie up loose ends. Marshall has learned to artfully weave her career into life with her husband and daughter by working while they are busy themselves.

"Being a lawyer is a crisis job," she said. "You never know when you're going to have to work nights, or when you're going to have to get on the next plane to California, Washington, or wherever."

One of the more challenging and rewarding aspects of her job is running the legal department, said Marshall. A self-made manager who learned the ropes by reading literature and by watching others in action, Marshall is constantly striving to strengthen her managerial skills by analyzing what qualities make some people better managers than others.

"Most of my job is bringing out the best in everybody," she said. Marshall tries to instill confidence in her staff and encourages top-notch performance—not just for the good of her

Siri Marshall

department and the company, but because she believes it contributes to a person's sense of well being. "It's a corny way to look at the world, but people spend so much time at work," Marshall said, "and good managers really can influence the quality of

132

their lives. They can make them happy to come to work, or they can make them totally miserable."

Marshall makes it a point to see people as individuals, both those who work for her and those she reports to. "They're all different. They all bring something different to the party."

This respect for individuality is inspired in part by her name. Born Siri Swenson to American parents of Swedish descent, her first name means "she who desires victory." Although Marshall didn't know the meaning of her name until she was in college, her parents selected it intentionally. "It's considerably more inflated and pretentious than I had ever thought," she said, smiling. "I just had to live up to my name."

That she has may explain why Marshall feels so strongly about women assuming responsibility and why she is eager for her twelve-year-old daughter, Serin, to see female role models. It's not necessary for Serin to be the most ambitious person on the planet or even to set goals right now, Marshall said. But she wants her daugher to be aware—at a much younger age than she was—that her career options go beyond teacher or nurse.

"I want her to think it's just natural that she should be able to do all sorts of things," Marshall said. "The important thing for girls as they grow up is to think that anything is open to them. And to try. There are so many ways you can put the pieces together today. You can work part time; you can work at home. The important thing is thinking you can do it."

Equally important, Marshall said, women should ask: Are things working in my life? If not, they should make changes so goals become possible. "The pity about when we grew up is that we thought so many things weren't open to us or weren't appropriate for women, so we never even thought of trying."

Fortuately for Marshall, her mother paid little attention to the social sanctions of the time, and set the same standards for her daughter that she did for her son. "One thing that my mother always insisted on is that my brother and I be treated exactly the same," Marshall recalled. "We always had the same chores, the same summer activities, and the same allowance." Both kids were encouraged to excel in school, in sports, and in music. And their achievements were equally recognized.

Marshall was the first person from her high school to attend Harvard. When she started college in the mid-sixties, the country was in turmoil: a war raged in Vietnam, campuses were highly charged politically, and women were poised to change their destiny. As a young woman embarking on adulthood, Marshall had little idea of what was in store for her generation.

"My class, the class of 1970, at least at Harvard, was the pivotal class," said Marshall, explaining how her expectations suddenly changed from becoming a suburban housewife who would raise a family to being a professional woman pursuing a traditionally male career. "I look at the class of '69, and those women are way behind where we are in terms of the decisions we made about our lives and what we achieved. But the class of '71 is light-years ahead of us."

Marshall majored in English history and literature, but as late as her senior year, she didn't know exactly what she wanted to do with the rest of her life. She knew she was going to be working, and wanted to find something stimulating. After having dinner one evening with friends who were going to law school, Marshall woke up in the middle of the night and decided to do the same.

"I had no idea what lawyers did," she recalled. "I think I went to law school because I didn't know what else to do."

Because she didn't take the law boards until the second semester of her senior year, Marshall was too late to apply to many law schools, so she took a year off from studying. "I came down to New York City and just walked around until I got a job," she said. She found one with a small law firm, where she worked for a year before entering Yale Law School.

Marshall remembers that when she told her father about her decision to go to law school, he clearly hoped it was a passing phase and even suggested she attend night school to get the idea out of her system. "He said I should be a teacher so that I could get my summers off," she recalled.

Back then people just couldn't imagine a female corporate attorney, Marshall explained. And from a parent's perspective, it was the worst thing that could happen to a daughter—because it meant that she would never marry. "I know my mother thought I was going to be an old maid," said Marshall, who met her husband at Harvard during her freshman year. They dated on and off, and married when she was twenty-six.

But even after she entered law school, Marshall didn't have lofty expectations. She worked hard at her studies because she wanted to do a good job, but her ambitions ended there. "I never really looked beyond the next step," she said.

In spite of that, she has been tremendously successful because it's just in her nature to search for something new and challenging to do. But she doesn't necessarily recommend this approach, believing that it's better to set long-term goals.

"I look at the men of my generation," she said, "and they grew up thinking they were going to be the titans of business, running companies, or being political leaders." By the time she saw herself in a comparable role, Marshall said, she was in her late twenties.

Marshall went to law school with Supreme Court Judge Clarence Thomas and Secretary of Labor Robert Reich. The present administration is full of Yale Law School grads from her era. "I was in the class behind Bill and Hillary," said Marshall, who laughs good-naturedly when asked why the president didn't pick her to be attorney general. Her classmates are the ones making decisions today in Washington. "Even though I'm not close to them, I feel like I'm part of it—it's fun."

For five years after graduation, Marshall worked at a large New York City law firm. Though the job was rewarding, she felt something was missing. "I really wanted to get into business," said Marshall. She longed for a sense of teamwork and the continuity of being part of a company. "I felt that was a better way for me to make a lasting contribution."

In her job search, she interviewed at Avon but wasn't interested initially, because she felt that working for a cosmetics company was a cop-out for a woman, especially one like herself who had resisted wearing makeup. Also, because her previous job experience had been entirely financial, she thought she should move to a bank or an investment house. "If I was going to be a big-time lawyer," she said, "then I needed to tough it out in the world of finance."

But the more Marshall learned about Avon, the more appealing that job sounded. And the longer she thought about it, she came to the realization that a man simply wouldn't have the same reservations she did about joining a cosmetics company. So she started in Avon's legal department in 1979, and through a series of promotions worked her way into the executive ranks.

With her blonde hair, wide cheek bones, and the natural beauty Scandinavian women are famous for, Marshall could be an Avon model. Although she now wears a tasteful trace of makeup, she didn't convert to Avon products her first day on the job. "But something happens to every woman lawyer who comes to this company," Marshall observed. "You're here for a couple months, and you're in the elevator; all of a sudden you look around, and you realize these women look terrific. And you see yourself, and slowly you start wearing lipstick."

Now she's a big believer in wearing makeup. "I think it's great," Marshall said, "basically because it makes women feel better about themselves. It gives them more self-confidence."

For many reasons, Marshall considers herself lucky because, compared to some women, she's been able to combine a career and motherhood with relative ease. Her husband, a lawyer at *Time* magazine, is very supportive. He shares in household responsibilities and child rearing. "Perhaps because I knew him for so long, and I knew him when we were students, everything is fifty-fifty," she said. "It has always been that way."

It's also helpful that her husband's job doesn't require the kind of traveling Marshall's does and that her daughter is a healthy, happy child who excels in school. "My daughter is an easy kid," said Marshall.

Although Marshall avoids working at home when her daughter is around, sometimes it's necessary. When Serin was a tot, she would lay on the bed, watching her mom make business phone calls "and she'd ask me, 'are you almost done mommy?'" Marshall recalled with a smile.

Though Marshall's job can at times become all-consuming, her career has never been an issue—because Serin also has a full life while her mom is at the office. And she plans to follow her mother's example and have a career when she grows up.

While Marshall makes juggling her roles of corporate executive, wife, and mother look almost effortless, she candidily acknowledges, "it's not a piece of cake. I wouldn't say it's difficult, it's challenging."

So how does Marshall manage to "have it all" personally and professionally? For one, she extols in being organized and she's always had a high energy level. But just as important, Marshall said, "You need to love your job, because if you don't, you resent the time you spend away from your family."

She feels no guilt for being passionate about her career because, Marshall said, "When I'm with my daughter, I'm completely with her." She can afford to give her daughter undivided attention because the family has live-in help. "I don't do what a lot of women do," Marshall said, explaining that when she walks in the door at night, she doesn't have to contend with cooking, cleaning, and laundry. Instead, her family has fun over dinner as they catch up with each other's day.

"Although I have a more difficult juggling act," Marshall said of her demanding career, "when Serin and I are together, it's usually very happy." Still, like most working moms, she must make choices about where to invest her time and energy. So Marshall analyzes everything in terms of: Will Serin care if I don't do this personally? That's why the housekeeper makes cookies for class bake sales and fills out school forms while Marshall gets into the more intimate parts of mothering. She and Serin pack for camp together. They run errands and spend time talking about everything. "I find her life very interesting," Marshall said. "I love to hear about her friends."

Yet Marshall admits some of the choices she must make aren't easy for a mom. For example, she regrets that she can't be there for every concert and softball game. But such regrets are just part of the bargain, Marshall said, because every woman must set the right balance in her life and know what's important to *her*. "I don't think that everyone has to work," said Marshall, who believes raising well-adjusted children who will live meaningful lives and will contribute to the world is a major achievement.

"Success is doing what is really important to you and doing it in the best way you can," she said. "It's trying hard. Women need to realize that there is success in every day." It could be baking a great batch of cookies with your kids, or winning a tennis game, or being president of the PTA. The important thing is that every success builds confidence and fosters future success, she said.

Marshall and her husband often travel to France, and they love to relax over long, leisurely dinners at fine restaurants. Between her career and family life, Marshall does indeed feel lucky that she found a way to have it all. "I wish girls could see my life," she said, comparing it to the 1950s of her youth. "It should be the new all-American story."

Lynn Martin

*～I realize now it is the style to say 'Let's let people
be what they want to be,' but I think that misses
the point of people later in their life being all
that they can be. I wish people had said, 'You
can do it, you will do it, and you can do it
sooner rather than later.'*

Lynn Martin learned early about the harsh realities of politics
when she lost an election for eighth-grade class president by one
vote. The vote was her own and the winner was her boyfriend.

"You see, I voted for my opponent because I thought it was
polite," Martin said. "Well, he voted for himself, and I learned
my lesson: If you believe in yourself, vote for yourself."

Martin, a fifty-four-year-old former high school teacher and
U.S. secretary of labor under George Bush, has been voting for
herself ever since. First, for a spot on the local board in
Winnebago County, Illinois. Then for the Illinois state legislature. For five terms in the U.S. House of Representatives. And
finally, for the U.S. Senate, the only other election she lost.
Rumor has it Martin hopes to vote for herself once more in
1996—this time, for president of the United States.

If she decides to run, she may have a lot of people casting their
ballots with her. In eleven years in Washington, Martin accomplished what very few politicians can manage: She made friends
on both sides of the aisle. Republicans like her because she is one
of them. Many Democrats like her because she was willing to

oppose her party and her president, if necessary, to stand up for what she felt was right. Fiscal conservatives like her because she favors reigning in government spending. (In Illinois, her budget-cutting tactics earned her the nickname "the Axe.") And social moderates like her because she supports civil rights, family leave, and a woman's right to have an abortion.

Martin has made some enemies, too. But more people seem to respect her intelligence and pragmatism. They also admire her earthy style, quick wit, and searing sarcasm—qualities that have earned her a second nickname, "the Joan Rivers of Politics." The tall, angular former homeroom teacher once compared her cranky colleagues in Congress to preschoolers and suggested they "would all do a little better after a nap." She supports women's issues but dislikes being labeled a feminist. "I don't walk into every meeting humming, 'I am woman,'" she joked.

Martin credits her sense of humor with contributing the most to her success. "I'm not sure where one gets it," she said. "But if one doesn't have it, life is a lot less pleasant."

Picture this: It's 1980 and George Bush, a patrician blue blood with the demeanor of a basset hound, was about to debate his vice-presidential opponent, New York congresswoman Geraldine Ferraro, who came on more like a well-trained German shepherd. This was no time for jokes. Bush advisors apparently feared the vice president would take a hit to the jugular and bleed to death before he even knew he'd been bitten. He needed a worthy sparring partner to whip him into shape. Enter Lynn Martin.

Before the first mock debate, Barbara Bush pulled Martin aside and told her, "You get him. You go after him." Martin took her advice and showed the vice president no mercy. When Bush tried to warm things up, she stared back icily with her steel-gray eyes. Her aggressive style and complete mastery of the issues convinced him that he needed more practice.

Jack Davis, a former Illinois congressman and state legislator, doesn't find that scenario the least bit surprising, knowing Martin. "She has the ability to grasp complex topics and reduce them to their essentials and to bore through all the shading, the screening material, and get right to the heart of it—and drive a sword through your heart," Davis said. "There is a time when the hard line comes through and the laughter stops and she nails you right to a tree."

Bush apparently didn't hold Martin's sharp aim against her. The two became close friends and in 1988, he named her as the only woman to be a national co-chair of his presidential campaign. In 1991, after she lost the Illinois senate race to Paul Simon, Bush picked her to replace Elizabeth Dole as secretary of labor. And at the 1992 Republican convention, she returned the favors by giving the speech that nominated Bush for a second term as president.

Martin didn't always want to be a politician, but she was always ambitious. As a young child growing up on Chicago's North Side, she set her sights on becoming a nun, a scientist, or a space traveler to Mars. She was so eager to learn that the teachers at her parochial grade school asked her parents, Lawrence and Helen Morley, to encourage Lynn not to monopolize classroom discussions. At the University of Illinois at Urbana-Champaign, where she majored in English, Martin graduated Phi Beta Kappa in three years—despite the fact she often cut classes. After college, she did what many bright women of her generation did: She got married and got pregnant.

Martin had two daughters, Julia and Caroline, with her first husband, John Martin, who owned a successful printing equipment business in Rockford, Illinois. They were divorced in 1978. In 1987, she married Harry Leinenweber, a U.S. district judge in Illinois. Their family includes Martin's two daughters and Leinenweber's five children from a previous marriage.

Having children relatively early in life limited some of the things she could do, Martin said. For instance, she had to postpone her teaching career because she was pregnant with her first daughter. She quit teaching completely after the birth of her second child. But motherhood "also opened a change and a choice in my life," she said. When asked to list her most important achievement, Martin names two: being secretary of labor and raising two children with "good heads and good hearts. I have always loved them," she said. "But I also like them very much, too."

Lynn Martin   Photo by Bachrach

Until 1969, Martin taught high school English, economics, and government in various public and parochial schools in and around Chicago. Then in 1972, on a whim, she ran for the Winnebago County board. She was elected and served on the finance and public works committees, despite complaints by the road supervisor that women had no business messing around with potholes and sewage. In 1976, she recruited her daughter's junior high class to help her campaign for the Illinois House of Representatives. She beat the Democratic incumbent and two years later was elected to the state Senate.

As a senator, Martin is perhaps best remembered for cosponsoring a bill imposing tougher controls on nursing homes and establishing a bill of rights for residents. Her concerns were prompted in part by memories of her own mother, who died of Alzheimer's disease in 1974. The devastating illness took a toll on the family and taught Martin a valuable lesson: It "provided me the recognition that one cannot control everything about one's life," she said, "and that love does not stop even when someone cannot return it."

Throughout her career, Martin has let her conscience be her guide, even when it was not politically advantageous. A Catholic educated in parochial schools, she supports a woman's right to have an abortion and believes the federal government should make abortion funding available for poor women. In Congress, she voted for the MX missile, the Star Wars defense system, and aid to the Nicaraguan Contras. But she also supported a nuclear freeze and a ban on chemical weapons, and opposed massive military spending at the expense of social programs. After a trip to South Africa, where she saw firsthand the effects of apartheid, she voted for economic sanctions—even though the Reagan administration staunchly opposed them.

Martin's ability to be tough on issues of government spending but compassionate toward those in need appealed to Illinois residents, who voted her into the U.S. Congress in 1980 by a two-to-one margin. Once in Washington, she immediately began to make her mark. She was the first freshman appointed to the powerful Budget Committee. The schoolteacher in her came out when she remarked that getting such a plum assignment so early was like "getting sex education at age six. It's a little too soon to understand—there's a lot of stuff you really shouldn't know until a lot later."

But she was a fast learner. In 1984, she was elected vice chairman of the House Republican Conference, a policy-making caucus. She was invited to weekly White House strategy sessions to help determine budget priorities. In 1986, when she temporarily took over for the ranking Republican on the Budget Committee, who had become ill, she proved herself to be an able negotiator and won the respect of her Democratic colleagues. Her success prompted *U.S. News & World Report* to name her one of the "Ten Rising Stars of American Politics." She also was named "Republican Woman of the Year" in 1989.

Martin was re-elected four times by comfortable margins, although she once confessed that "deep in my heart of hearts, I never believed I was going to win any election." In 1990, President Bush and other Republican leaders urged her to give up her safe House seat and challenge Illinois Senator Paul Simon. Simon, a Democrat, beat her by more than a million votes. Martin's mouth had gotten her into trouble when she made wisecracks about Illinois "rednecks." She also had supported Bush's promise, which he later broke, of "no new taxes."

Martin decided her political career was over and announced that she would spend more time with her husband at their century-old English-style cottage in Illinois. However, friends convinced her that she still had a lot to give. With their encouragement, she let Bush know she was interested in the secretary of labor post, which had been vacant since Elizabeth Dole left to become president of the American Red Cross. Bush offered her the job in December 1990. Although organized labor opposed her, saying she had shown little sensitivity to the needs of workers, Martin was easily confirmed. Several prominent Democrats, including her former opponent, Paul Simon, endorsed her nomination.

Not surprisingly, Martin took a unique approach to her new job. To prove her union opponents wrong, she decided to find out firsthand the problems facing the average American worker. She spent a day selling women's suits and blouses in a department store; worked as a plumber and pipe welder in Chicago; cut sugar cane in Florida; and made French fries at McDonald's. She didn't invite television cameras along to publicize her efforts. She just worked, observed, and listened.

Martin discovered that workers were most concerned about issues related to job security: how to pay for health insurance if they lost a job, where to find the skills for a new one, and whether they would live comfortably in retirement. She supported a proposal to allow workers to carry pensions and health insurance with them when they change jobs, something the average American worker does six times in a lifetime. She proposed a job-training initiative and a national youth apprenticeship system. And she conducted a well-publicized campaign to bring down the "glass ceiling" that keeps many women and minorities from reaching their potential.

Martin's labor agenda included cleaning her own house. She reviewed department policy and practices to make sure there were no barriers to qualified women and minorities seeking advancement. Department employees also received training about sexual harassment and cultural diversity.

She has continued working to improve the status of women in the private sector. After Bush lost the 1992 election, she was named an advisor to the Big Six accounting firm, Deloitte & Touche. She currently chairs the firm's Council on the Advancement of Women. She is a regular business commentator on National Public Radio as well as public television. She advises businesses and universities on the changing global economic and political environment. And she serves on the board of directors of Ameritech; Harcourt General; Dreyfus Funds; Ryder Systems, Inc.; and Chicago's Lincoln Park Zoo. She also has assumed the Davee Chair at the J.L. Kellogg Graduate School of Management at Northwestern University.

From her own experience, Martin knows that being a woman limited her choices, at least early in her career. "Interestingly enough," she said, "I don't remember rebelling against those limitations, as maybe I should. But as opportunities opened up, because I at least had the opportunity to be educated (something still not available or even forbidden to many women in this world), I was at least more ready to take advantage of those open doors."

She also was lucky to have had lots of people who helped and supported her along the way. "My neighbors who came out to vote for me, the people who helped me raise money when others said a woman couldn't win, my father who kept telling me I could do anything, and the memory of my mother and her quiet strength all made a difference," she said. "Unlike many young people today, I was surrounded by the kind of love and imperative to try that made a difference."

Martin wishes even more adults were willing to push young women to excel. The early lesson she learned about believing in herself was not lost, even on an eighth grader.

"I realize now it is the style to say 'Let's let people be what they want to be,' but I think that misses the point of people later in their life being all that they can be," she said. "I wish people had said, 'You can do it, you will do it, and you can do it sooner rather than later.'"

Marlee Matlin

*~I grew up thinking that I'm going to be
independent, deaf or not; that no one's going
to control me. I fought. I never hid anything.*

Award-winning actress Marlee Matlin knows the pain of growing up defined by other people's labels, stereotypes, and misper-
ceptions. When she was a child, neighborhood kids called her
"Deafo." Even now, the stigma sometimes still stings. Despite
being the youngest woman ever to have earned one of
Hollywood's most coveted kudos—she won an Oscar for Best
Actress when she was only twenty-one—Matlin strives to find
acceptance as an actress first, a deaf person second.

"I'm an actress who happens to be deaf," she said. "I think my
biggest advantage in some respects is to be deaf, because I can
translate the art by seeing it instead of listening to it."

Illness stole Matlin's ability to hear at an early age. She was
born with normal hearing in 1965, the youngest of three children and the only daughter of Donald and Elizabeth Matlin,
owners of a used car dealership in a Chicago suburb. Matlin was
only eighteen months old when she suffered a tough bout with
the virus roseola, a form of measles. By the time she recovered
from a high fever and other complications, Matlin was totally
deaf in one ear and eighty percent deaf in the other (she can hear
some sounds with the help of a hearing aid).

Fiercely independent, even as a young child, Matlin refused to
be cowed by roseola or the silence it left behind. By the time she

was five, she could read lips. She soon learned sign language as well, along with the rest of her family. Always supportive, her parents did everything they could to ensure deafness would not deter their daughter from living life on her own terms.

"I dealt with the outside world from the age of three. I was not shut out," Matlin said. "I grew up thinking that I'm going to be independent, deaf or not; that no one's going to control me. I fought. I never hid anything. My mother was very strong and very feisty, and that's probably where I picked it up from."

Her parents searched out the best schools, eventually deciding to enroll Matlin in public schools with special programs for hearing-impaired students, rather than placing her in specialized academies. As Matlin grew up, though, deafness sometimes proved difficult for her to cope with. Teasing from other children compounded her own frustrations over her deafness, filling Matlin with anger that often erupted into childhood temper tantrums.

"The children in the neighborhood didn't accept her," Matlin's mother recalled. "She became angry at everything."

Hoping to give her daughter a creative outlet for that anger, Matlin's mother introduced her to the theater and acting. At age eight, Matlin began performing in productions at the Center on Deafness in Des Plaines, Illinois, a school her mother helped establish. Matlin's first role: Dorothy in *The Wizard of Oz*, the center's first production in 1974.

"We all knew from the start that she was something special," Patricia Scherer, the center's founder, said of Matlin's earliest stage performances. "We had lots of talented kids, but she shone above the rest."

For the next seven years, Matlin traveled with the theater company throughout the Midwest. Once she was in high school, though, Matlin decided simply being a teenager was more fun than acting, and she quit the theater. "I had a boyfriend, I had a car, I had everything a high school student wanted," Matlin recalled. "So I didn't need to act."

Her break from acting proved only an intermission. Since deafness brought Matlin to the theater, it's not surprising that deafness would soon call her back. After graduating high school, she enrolled in Harper Junior College in Palatine, Illinois, with plans for a degree in criminal justice and dreams of becoming a career police officer. But Matlin quickly dropped out after learning that her hearing impairment would restrict her to a precinct desk job. Before leaving Harper, though, Matlin learned of auditions for *Children of a Lesser God*, a play centered around an angry, stubborn deaf woman.

Auditions were being held for a production of the play at the Immediate Theater in Chicago. The Tony Award-winning play by Mark Medoff focuses on the politics of deafness and the discrimination experienced by deaf people. Matlin decided to try out for the production and landed the role of Lydia, one of the play's secondary characters.

At the same time, an international casting search was underway for the film version of *Children of a Lesser God*. Randa Haines, the film's director; Candy Koethe, assistant producer; and Gretchen Rennell, casting director, were busily contacting institutions for the deaf throughout the United States, Canada, Great Britain, and Sweden, and considering every actress who had ever performed the lead female role of Sarah Norman in any stage production of the play. *Children of a Lesser God* represented the first time that deaf characters would be played on film by deaf or hearing-impaired actors.

"We rejected thousands of photos, including one of Marlee Matlin," Koethe recalled.

But Matlin wasn't rejected the second time Koethe and partners saw her. While reviewing a videotape of the Chicago production, the trio noticed Matlin in the secondary role of Lydia. Impressed by her stage presence, they decided to fly Matlin to New York City for a reading with actor William Hurt, who was already slotted to play the part of James, the lead male role in the film. That reading, followed by two more in Los Angeles, convinced the movie's producers that they had found the actress to portray Sarah. Instead of becoming a police officer, Matlin was on her way to stardom.

Matlin connected immediately with Hurt, who had learned sign language for his role. From their first script reading together in New York, sexual chemistry was evident between the pair.

Marlee Matlin   Photo by Greg Gorman

That chemistry not only added intensity to the film, it led to a full-blown romance. Matlin lived with Hurt for almost two years in his Manhattan apartment near Central Park. The romance ended in late 1987, reportedly because Hurt was upset over Matlin's overnight success as a movie star.

Their off-screen romance wasn't far removed from their on-screen relationship. While the stage version of *Children of a Lesser God* focuses on the politics of deafness and discrimination against the deaf, the movie takes a different tack, focusing on the relationship between James and Sarah, with Sarah's deafness serving as a metaphor for the communication problems inherent in all relationships.

"It's about talking and listening," Matlin said of the film. "It's about deaf people and it's about love and it's about communication. It's about rejection, about giving and taking, about patience."

But Matlin maintains she has little in common with Sarah, who refused to communicate except through sign language. "I'm more outgoing, more open-minded. I have hearing friends and deaf friends. And I can talk. Unlike Sarah, I didn't go to an institution for the deaf, in a world run by people who didn't understand me. Sarah was emotionally scarred because her hearing family treated her like an embarrassment. My family is supportive."

The film was released in October 1986 to mixed reviews. But critics raved about Matlin's performance, describing her as "an actress of awesome gifts" who brought an "intense, burning presence" to the film. At the Academy Awards ceremony the following year, Matlin beat out veteran actresses Jane Fonda, Sissy Spacek, Kathleen Turner, and Sigourney Weaver to win the Oscar for Best Actress.

Matlin followed the acclaim with a movie role that she had unfortunately accepted before winning the Oscar. The movie, *Walker,* based on the life of William Walker, an American adventurer who led a takeover of Nicaragua in 1855, proved box-office disappointment—not a career-boosting encore for an Oscar-winning actress.

Matlin bounced back with a starring role in the 1989 television movie, *Bridge to Silence,* the story of a deaf woman whose mother battles her for custody of her hearing child. In negotiating the role, Matlin demanded that the movie be close-captioned for the benefit of hearing-impaired viewers. (She also refuses to be interviewed on programs that are not close-captioned.)

Since *Bridge to Silence,* Matlin has been featured in *The Man in the Golden Mask,* a European film not released in the United

States, and appeared in small parts in the movies *The Linguini Incident* and *The Player.*

Matlin returned to TV in 1991, portraying a hearing-impaired district attorney in the series *Reasonable Doubts.* She was nominated for a Golden Globe award for best actress in a dramatic TV series for her portrayal of the show's Tess Kaufman, a liberal, opinionated Chicago prosecutor. That role originally was conceived for a hearing actor, but Robert Singer, the show's executive producer and creator, couldn't find anyone he liked to play the district attorney character. Something clicked, though, when Singer met Matlin—so much so that he rewrote the character to be deaf and gave Matlin the role.

"She has a star quality that's unmistakable," Singer said. "She's direct. She's very self-assured. Though the show wasn't conceived with Marlee in mind, from my first writing," Singer adds, "it was always for her."

Changing Tess Kaufman into a deaf prosecutor was done with fairly simple script changes. The show's other main character, a maverick cop turned investigator, was given a deaf parent so he would know sign language. Matlin's character was provided an interpreter for courtroom sequences. And because Matlin has limited speech abilities, the character could still speak some lines.

Matlin and Singer say the biggest challenge has been turning Kaufman into a character who happens to be deaf—rather than a deaf character. Both worked hard to integrate deafness into the role of Kaufman, instead of focusing on deafness as the character's main feature.

"At first, I could see that the writers were caught off guard," Matlin said. "It takes time for people to assimilate ideas about deafness. But I'm not only teaching them about deaf things. They're teaching me about the real things when it comes to writing—things that I don't hear, things that I don't necessarily see."

Despite her experience with *Reasonable Doubts* and the critical acclaim she has earned as a TV and film actress, Matlin still finds there are few good roles available to deaf actresses. For example, she was once offered a TV role that would have had her co-starring with a dog. She promptly turned it down.

Characteristically, Matlin isn't giving up on herself—or

Hollywood. She has set up her own production company, Solo One Productions, to develop her own projects.

"I'd like to play roles that any actor has the opportunity to play. Something that Sally Field, Meryl Streep, or Julia Roberts could play. If it's a good actor that's required for the role, then I can play it," she said.

"I hope that Hollywood will be more flexible toward me and other deaf actors. I don't want to play victims anymore. Some people think that's the only thing I'm good at."

As she searches for the right roles and projects, Matlin has found the right man in her life. In August 1993, she married Kevin Grandalski, a Los Angeles-area police officer, in a ceremony at the home of actor Henry Winkler, who is a close friend of Matlin's.

She continues to be a strong advocate for the rights of the hearing-impaired. Matlin has testified before the U.S. Senate on behalf of the National Captioning Institute, and she appeared as a guest on ABC's *Nightline* news program in 1988 regarding a student rebellion at Gallaudet University, the nation's only liberal arts college for the deaf. The students had rebelled over plans to install a hearing president who couldn't sign.

"If I meet someone who's isn't deaf and doesn't make any effort for me to understand them, from my point of view, it's very selfish," Matlin said. "People who know that I'm deaf should be able to acknowledge the fact that I have a deafness."

If Matlin had her way, the whole world would know sign language. "We deaf people have to learn how to speak—not necessarily in the verbal sense—but we have to learn to cope with the world we live in. Why not everyone?"

Terry McMillan

*⌒I'm not just going to sit back; I've never been
passive, and I'm not going to start now.*

When her first novel, *Mama,* was slated for publication in 1987,
Terry McMillan didn't sit back on the couch, open a bottle of
champagne, and toast her success; she started writing letters to
promote the book. McMillan was afraid *Mama* would suffer the
fate of most first novels and be left to languish on the publisher's
list without reviews, publicity, or sales.

"I had seen it happen before to friends of mine, really fine writers, whose publishers did nothing except send out a little press
release and the galleys," said McMillan, the best-selling black
author of *Disappearing Acts* and *Waiting to Exhale.* "My publisher
had come right out and told me what they couldn't do."

But McMillan was not one to accept the status quo. She
believed in her work and resolved that it should have the attention it deserved—even if she had to become her own press agent.
McMillan said she told herself, "I'm not just going to sit back;
I've never been passive, and I'm not going to start now."

So she got busy on the word processor at the law firm where
she worked as a night typist, and eventually sent out more than
three thousand letters to bookstores, universities, and the news
media, focusing on black organizations. "I did it all summer
long: my friends were at the beach, and I was licking envelopes,"
she recalled.

"I got a load of readings, so I set up my own tour because the publisher wasn't going to send me anywhere. Every week I sent my itinerary to my publicist—and it should have been the other way around."

McMillan showed the publisher how it should be done. *Mama* sold out its first printing before the publication date, an unusual success for a first novel. But then Terry McMillan is not your usual writer.

It's not just that her most recent novel, *Waiting to Exhale,* is a commercial triumph (the novel's paperback rights alone sold for $2.64 million, one of the highest prices ever paid for a reprint), or that women line up for hours to hear her speak, then nearly drown out her readings shouting, "You can say that again, sister!" and "Amen, amen."

McMillan has done more than write stunningly popular fiction; she has destroyed the conventional publishing wisdom that maintained there was no market for books in the black community. As *The New York Times Magazine* put it, "Publishers agreed that blacks don't buy books. Author Terry McMillan is making a fortune by proving them wrong."

McMillan grew up in a home in which the only book was the Bible. She was born in Port Huron, Michigan, in 1951, the oldest of five children. Her father was a laborer and an alcoholic whose tendency toward violence made family life turbulent. Her mother, who McMillan describes as a "survivor," supported the family by working at factory jobs. McMillan credits her mother with "teaching me and my siblings how to be strong and resilient. She taught us about taking risks."

McMillan's father died when she was sixteen. By that time, her parents had been divorced for three years, and McMillan was shelving books at the local library to make extra money for the family. She earned only $1.25 an hour, but the payoff was far greater: She discovered books.

It took this young library worker awhile to discover black writers—and even then, she didn't rush to read them. After coming across a novel by James Baldwin, she said, "I remember feeling embarrassed and did not read his book because I was too afraid. I couldn't imagine that he'd have anything better or different to say than Thomas Mann, Henry Thoreau, Ralph Waldo

Terry McMillan   Photo by Marion Ettlinger

Emerson. Needless to say, I was not just naive, but had not yet acquired an ounce of black pride."

She did know, though, that she wanted more opportunity than a factory town like Port Huron could offer. When McMillan was seventeen, she moved to Los Angeles and found work as a secretary. She took a course on black literary classics—and she wrote a poem. "I fell in love and wrote this poem because he broke my heart," she recalled. "That is how it started. It kept going and it started turning into sentences."

McMillan's sentences impressed Ishmael Reed, a novelist and promoter of little-known ethnic writers, whom she met when she transferred to the University of California at Berkeley "on some kind of minority type program." Reed published McMillan's first short story, "The End," in 1976.

McMillan earned a bachelor's degree in journalism from Berkeley, then moved to New York City to study screenwriting at Columbia University. But she was disappointed with the program, dropped out, and found work as a word processor.

Still, she didn't stop writing. She became a member of the Harlem Writers Guild and met regularly with a group to read her short stories. She recalled one meeting: "After I finished reading, the room got real quiet. Finally, somebody said, 'You sure can write!'"

Despite the encouragement of her writing group, these were troubled times for McMillan, who began drinking heavily. "I didn't drink every day, you didn't see me stumbling," she said. "But it was a problem, and I couldn't handle it."

She knew she had to overcome the addiction before it overcame her, just as it had her father. She gathered her strength and quit. Since the early 1980s, McMillan has been alcohol-free.

In 1983 she was accepted at the MacDowell Colony, a retreat where writers can work uninterrupted by the stresses of day-to-day life. During a two-week stay, she completed a first draft of *Mama.*

Back in New York, McMillan reworked the manuscript in the only time she had—on the subway commute to her word processing job. At the time, she was balancing work, writing, and single motherhood, caring alone for her young son, Solomon, who was born to her in 1984.

Mama, the story of a strong-minded black woman who brings to mind McMillan's mother, was published in 1987 to warm reviews. After McMillan completed her whirlwind promotional campaign, she left New York to take a teaching job at the University of Wyoming at Laramie.

There she began work on *Disappearing Acts,* the story of the painful love affair between Zora Banks, an aspiring singer, and an unemployed, frustrated-with-life contractor named Franklin Swift. The story is told from both points of view, shifting from Zora's account of the relationship to Franklin's.

McMillan's publishers were so impressed with her portrayal of Franklin that they asked her to rewrite the manuscript from his point of view. But that wasn't how McMillan saw the novel.

"It was going to be this coup: black woman writes story from black man's point of view, it's never been done, blah, blah, blah, blah, blah," she recalled. "Well, I didn't write *Disappearing Acts* to prove anything; that was the way the story had to be told. When my editor told me that Zora sounded kind of preppy, I said 'Look, she's not barefoot and pregnant, living in the projects. I cannot apologize because some of us have been to college, okay?'"

When the publisher added insult to McMillan's injury by asking to see the completed book before making an offer, McMillan withdrew her manuscript. Women, who are so frequently taught compliance, often don't have the courage for such audacious moves. But McMillan's mother had taught her to take risks. And the lesson paid off: another publisher promptly bought *Disappearing Acts*—and McMillan's view of the project. The novel was published in 1989, sold several hundred thousand copies, and is expected to be released as a movie, with the screenplay by McMillan.

By the time *Disappearing Acts* hit the bookstores, McMillan was teaching at the University of Arizona at Tucson, and she had another novel in her head. It started out as a personal essay about her dating woes and became *Waiting to Exhale*. The story of four accomplished black women who have it all but can't find men worth sharing it with, *Waiting to Exhale* burst into the publishing world and zoomed right up the bestseller list.

McMillan's portrayal of the foursome with their smart, sassy mouths, good jobs and bad dates had readers across the country saying, "Hey, that's me!" One fan put it best when she wrote McMillan saying that before *Waiting to Exhale*, she hadn't "read anything that was even close to my life."

For the first time, educated, middle-class black women saw their lives in a novel. But it was not just black women who responded to McMillan's writing; women of all colors identified with the novel's characters. Indeed, any woman who has dated too much will echo *Waiting to Exhale's* Savannah Jackson as she prays to the Lord for a "decent" man: "Could he be full of zest, and please, a slow, tender passionate lover—and could he already be what he aspired to?"

Here's how McMillan explains the book's broad appeal: "A lot of our circumstances and background may lend themselves to our own ethnic groups, but when you get right down to it, we all tick to the same beat. Women—human beings in general—all basically crave the same things in terms of affection, love, companionship. Nobody likes being lonely, and there's no color on that."

When this novelist says she had a good time writing her book, one is tempted to respond, "I *know* you did, girl!" According to McMillan, "Sometimes it got so hot, I had to fan myself while I typed it. Whoo! I write what I like to read."

Whoo again! By the end of 1992, more than 700,000 hardcover copies of *Waiting to Exhale* had been sold, and McMillan was outselling the popular thriller writer John Grisham at Waldenbooks, a national chain with over 1,150 stores. "We have really begun to pay attention to this," said Jeff Rogart, vice president for merchandising at the chain. Waldenbooks now has African-American sections at more than a quarter of its stores and plans to add more.

McMillan made booksellers sit up and take notice of a market they had traditionally ignored. The black middle class has grown, and *Waiting to Exhale* made it clear that they will buy books—if stores offer books they want.

McMillan made another point: publishers should rework their marketing plans if they want to sell to African Americans. As *The New York Times Magazine* concluded, "What McMillan did with her letter-writing campaign, her endless reading tours, which included not just colleges but also jazz clubs, community centers, and smaller black bookstores, was to create a paradigm of how to sell to black American readers."

Waiting to Exhale made the girl from Port Huron, Michigan, a millionaire. Today she and her son live in an art-filled Southwestern-style home in an affluent suburb outside Oakland, California.

One can't help but think that there's a lot of McMillan in the

Waiting to Exhale character Savannah Jackson, who tells her lover, "Well, one of my biggest hopes is that people in general, but all colors specifically, treat each other with kindness and respect. But I wish I had the power to wipe out poverty, and especially drugs."

McMillan would like to lead workshops with young blacks to help them tell their own stories. And she waived her lecture fee (which can run up to $5,000) to speak to a fiction-writing class at an adult education program in East Harlem. She urged the students to write for their own satisfaction and told them, "I'm not a star; I'm a writer."

But McMillan doesn't object to using her prominence where it will do the most good. She's not forgotten her library days and wants young black men and women to be proud of African-American writers. In an effort to promote the work of black novelists, she compiled and edited *Breaking Ice: An Anthology of Contemporary African-American Fiction.*

She used her position on the selection panel for the 1990 National Book Award to urge that *Middle Passage,* a novel by the black writer Charles Johnson, be chosen for the prize. Her advocacy stirred up controversy (one magazine accused her of calling a white judge a racist), but McMillan, armed with the strength her mother bequeathed her, fought for what she believed was right. She pointed out that no black man had won the award since Ralph Ellison in 1953, and she prevailed. When the award announcement was made, McMillan waved her arms over her head and cheered.

Similarly, McMillan views her foray into filmmaking as an opportunity to express her black pride and to make a statement: Blacks should be portrayed in films not as stereotypes but as ordinary human beings. "What's important to me is that a movie like *Disappearing Acts* gets onto the screen because we black people have to see ourselves as sensuous, erotic, passionate beings on the screen like white people do. We never get that opportunity," she said.

Despite her strong identity as an African American and her efforts on behalf of black writers, McMillan's work has not been recognized by black intellectuals. It may be that the very qualities which make McMillan's novels popular—their accessibility and their subject matter—keep them from garnering the critical acclaim reserved for more abstract or ideological literary works.

The poet Thulani Davis dismisses McMillan's novels as art for black yuppies. And McMillan doesn't hide her disappointment that "serious" black writers like Alice Walker and Toni Morrison have not expressed their regard for her work.

"I've gone out of my way to show respect for other black female writers," she said, "but I've yet to be acknowledged by some of the more successful ones, and it hurts."

McMillan expected criticism from black men because *Waiting to Exhale's* male characters are, at best, noncommittal and immature and, at worst, deceitful cocaine dealers. Although she'd been accused of "black male bashing" in *Disappearing Acts,* prominent black artists like Spike Lee and Ishmael Reed have been supportive of her work.

"I've been braced, but I really haven't gotten bashed," McMillan said. "Anyway, I don't apologize for my story. I told the story I wanted to tell."

Surprisingly, in this age of "anything goes," McMillan has raised eyebrows by liberally sprinkling her prose with four-letter words. She responded to the criticism typically, with four-letter words, then said, "So what? That's the way we talk. And I want to know why I've never read a review where they complain about the language the male writers use!"

Today McMillan has a new novel in progress. "It's like a picture that's out of focus," she said. "I don't force things on my characters; I wait and watch them grow."

One thing is certain, though, McMillan's new work will show black Americans working and loving and living their lives: gabbing with their friends and fighting with their lovers, buying new cars and closing big deals, stopping for milk at the 7-Eleven. McMillan once again will be writing her own story, for that has been her real accomplishment. She took her feelings and experiences, transformed them into fiction, and made it possible for African-American women to see themselves in print, just as the white women they work with can. There they are in a novel: smart and sexy and proud, laughing and struggling, living the

American dream, with all its flaws and delights.

McMillan has paved a way through the craggy landscape of publishing. Now it will be easier for black women—and black men, too—to write their stories and see them published. McMillan started as a writer, but she became a phenomenon. Writing, reading, and selling books will never be quite the same. As her agent, Molly Friedrich, put it, "Terry has become a force of nature."

Josie Natori

~I play many roles. I'm head of this business, a wife, a daughter with family obligations, and a mother...I have a lot of jobs, but each has been by my own choice.

Everybody knows the stereotype of the buttoned-down Wall Street businesswoman who wears sexy lingerie under her Brooks Brothers suit. Josie Natori has turned that fantasy upside down.

Natori, a former investment banker, has made a fortune convincing women to wear their underwear on the outside. As head of The Natori Company, a $35 million fashion empire, she designs seductive sleepwear that is just as likely to be worn out on the town as under the covers.

Natori's success is built on a simple idea: that working women want to indulge themselves. Her customers include everyone from Madonna to Fortune 500 executives. But she is perhaps the best proof of her own philosophy.

A former vice president at Merrill Lynch, Natori favors French couture over corporate tweeds. She's a working mom, with all the routine responsibilities that go along with raising a teenage son. At the same time, her glamorous lifestyle as a high-profile executive regularly takes her from the boardroom to limousines and charity balls.

Balancing the many roles in her busy life has given Natori an insight that accounts for her company's continued growth. "Women have spent so much time in the last fifteen years trying to go up the corporate ladder, trying to conform," she observed. "The point is that this underwear phenomenon is an affirmation. It means you can say, 'Hey, I want to be sexy, and it doesn't just have to be in the bedroom.'"

Over the past seventeen years, this diminutive dynamo—Natori stands a mere 5 feet 2 inches and weighs 94 pounds—has become an imposing force in the fashion industry. Starting with a small business that operated out of her apartment and offered only one item, a hand-embroidered peasant blouse, she now sells a wide range of products in forty countries. Several years ago, The House of Natori launched a collection of haute couture eveningwear, dresses and separates, as well as a line of moderately priced sleepwear and daywear sold under the "Josie" label.

More recently, the company announced that in 1994, it will begin offering shoes and in 1995, it will globally distribute fragrances through a licensing agreement with Avon Products, Inc. Such items will be sold in boutiques that market the Natori "lifestyle," in much the same way that Ralph Lauren and Laura Ashley have brought English club and country styles to the masses.

What is the Natori style? Like Natori herself, it's seductive without being sirenish, glamorous without being glitzy. It isn't the pink frills and potpourri of Victoria's Secret. But neither is it Frederick's of Hollywood. Gliding into a crowded Manhattan department store for one of her many public appearances, Natori stops traffic in a chic black wool suit with big pearl buttons. Her jet-black hair swings stylishly at her chin. The only touch of color: fire-engine red lips and nails.

With no design background—she doesn't sketch or sew—Natori has redesigned the lingerie and evening wear industry with her beaded bustiers, embroidered leggings, and stretch slip dresses, said Lynn Manulis, president of Martha International, which carries the Natori line. "Everyone is copying her look."

Ironically, Natori had business—not underwear—in mind when she left her home in Manila for New York City at the age of seventeen. A native of the Philippines, Josefina Cruz Natori was raised in an aristocratic home and schooled by nuns. For many years, she couldn't bring herself to describe her designs as sexy. "I'm a devout Catholic," explained Natori, the oldest of six children, "and I believed it was sinful to talk about sex."

Her parents, while strict, passed down to her an entrepreneurial spirit. Natori's father was a self-made man who ran his own construction company and eventually would build his daughter's manufacturing plant in the Philippines. Her mother was a strong-willed woman nicknamed "The Commander." But when Josie first told her parents that she was leaving her $100,000-a-year Wall Street job to sell lingerie, they were less than thrilled.

"They fought me in the beginning," she recalled. "They couldn't understand why I would leave such a prestigious job and go into an unknown business." But she was ready for a change.

Natori had come to New York in pursuit of a business degree and ultimately, a career on Wall Street. After graduating with straight As from Manhattanville College in 1968, she was offered a job in the corporate finance department of Prudential-Bache, Inc. Within months, she was helping run the firm's new Manila office.

"I found myself having to hire twenty people at once," she recalled. "It was instant exposure to the business world."

By 1975, Natori had become the first woman investment banker to be named a vice president at Merrill Lynch. She also had met and married Ken Natori, a Japanese American and former managing partner at Shearson Lehman Hutton. After the birth of the couple's first and only child, Kenneth Jr., in 1976, she began to reevaluate her career choice.

"I was making tons of money, but there was something missing," she said. "I could have kept going on and climbing the corporate ladder, but I wasn't happy deep down inside. I just wasn't challenged anymore."

She always had dreamed of starting her own business; the only problem was deciding what kind. She briefly considered opening a car wash, which she'd heard was profitable. She and her husband even spent weekends parked outside New York car washes, counting customers. But Natori soon realized she had no aptitude for soap suds and hot wax. She needed something that tapped more of her creative talents.

Ultimately, Natori focused on what made her unique: her eth-

Josie Natori

nicity. She went back to the Philippines and began looking for native products to import to the United States. First, she tried reproduction Queen Anne furniture. She sold a few loads, then the factory burned down. Next, it was wicker baskets, most of which ended up in her attic. Even with two strikes against her, she wasn't willing to give up her dream. When a relative sent her several embroidered cotton peasant blouses in 1977, Natori sensed she was about to get a hit.

Carrying the blouses around in a shopping bag, Natori began to visit stores, drawing on the cold-calling sales skills she'd learned as a stockbroker. When a buyer at Bloomingdale's saw the blouses and suggested she turn them into nightshirts, Natori seized the advice. Within three months, she had $150,000 worth of orders—and confidence enough to quit her job at Merrill Lynch and go into the lingerie business full time.

For the first year, Natori sold her products out of her home, sometimes even packing the orders herself. "Buyers would go to Josie's home, and she'd have her baby in his crib, and she'd go through her line," recalled Mary McMahon, then a vice president of intimate apparel at Macy's. "Even then, it was clear that she had something special. You could tell she was a real comer." Natori's husband would pitch in on his days off, acting as the butler and serving wine to buyers.

By 1978, the business had outgrown the couple's apartment, so they invested $200,000 of their savings in a small showroom on East 34th Street in Manhattan. Today, The Natori Company occupies an entire floor, as well as a design studio in a building around the corner. Ken Natori became his wife's business partner in 1985. As the company's chairman and chief financial officer, he is in charge of operations, finance, and licensing. As president and chief executive officer, she provides the company's public image and focuses on the creative side.

Everything about the Natoris screams success, from her Pierre Cardin suits to his pinstripes, bow ties, and suspenders. They share a sleek, walnut-paneled office at The Natori Company headquarters. She works at a modern desk carved from a giant slab of black granite; he prefers an ornate Louis XIV reproduction. On the rare occasions when they're in the office at the same time, they celebrate by sending out for a lunch of white wine and seafood salad.

Away from work, the Natoris divide their time between three homes—a Park Avenue apartment, a pied-a-terre in Paris, and a country retreat in Pound Ridge, New York. They are familiar faces on the New York social scene, attending as many as three functions a week. Josie Natori also sits on several charitable boards and is an active member of the Committee of 200, a group of women entrepreneurs who head multimillion-dollar companies. In 1990, she helped raise money for victims of an earthquake in her homeland.

Natori confesses that her wide-ranging obligations often stretch her thin. "I play many roles," she said. "I'm head of this business, a wife, a daughter with family obligations, and a mother...I have a lot of jobs, but each has been by my own choice."

When she manages to find a little time for herself, shopping is her favorite form of relaxation. When in Paris, she browses flea markets for inspiration and visits the couturiers. But running a $35 million business leaves little time for such pursuits. Unlike many CEOs, Natori believes in making as many personal appearances as possible, getting into stores and meeting her customers, finding out what they want. "It's the most important thing I can do," she said.

Watching Natori work the crowd at a Lord & Taylor lingerie show, it's difficult to imagine that when she started her business almost two decades ago, she had no experience and no connections. "I knew nothing about the rag trade. I wore brown polyester dresses, and my hair was down to here," she said, pointing below her waist.

Yet her naiveté may have been her strong suit in the beginning. "I had no preconceived ideas," she explained. "I came in and said, 'Who cares what color lingerie is supposed to be? Why can't it look like an evening gown? Why should it look like all that granny stuff?' I wasn't bound, I followed my instinct."

Because of her inexperience, she also learned many lessons the hard way. Designing clothes to fit her own petite frame, she quickly discovered that she had to hire standard-size models. She also faced problems with poor workmanship in her early days as an entrepreneur—until she figured out she could send defective goods back.

"I didn't know there was any such thing as a reject," she explained. "We got an order from Horchow's for a thousand scalloped-neck nightshirts and they came from Manila without scallops. Mother and I cut them ourselves all night long. If garments came in dirty, we washed them in the bathtub. Then they would shrink. It was a nightmare."

In 1980, Natori gained control over the manufacturing process by having her father build her a factory in Manila, which now employees six hundred people. But some nightmares were beyond her control. The hardest lesson Natori had to learn: in the fickle fashion world, few things are ever certain. For instance, she once received a $25,000 order from a major New York store, which was later canceled—but not before all the garments had been made. The incident initiated Natori in a new style of business. "On Wall Street," she said, "you cement a deal over the phone. But in fashion, you can sign in blood and it doesn't mean a thing."

Several things did work in her favor, though. Timing, for one. Natori's rise in the business world coincided with that of many women of her generation, so she was perfectly poised to understand their need for respect in their professions and romance in their personal lives. She also was savvy enough to pick up on fashion trends in pop music and street culture. When teenage Madonna-wannabes started showing up in downtown music clubs wearing bustiers, lace bras, and leggings, Natori translated the look for her uptown, upscale customers. Now when Madonna wants to get dressed up, she often dons a Natori design.

Natori also believes that being a woman and a member of a minority group have worked for her, not against her. "Being female and Filipino have been my biggest assets. The two cultures (Asian and American) gave me a certain mystique." And her size undoubtedly has had its advantages. "I may look vulnerable," she acknowledged.

But make no mistake, underneath the satin and lace lies a razor-sharp mind for business—and that is what's given Natori an edge in the extremely competitive $7 billion lingerie industry. "I go straight in there and find my way through," she said. "On Wall Street, they used to call me 'small but terrible'—in a joking way, you know."

Assunta Ng

~*Being a woman makes me more
determined to survive, succeed,
and enrich the lives of other people.*

"Don't ever look back." That's the advice Assunta Ng, founder of
the *Chinese Seattle Post,* the first Chinese-language newspaper in
the Pacific Northwest in half a century, likes to share in her many
speaking engagements to diverse audiences ranging from professional women to Asian-American entrepreneurs.

While Ng's simple message may have the ring of pat podium
philosophy, her admonitions are heartfelt and her wisdom hard-
won, for she's overcome obstacles that surely would have
defeated a less daring soul. Born in Canton, China, and raised in
Hong Kong, Ng had little hope of spreading her wings: as far
back as she can remember, she felt stifled by the traditional
expectations her Asian culture placed on girls. "I was not
encouraged to dream about anything," she said. "If I expected to
get out of the house at all, I could be a teacher, nurse, or secretary. Nobody ever encouraged me to do anything more."

In fact, Ng was considered the "least likely to succeed" among
her peers at school. The stressed-out lifestyle of young Chinese
students, marked by the constant fear of failure on exams, all but
destroyed Ng's self-esteem. "I was shy and did not get involved
in a lot of extracurricular activities," she said. "I was not well-
liked by the teachers, and I simply did not stand out."

But all that changed when Ng took the national standardized

test required for Chinese high school seniors. She scored in the top 100 of the 35,000 students who took the exam. Stunned by her outstanding performance, Ng began to think beyond the secretarial courses she had been taking. She began to think of college—in the United States.

"Of course my parents were very upset," she said. Her desire to move abroad seemed so sudden because they never suspected their quiet, obedient eldest child felt confined and sheltered at home. "My childhood was not a happy one, but I didn't realize it at the time," Ng recalled. "I did what was expected of me. Consideration of happiness is not a priority in Chinese culture. Nobody was happy. You just didn't think about it. Fathers worked to put food on the table. Mothers were subservient to men. No one thought about child rearing as a joy, like today's baby-boom parents."

Her parent's fears were the least of it. She also faced very real financial constraints. The Ng family did not have the means to support her while she studied abroad. So she finally struck a deal with them: They would provide enough money for one year; she would be responsible for the rest.

So with no money to speak of, no friends and family to turn to, and no definite plans beyond continuing her education, Ng turned her sights to the west and landed in the Seattle, Washington, area on the picturesque campus of the University of Washington. At the time, she had little awareness of or appreciation for the fact that she had single-handedly changed the course of her life.

Unlike many other students who struggle to fit into a new culture, Ng felt at home immediately. "For the first time in my life, I felt free," she said. "My life had been shallow and limited. I wanted to see the world and there I was—young, naive, poor, but ready."

Ng thrived in the American educational system, which she feels encourages more free thinking and creativity than the rote memorization demanded in Chinese schools and universities. She was interested in everything but concentrated on history, education, and journalism. "I was finally on my own, doing things I liked. It was very healthy for me psychologically."

Assunta Ng   Photo by Alan Abramowitz

Not that her life was fun and games. Ng often worked three jobs during the summers, saving every penny for tuition and board. She moved from apartment to apartment, always on the lookout for the cheapest living quarters available, no matter how small. The way she figured it, she didn't need much space since she was out working most of the time. In spite of—or maybe because of—such hardships, Ng's self-confidence and determination were growing.

That period in her life is best illustrated in this story Ng shares about a conversation she had with her oldest son, Ho-Yin, who's now fifteen. "I was telling Ho-Yin how I had written to Pearl Buck, the Nobel Prize-winning author, for a term paper. I wanted to do something special so I could stand out, and of course, get an A. She even wrote back. But when my son asked if I still had the letter, I said of course not. He simply could not understand how I was living, moving so often that I could have no extra baggage. I was mobile—but I was *free.*"

Ng graduated, married, and moved into teaching, an occupation she loved but found frustrating at times. Many of her public school students were immigrant children—from Germany, Mexico, the Philippines, and China—so Ng felt a special affinity with them.

After several successful years as a teacher, she reached a turning point when the teachers in her district went on strike. Ng crossed the picket line because she felt that no matter what, her place was in the classroom. "Yes we were severely underpaid and worked too hard for too little money," she recalled. "But I strongly believe teachers should spend their time teaching, not picketing." When the strike was finally settled, Ng sensed subtle hostility from her once-friendly colleagues. She decided her "heart was no longer in teaching," even though she had no back-up career plan.

Indeed, Ng feels strongly about acting on decisions once they're made. "I didn't have a 'Plan B.' I just knew I was ready for a change." True to her own words, Ng didn't look back.

She found herself in graduate school, again at the University of Washington, this time studying business administration and speech communications. She received her master's degree in 1979.

But the question of what to do next was a daunting one. Her husband, George Liu, encouraged her to find something she truly loved, for he had already learned that working simply to make a living lead to an "empty life."

After months of career counseling and soul-searching, Ng decided she was going to start a Chinese-language newspaper, a communication vehicle she found was sorely lacking in the greater Seattle area. Sensing this strong need, she decided to forgo her traditional business school training—which stipulates the need for extensive research and analysis before undertaking such a project—in favor of her own gut instincts. The decision took courage, for Ng knew full well she would face detractors in every corner.

"The newspaper industry is tough and male-dominated, the Asian business community was not ready to take a woman seriously, and banks were not forthcoming with financial backing," she recalled. Despite numerous warnings of failure, Ng stuck with her decision and plunged full speed ahead by using her own savings to finance the start-up. "I couldn't back down just because some people said 'no,'" she explained.

Once again the daring Ng put herself in a situation that demanded nothing short of body-and-soul commitment if she was to succeed. "Printing newspapers is very labor-intensive. It's challenging and stimulating, but also physically draining," Ng said. Alongside her full-time staff of three, she worked practically around the clock for months until finally she fell ill from sheer physical exhaustion.

Today Ng continues to work long, hard hours but feels less inclined to do "every little thing myself." But make no mistake, she's still very much in charge of her increasingly diversified business, which now includes the *Northwest Asian Weekly,* the only English-language Asian weekly in the Pacific Northwest, and several annual publications—the *Seattle Chinese Business Directory, Asian Magazine,* and *Discover China in Seattle.*

In addition to publications, her company, the Seattle Chinese Post, Inc., offers translation, printing, and typesetting services in Chinese, Cambodian, Korean, Japanese, Laotian, and Vietnamese. Ng has been able to expand the business primarily by learning how to operate more efficiently: although the number of publications her company offers is growing, the time involved in writing and producing them actually has been reduced. This progress she attributes to her husband, George, who eventually left his "predictable career track" to help Ng computerize her business. "We have a very sophisticated system that allows us to do much more than a few people could really do. George has done a thorough job," Ng said proudly.

At the same time, she acknowledges that having her spouse at the office did require some adjustment on everyone's part. "All of a sudden there were two bosses, which was very confusing and sometimes stressful for the staff," she explained. The couple decided that only one of them should have the authority for final approvals—Ng, naturally. However, she is careful to stay out of matters involving the computer system, which is entirely George's domain.

With circulation topping 15,000 and annual sales of $600,000, Ng's *Chinese Seattle Post*—which is still the only bilingual Chinese newspaper in the country—is by all accounts a solid success. That's why recently Ng has been able to devote more attention to her deep-rooted interest in serving women, children, and the Asian community. For instance, one dream she has yet to fulfill: starting a cross-cultural program for youths. "There is so much racial tension today," said Ng, who believes much of the problem can be attributed to a lack of understanding and exposure to other cultures. "If we bring African-American and Hispanic children into Chinatown to learn how to make dim sum or practice kung fu, they will have a greater understanding of our culture," she observed. She hopes to bring about this cross-cultural exchange through a foundation she is working to create—the Asian Weekly Foundation—and by continuing the many projects and programs her business already supports.

Ng also devotes time to women's issues, mostly through her many board memberships and speaking engagements. She is actively involved with groups such as the YWCA, Women's Network, Women's Forum, and others. "Being a woman makes me more determined to survive, succeed, and enrich the lives of other people," she said.

The fact that she has already achieved much of this is evidenced in the number of awards she has received, chief among them the Women of Enterprise Award sponsored jointly by Avon Products, Inc., and the U.S. Small Business Administration. She's also received the Women Making a Difference in the Corporate World award sponsored by the International Women's Forum.

Most of the awards Ng receives recognize her success as an entrepreneur—an experience she encourages women everywhere to try. "Because I am running my own business, every day is exciting and new. I wouldn't want to work for anybody else. I am shaping my own destiny." Her message to other women: "You can do it too."

Ng's other community activities center on helping "people of color." She does not like the term "minority," which she feels is dangerously misused. "It's a label that affects how people perceive themselves. It's degrading," she explained. To further her own desire for greater understanding and communication, Ng supports such organizations as the Northwest Minority Publishers Association, Chinese Information and Service Center, and the Chinatown Chamber of Commerce, to name a few.

But with all her accomplishments and professional accolades, Ng still considers motherhood her greatest achievement—because she never expected to have children. When she was growing up, Ng recalled, her mother often chided her for not having any maternal instincts because, unlike most young girls, Ng shunned dolls. Today, as the mother of two teenage sons, Ng knows nothing could be further from the truth.

"It's very difficult to raise children in the right way," she said. "Being a mother is such a huge job." Yet whenever her sons are asked whether they mind having a mother who's so busy and who works so hard, Ng said, their usual reply is, "No, she makes it up to us in so many ways." Naturally, she finds this very rewarding.

But in raising her own children, Ng is careful to foster their sense of freedom and curiosity, because she wants them to have the self-confidence that was missing from her own childhood. "I do not limit my sons," she said. "They have developed their own interests and ambitions, and my job is to encourage them to go as far as possible."

That Ng shares a similar perspective about the community at large is apparent. Whenever she's asked to speak to groups, Ng often admonishes the audience to seek their own challenges and take risks: "If you do not have goals, if you do not embrace challenge, if you do not dream of more, if you always look back, you are just existing—not living."

Anna Quindlen

∽I think this is what feminism has always looked like—ordinary women who want the best for themselves, the best for their daughters, the best for their sons. Women who want to decide what that best is and don't want anybody saying, 'You can't stay home because that's not cool,' or 'You can't be vice president because you'll just leave and have babies,' or 'You can't grow up and collect trash, because women don't know how to collect trash.'

"Whenever my response to an important subject is rational and completely cerebral, I know there is something wrong with it," Anna Quindlen has written. "I have always been governed by my gut."

It is Quindlen's gut and her ability to translate her feelings into the written word that have made her one of the best known newspaper columnists in the country and one of the few female luminaries in American journalism. Whether she is writing about homelessness or abortion, grocery shopping or watching her son discover a lightning bug, Quindlen uses her own experiences and visceral responses to touch her readers and make them think.

"The only thing that makes writing good is giving it our own voice, our own personality," Quindlen said. "Writing is always an act of faith in your own character."

Quindlen's ruminations about such topics as the Clarence

Thomas hearings, abortion, and the Persian Gulf War in her "Public and Private" column, syndicated by *The New York Times*, won her the 1992 Pulitzer Prize for commentary. She was only the third woman in the history of the prize to win this particular award.

But her greatest achievement is found in those gut feelings so artfully expressed. First, with her "Life in the 30s" column where she wrote about motherhood, being a Catholic, dealing with the painters, and the other things, both large and small, that make up our lives, and then with "Public and Private," Quindlen has brought a personal—and some would say, a woman's—voice to journalism.

"Public and Private" is not sober, analytic commentary. Quindlen's work has immediacy because she homes in on details, what she once called "the tiny dots that, taken together, make up the pointillistic picture of our lives." In a piece on the Persian Gulf War, for example, Quindlen wrote about three children who were left alone when their father was sent to the Mideast: "They were wearing dirty clothes because they hadn't figured out how to do the laundry, and their father had tacked a note to the wall, telling them how to get cash with his automatic teller card."

Quindlen's columns provide logical, well-thought-out arguments on important issues, but they also show, through vivid images like a child's dirty clothes, how these issues affect our day-to-day lives. "Anybody who tries to convince me that foreign policy is more important than child rearing is doomed to failure," Quindlen said. "The personal has become the political in what I think is the most positive way."

Quindlen also has achieved recognition as a book author. *Object Lessons*, her first novel, was published in 1991 and became a bestseller; she's now working on a second novel. In 1992, she published a children's book, *The Tree That Came To Stay*.

Anna Quindlen was born in Philadelphia in 1953, the oldest of five children. Her father, a management consultant, was of Irish descent; her mother, a homemaker, was Italian American.

"I really felt the mix," Quindlen said. "The Irish side was very loud and vocal, upwardly mobile. But my Italian mother was such a powerful figure. She was not the particularly intellectual type, but she had an unnerving nose for the truth."

As a girl, Quindlen had no lack of spunk and thought she would become either "pope or president." She was, she has written, "a textbook case eldest child—a leader, a doer, a convincing veneer of personality and confidence atop a bottomless pit of insecurity and need."

Quindlen went to parochial schools where she was required to memorize the entire Baltimore Catechism. But she was taught by liberal, intellectually rigorous nuns and priests. She remembers the nuns as "marvelous teachers and incredible role models." They showed Quindlen that women could do intellectual work.

Quindlen grew up at a time when society had many rules to follow, and in a religion where there were many more. But then in the late 1960s and early 1970s, powerful social changes swept the country and the rules went the way of white gloves and stay-at-home moms.

Seemingly, to Quindlen, at the same time, her mother died from cancer, "eaten alive by disease." Quindlen was nineteen when, on a cold January night, she and her father told her younger brothers and sisters that their mother was dead. Then she had to help care for the family and to find a way to shape her life, without her mother and without the rules.

"A kind of earthquake in the center of my life shook everything up," she has written, "and left me to rearrange the pieces."

Late adolescence is a time of inner turbulence for most young people. For Quindlen, who was moving into adulthood during a time of social turmoil, still reeling from the death of her mother, it was a particularly difficult period. She has written about that time in her life: "I felt orphaned, cut off from the past. It was many years before I would know that I had found both feelings liberating."

Instead of rules, Quindlen suddenly had choices. It was a situation infinitely more frightening, but one filled with possibility. Despite her grief and the aching pit in her stomach, Quindlen set out to discover what the changed world had to offer.

While she was a junior at Barnard College, she sent a story to *Seventeen* magazine with some hope but no expectation. The

Anna Quindlen

magazine sent back a check. "It seemed to me a miracle," she said, "a little like the loaves and fishes."

Although Quindlen wanted to write fiction, she also thought she would be a good reporter. She landed an after-school job at the *New York Post* by showing up at the homes of journalists who had registered with the Barnard baby-sitting service. "I needed a way to let them find out about me," she said. She accepted a full-time job at the *Post* when she graduated in 1974.

"I found that it was more fun than anything in the world," she said of reporting, "that it was an end in itself and also that it would be good for me as a fiction writer."

Within three years Quindlen had a job at the nation's most prestigious newspaper, *The New York Times*. In those days the *Times* was a male preserve, but Quindlen had found work she wanted to do and she was determined to do it, no matter the obstacles.

She started as a city hall reporter and didn't wait for her first promotion to come to her. She wrote well, worked hard, and then asked her editors to let her write the paper's "About New York" column. At twenty-eight, she was the youngest person ever promoted to what was considered one of the paper's best writing jobs.

Two years later, Quindlen became one of the highest-ranking women at the *Times* when she was appointed deputy metropolitan editor. She valued this job for more than its impact on her career: "I had the ability to assign women, to hire women, and to act as a role model in an institution that didn't have a lot women at role model level."

Still, after two years, it was time to move on. "I think the thing that has always motivated me in my work is to do something that I haven't done before," she said.

This time she aimed to do something completely different. In 1978, she'd married lawyer Gerald Krovatin, whom she'd met when they were both eighteen. By the time she was ready to leave the deputy editor's spot, she and Krovatin had two young sons, and Quindlen wanted to spend more time with them and work on a novel.

While she was home, she wrote a series of freelance essays for the *Times*. They attracted so much reader attention that several newspapers offered Quindlen her own column.

A.M. Rosenthal, then the executive editor of the *Times,* was horrified. "He said, 'Do the column for us,'" Quindlen recalled. "It took him about three minutes to come up with the concept:

'Let's see, how old are you? Okay, let's call it Life in the 30s.'"

Baby boomers took to her "Life in the 30s" column as they once had to hard rock and left-wing politics. Quindlen's weekly personal essays showed her readers the details of her life and her heart: loving her husband and children, buying junk food, missing her mother, and surviving birthday-party wars. She wrote about her life—and captured the lives of her readers.

"When you read her column, it's almost like you're reading a letter from Anna," Rosenthal said.

The column was syndicated in sixty newspapers by the time Quindlen decided that, once again, she should move on. She wrote her last column when her third child, a daughter named Maria, was born. As a postscript, the columns were collected in a book, *Living Out Loud,* published in 1988.

But the *Times* found yet another way to persuade Quindlen to return—by offering her a column on its highly respected Op Ed page. She would join journalistic superstars William Safire and Russell Baker, becoming the third woman and youngest writer ever to have a column in the space. It was an achievement she had earned with talent and determination, but one she hardly had dared to dream of: "If, when I first came to the *Times,* someone told me I would be writing a column alongside Russell Baker, I would have said 'Get outta here.'"

Dubbed "Public and Private" in honor of Quindlen's ability to bring the personal to bear on the collective, the column, which premiered in 1990, brought a refreshing brightness to the paper journalists call the "Gray Lady."

And Quindlen, without apology, brought her feelings to the job. "I don't believe in objectivity, I believe in fairness," she said. "A friend told me recently that she could never be a journalist because she would get too involved emotionally in the stories. I told her that when I stop feeling it, it's time to stop doing it."

Quindlen may have her heart on her sleeve, but her writing cuts to the quick. Hers is a voice filled with humor and warmth—and with the passion of indignation. Twice a week she speaks her mind in beautifully crafted prose. Here, for example, is Quindlen on the homeless: "Too much energy has gone into deciding where we do not want them to be and making sure we would not be there."

Quindlen keeps no sacred cows. When the *Times* broke journalistic tradition and published the name of a woman who said she had been raped by a member of the Kennedy family, along with a quote that described the woman as "having a little wild streak," Quindlen wrote a scathing response. What the paper had done, she said, was "beneath its traditions" and was "not informative, but punitive."

She refused to accept accolades for going up against the boss. "It was not courageous for me to write that column," she said. "It would have been cowardice if I had not."

"Public and Private" now appears in one hundred newspapers. In 1993, the columns were collected into a book, *Thinking Out Loud.* (Quindlen took a leave from the column while working on her latest novel.)

Not surprisingly, Quindlen's strong views have attracted criticism. Her columns on abortion (she is pro-choice) bring the most negative mail. And she is often accused of "Catholic bashing" because she is critical of the church's stand on abortion, birth control, and women priests.

Quindlen takes the flak without flinching. "I'm not afraid of being seen as a bad Catholic," she said. "I know I am a good Catholic. And I know I represent many, many Catholics out there who feel the same way as I do."

Her disagreements with the church have not turned her away from Catholicism. She attends church regularly. "I could no more say I am not Catholic than say I am not Irish, not Italian," she once wrote.

Quindlen's stand on women's issues in particular has attracted wide-ranging attention. She's been attacked for being too much a feminist, and she's been attacked for not being feminist enough. To her, it's a straightforward matter. "If I'm anything, I'm a feminist," she said.

When Quindlen was growing up, the world was run by men. Women stayed home or served as assistants. This was not the life she saw for herself. "I figured either life was going to be considerably different for me than it was for my mother or I was going to be angry all the time," she said.

Today Quindlen's column is her bully pulpit and she often uses it to take a stand on the cause of women's rights. Her daughter's birth has given new passion to her preaching. "I got pissed off all over again about how the world treats women," she said.

The way Quindlen sees it, feminism is not an abstract body of ideas, the province of political thinkers. It is for Everywoman— and for every day. The concept is simple: feminism means making sure that women have choices about how *they* want to live their lives.

"I think this is what feminism has always looked like," Quindlen said, "ordinary women who want the best for themselves, the best for their daughters, and the best for their sons. Women who want to decide what that best is and don't want anybody saying, 'You can't stay home because that's not cool,' or 'You can't be vice president because you'll just leave and have babies,' or 'You can't grow up and collect trash, because women don't know how to collect trash.'"

Quindlen has practiced her own philosophy and used the choices feminism has won for her to structure her life. But making choices is sometimes more difficult than following the rules. Quindlen agonized over her decision to resign her position as deputy metropolitan editor after her second son was born. "When I decided I was going to do that, I thought, 'This is bad for women,'" she recalled. She was painfully aware of the old saw that a woman can't hold a position of responsibility because she will leave to have children.

Yet she also knew the strain a pressured job brings to family life. "I could have done it," she said, "but I felt I would have been missing so much good stuff at home, it just wouldn't have been worth it to me."

Now Quindlen, who lives with her family in a brownstone in Hoboken, New Jersey, takes her children to school in the mornings, spends evenings and weekends with the family, and works in between. It's not easy moving between two worlds, balancing newspaper deadlines and carpool schedules, but Quindlen wouldn't have it any other way.

She is clear about why maintaining the balance is so important—not only for her children, but for herself. "A good job doesn't warm you on Christmas Eve," she said. "And twenty years from now my kids won't remember a commencement speech I gave, but they might remember a good game of Scrabble."

These are unusual words for a Pulitzer Prize-winning columnist. But Quindlen values her private life as much as her public presence, and she won't compromise one for the other. Few have fought harder than Quindlen to make an equal place in the work force for women, yet she resists any attempt to hold up her career as an example for future generations. "For younger women," she said, "I'm happy if they see my life and, knowing I give equal shelf space to my personal life, consider me a role model."

But Quindlen doesn't kid herself—or the women who read her columns. Arranging "the shelf" so that everything fits is always a struggle and sometimes impossible. "Women were freed to have wonderful jobs, but for most of us it turned out to be the right to have two jobs," Quindlen has written. And she argues that unless sex roles are "overhauled in some primary, radical way, it will turn out to be an incomplete revolution—one that is essentially meaningless to working-class and poor women."

It is probably no coincidence that Quindlen, the master of balance in her personal life, won the Pulitzer Prize for a column called "Public and Private." Over the years, she has learned to harmonize, to make elements into a whole. Her ability to bring together the individual story and the broad issue, and to marry her feelings with her intellect, have earned her professional acclaim, not to mention public admiration. And her decision to equate work and family has made her life rich.

But Quindlen does not believe in happily-ever-after. The young woman who mourned her mother's death on a cold winter's night, then braved a new world and conquered it, came of age along the way. She came to understand that living is a life-long process.

As Quindlen wrote in the introduction to the collection of her "Life in the 30s" columns: "Oddly enough, what I have learned since that January night many years ago is that life is not so much about beginnings and endings as it is about going on and on and on. It is about muddling through the middle. That is what I am doing now. Muddling through the middle. Living out loud."

Janet Reno

~I think the problem of drugs in America, youth violence, teen pregnancy, and youth gangs are symptoms of a deeper problem in America... that too often we have forgotten and neglected our children.

One aunt was a World War II nurse who landed with General Patton's army in North Africa and marched on Italy. Another tested combat aircraft and trained pilots. Her mother wrestled alligators and was named an honorary Indian princess.

So it's little wonder that Janet Reno has boldly tackled her role as the nation's top crime fighter.

Reno, fifty-five, comes from a long line of fearless, spirited women. Raised on the edge of the Everglades, she spent fifteen years as the state attorney in Miami, where she earned a reputation as a tough opponent of drug dealers and deadbeat dads. As the nation's first female attorney general, one of her first jobs was ending the standoff between law enforcement officers and cult members in Waco, Texas. The FBI assault on the Branch Davidian compound ended in tragedy. But Reno was quick to take the blame.

"She stood up and took a bullet for us," one veteran agent later observed with obvious admiration.

Standing 6 feet 1½ inches, Reno has a larger-than-life image that has made her perhaps the most popular member of the Clinton administration. Jay Leno personally called to ask her to be on *The Tonight Show.* Schoolchildren chant her name and fans have lined up for her autograph—even when she was dining with Barbra Streisand. In a town where politicians routinely test the political winds before taking a stand, Reno is admired for her honesty, bluntness, and courage.

"She isn't just a breath of fresh air," said New York Congressman Charles Schumer. "She's a hurricane of fresh air."

Janet Reno was born July 21, 1938, to a family that already was legendary in Miami, a city with more than its share of colorful characters. Her father, Henry Reno, was a police reporter for the *Miami Herald* for more than forty years. A Danish immigrant, he reportedly got tired of people mispronouncing his last name, Rasmussen, so he pulled out a map of Nevada and picked a new one.

Her mother, Jane Wood Reno, also was a reporter, who relished her reputation as a tough-as-nails outdoorswoman. She hunted and wrestled alligators, kept peacocks and boa constrictors as pets, and was made an honorary princess by the Miccosukee Indians. It was from her mother that Reno learned her love of nature. "When Janet Reno needs to be alone, she will get in a canoe and paddle thirty or forty miles," said Miami Mayor Seymour Gelber, a former judge and prosecutor who hired Reno to the state attorney's office.

Reno spent her childhood on the family's twenty-one-acre homestead near the Everglades with her sister, Maggy; her two brothers, Robert and Mark; and a host of exotic co-inhabitants. Never married, she continued even after she became state attorney to live in the cypress log house her mother had built. Reno helped nurse her mother through a fatal bout with cancer in the fall of 1992. Then in February 1993, she got a call from the President, asking her to come to Washington.

Reno was not Bill Clinton's first choice for attorney general. (His first two, Zoe Baird and Kimba Wood, were scratched for hiring illegal immigrants as nannies.) But by most accounts, she should have been. In fifteen years as Miami's state attorney, Reno weathered her share of controversy, but her integrity never was questioned. In fact, she was so careful about any appearance of impropriety that she fed the parking meters even while on official business and requested a special prosecutor to investigate complaints that her mother's peacocks were creating a disturbance.

She has been at the center of some of the most racially explosive legal battles in Miami's history. But she also has managed to build bridges to the city's divided ethnic communities. After four Dade County police officers were acquitted in 1980 of beating to death a black insurance man—an incident that set off days of deadly riots—Reno became the focus of the community's anger and disillusionment. She regained the public's trust by opening her office to blacks, Latinos, and women, and by becoming "the most accessible politician in the state of Florida, bar none," according to H.T. Smith, a prominent black attorney.

"I have gone from being one of her strongest and most outspoken critics to a strong supporter," Smith said. "There may be a better choice for attorney general, but I don't know that person."

One measure of her popularity is the fact that Reno, a liberal-leaning Democrat, was reelected four times in a heavily Republican county. In 1984, she campaigned for her second term by marching through riot-torn neighborhoods with an eight-piece Boy Scout band. Her office helped residents of a housing project open a convenience store to create jobs and boost morale. She used citizen grand juries to investigate poor conditions in public housing, as well as issues such as foster care, school dropouts, and gun control. She cracked down on child abusers. And she became a "hero in the inner city," Smith said, for tracking down absent fathers and forcing them to support their abandoned children. Under Reno's administration, annual child support collections in Dade County jumped from $16.9 million to $33.6 million, a feat that earned her the distinction of being the only future attorney general to be eulogized in a rap song.

Reno's emphasis on children's issues sets her apart from her tough-talking, macho predecessors, who seemed to take a "Dirty Harry" approach to crime control. While she believes that dangerous criminals should be dealt with severely, she also expresses compassion for "the angry young man who lashes out in violence because he never had a childhood." She has been described as "part social worker, part crime fighter." In Dade County, she helped set up an innovative drug court that routes low-level

Janet Reno

offenders into rehabilitation and education programs, rather than prison. Nine out of ten people who finish the program remain drug-free a year later.

"It doesn't help to send someone off to prison for three years, pluck them out of the community, and then plunk them back down, if they've got a drug problem—without having provided treatment," she said. "Better that we use our resources to provide alternative sanctions that allow them to come back to the community with a better chance of being law-abiding citizens."

Reno has been criticized for being "soft on crime" because of her opposition to the death penalty and her questioning of mandatory sentences for drug offenses. But she's proven that she's no lightweight. Although she is philosophically opposed to capital punishment, she has obtained more than one hundred death penalty convictions. She also held her own for fifteen years in a city notorious for its drug cartels, corruption, and organized crime.

And she has personally given crooks a reason not to mess with her. One night when she and her sister, Maggy, were walking through the streets of New York, a mugger grabbed Reno's purse. But he didn't hold onto it for long—apparently the sight of two six-foot women in high heels chasing after him was so disconcerting the mugger dropped the loot.

When *Miami Herald* reporter Edna Buchanan heard of Reno's appointment to attorney general, she predicted Reno would have no problem handling the slippery characters that prowl the corridors of power. Reno had played hardball "in one of the toughest cities in America," observed Buchanan, also a veteran of Miami's mean streets. "If she can survive in Miami, Washington will be a breeze."

Ultimately, Reno believes that money spent on treatment and on children's programs such as health care, day care, and job training will be money saved on prisons. She has advocated workdays that end at 3 P.M., so parents can be home when their children get out of school.

In Miami, she nagged her staff to get home early to be with their families. "This is the most important experience of your life," she told them. Her admonishment was undoubtedly prompted by Reno's memories of the strong guidance her own mother provided as she and her siblings were growing up. "It was my mother who worked in the home, who taught us to bake cakes, to play baseball, to appreciate Beethoven symphonies," she said. "She spanked us hard, and she loved us with all her heart. And there is no childcare in the world that will ever be a substitute for what that lady was in our life."

Much has been made of the fact that Reno has never married or had children of her own. Early on, she was busy building a career in public service. After graduating with a degree in chemistry from Cornell University, she studied law at Harvard, where she was one of sixteen women in a class of more than five hundred men. She worked for several years in private practice before joining the Dade County State Attorney's office in 1973. Five years later, she became Florida's first female state attorney.

As the first woman to hold the office of U.S. attorney general, she is more concerned with fighting crime than responding to comments about her gender. When asked if she's a feminist, Reno responded, "My mother always told me to do my best, to think my best and to do right, and to consider myself a person."

In Washington, where image is everything, Reno comes across as a woman whose personal habits are as sensible as her sturdy shoes, owlish eyeglasses, and no-fuss hairdo. She moved into an apartment furnished right down to the coffeepot and ironing board. She walks to work, eats lunch with the rank-and-file in the department cafeteria, flies coach, and never reads prepared speeches.

"We talked about getting her a speechwriter, but we couldn't figure out what they'd do," said Reno's spokeswoman, Caroline Aronovitz. "Everything she says comes from her head and her heart."

Reno doesn't seem to mind her image as a sort of doting spinster aunt. She adores her nieces and nephews, has devoted herself to the care of her ailing mother, and has been the legal guardian for the children of two friends who both died of cirrhosis of the liver. When the subject of marriage comes up, she deflects any sympathy or criticism by jokingly referring to herself as an "awkward old maid." Friends say she simply never found a man who could match her intellect and paddle his end of the canoe.

"Janet would have loved to have a relationship with a man and have children," said a close friend, Sara Smith. "But she's a very smart woman, and it was difficult to find a man who had both a sophisticated city mind and was an outdoor person—and was not threatened by a successful woman."

In appointing her to head the Justice Department, President Clinton said Reno possessed "one quality essential to being attorney general—unquestioned integrity." But some people wonder if he may have gotten more than he bargained for. In her first few months on the job, she criticized the White House for conducting an investigation of the White House travel office without consulting her. And she continued to support a nominee for assistant attorney general even after the president had rejected her.

Reno speaks her mind, despite the political or personal consequences. She makes no bones about her support for a woman's right to have an abortion, even though White House aides reportedly wanted her to soft-pedal the issue during her confirmation hearings. As attorney general, she fought for a federal law banning protestors from blocking abortion clinics. The story of how she once walked out on a group of juvenile court judges, calling them a bunch of "dunderheads," is classic Reno lore.

According to her brother, Robert Reno, a columnist for *New York Newsday*, it's not surprising that Janet is making waves in Washington. She simply is carrying on a family tradition. "Mother's mother and father's mother were absolutely indomitable. All the women in the family were," he said. "The men were strong too. They just had no talent for marrying spineless women."

Reno makes no apologizes for her opinions. She once candidly told a group of reporters, "I can be impatient. I do have a temper. My mother accused me of mumbling. I am not a good housekeeper. My fifth-grade teacher said I was bossy. My family thinks I'm opinionated and sometimes arrogant, and they would be happy to supply you with other words."

Nevertheless, she and the president seem to agree more often than not. They both support alternatives to imprisonment, including drug treatment and military-style "boot camps" where first-time offenders can clean up their act through hard work and discipline. They want more cops on the beat and fewer guns on the street. And they envision a national agenda for children that encompasses everything from prenatal care for expectant mothers to job training for teenagers.

Shortly after she was sworn into office, one of Reno's first official visits was to a school in the Washington neighborhood of Mount Pleasant, where a drive-by gunman was terrorizing the residents there. Reno tried to ease the children's fears by telling them a story about the brave boys and girls in Miami who had survived a terrible hurricane the year before. When she was finished, a little girl raised her hand and said, "We want to go outside without no shooting, no killing. We just want to go around having fun."

While it may be hard for that little girl's parents to see how better preschools could help make their neighborhood safe once again, for Reno, the connection is absolutely clear. "I think the problem of drugs in America, youth violence, teen pregnancy and youth gangs are symptoms of a deeper problem in America," she said. "And that is that too often we have forgotten and neglected our children."

Ann Richards

*I can remember a time in my life when I
wouldn't give a recipe to a friend because
that was the only form of power I had.*

Ann Richards is more a shining star than a lone star. As the first woman governor of Texas in more than fifty years, she has impressed fellow politicians and the public alike with her quick wit and warm, folksy style. Yet her rise to power, which has earned her a reputation as one of the country's most admired public figures, has been more arduous than her Texas-size smile lets on.

Richards first gained national prominence on the platform of the 1988 Democratic National Convention in Atlanta, where she delivered the keynote address. Then the second-term Texas State Treasurer, the charismatic Richards won over the audience of five thousand Democratic delegates when she chided incumbent President George Bush for being born "with a silver foot in his mouth." He later sent her a silver pin in the shape of a foot, which she wore when he visited the Texas legislature.

That she can poke fun at herself, other politicians, and life in general has contributed greatly to Richards' success. Says Jane Hickie, a former aide: "Her timing, her delivery, her wit, her comedic sense, it's all one of the most powerful aspects of her personality. She makes us laugh at ourselves. It's part of the tremendous charisma she has, which makes people around her be more than they thought they could be. She has learned to be the quintessential good ol' girl."

194

Being dubbed a good old girl is a label to be held in high regard, for it means Richards has broken the barriers to the good old-boy network, which is especially impenetrable in Texas where white-collar businessmen and oil tycoons have dominated the political scene for generations. When asked to explain this rare acceptance of a female into their fraternal circles, Richards cites her affability, flexibility, and sense of humor. "Men were willing to work with me because," she said, "after an initial period of 'getting to know you,' they saw I was someone who wasn't going to try to put them on the spot—that I appreciated their point of view."

While Richards may be smiling now, her life has been anything but a bed of yellow Texas roses. A native Texan, she was born Dorothy Ann Willis in 1933, in Lakeview, a small, rural town outside Waco that still was haunted by memories of the Depression. Her father, Cecil, was a truck driver for a pharmaceutical supply house; her mother, Iona, was a homemaker.

An only child, she was adored by both parents. Yet they gave her mixed messages that would prove troubling for Richards later in life. On one hand, her father encouraged her to believe that there were no limits to what she could achieve. "He always told me I could do anything I wanted to do if I was willing to work hard enough. The reiteration of that message went on throughout my growing years and prepared me for any career I wanted to pursue," Richards recalled proudly. She believed her dad so much that she once tried to emulate her childhood heroine, the fictional Wonder Woman, by flying off the garage roof with a "magic lariat."

Encouraged to reach for the stars, she was also taught to believe "a woman's greatest fulfillment is to get married and have children," Richards said. Her mother was an awesome example. A woman whose life was dictated by the ethos to work hard and work flawlessly, Iona Willis expected her daughter to perform each and every chore perfectly. When she fell short of her mother's expectations, young Richards would have to repeat her chores from the very beginning.

So her parents' constant counsel to be her absolute best came at a price: Richards often interpreted the message as a mandate to be infallible and perfect. "Mama and Daddy had high expec-

Ann Richards

tations, but exactly what they were neither they nor I knew,"
Richards wrote in her autobiography, *Straight From the Heart*.
But this much was certain: she accepted their expectations as her
own, and lived in constant fear of failure. Indeed, by her teenage
years, she had lost all confidence in herself and abandoned the

belief that she could be Wonder Woman. Looking back, she now realizes, "My standards were way beyond me. Way beyond me. It seems like I was scared all the time."

Richards hid those fears, unwilling to share her secret self even with her closest confidantes. For a long stretch, she managed to create an aura of perfection—closeting her feeling of being "kind of pathetic and inadequate" to all but herself.

After a short stint in San Diego, where Cecil Willis served with the U.S. Navy in World War II, the family returned to their Texas roots. Her parents decided to move to Waco, where daughter Dorothy Ann could attend a superior high school. But unbeknownst to them, she dropped her first name when she enrolled, preferring to be known by her sleeker middle name. "Dorothy sounded 'too country,'" Richards explained.

With her newfound sophistication, young Ann began to excel in such subjects as English and speech. Having inherited her father's oratory gifts, she realized one sure way to win approval was to always have a good story to tell. Smart and personable, Richards had her first taste of politics in high school. She was elected to represent her school, and later all of Texas, at "Girls State," a mock government session sponsored by the Women's Auxiliary of the American Legion. At the national event, she and other student representatives met President Harry S Truman.

Richards' skillful debating style won her a scholarship to Baylor University. In her junior year, she married high school sweetheart David Richards. After graduation, the couple enrolled at the University of Texas at Austin—he for a law degree, she for a teacher's certificate.

For one year, she taught government and history at an Austin junior high school. "Teaching was the hardest work I had ever done, and it remains the hardest work I have done to date," she said of the experience.

Meanwhile, her husband, by then an up-and-coming lawyer, was starting to be noticed by the local political elite while Richards assumed the role of perfect wife and mother. The couple became parents in 1959 with the birth of daughter Cecile, the first of four children.

Richards describes this phase of her life as a time when she was trying to be "everything to everybody." Young and attractive, she was known as a consummate hostess and devoted most of her time to family life and volunteer work. She even spoke to women's groups on "how to have a perfect husband and a perfect family and a perfect career," she said sheepishly. "I can remember a time in my life when I wouldn't give a recipe to a friend because that was the only form of power I had."

This shouldn't suggest that Richards had no more on her mind than baking, for she was involved in a wide-ranging list of volunteer activities that began to consume more and more of her time. She helped found the National Dallas Democratic Women group and served as its president for a time. She also worked in the Dallas headquarters of the Kennedy-Johnson presidential campaign.

At one point, the family moved to Washington, D.C., to be part of the "New Frontier," after husband David was hired as a staff lawyer for the Civil Rights Commission. But disillusioned by the Washington bureaucracy, the family eventually returned to Dallas.

Richards resumed her work, first by helping to organize the Dallas Committee for Peaceful Integration and later, the local chapter of the National Association for the Advancement of Colored People. Though she, like her husband, claimed at the time to have grown tired of politics, Sarah Weddington, the lawyer who had successfully argued the infamous Roe v. Wade Supreme Court abortion case, asked Richards to become the campaign manager in her run for a state legislature seat.

Richards agreed, and after the election, became Weddington's administrative assistant. Likewise, in 1974, she helped Wilheminia Delco become the first black woman elected to the Texas legislature.

In 1975, local Democrats asked David Richards to run for Travis County commissioner. He declined, but encouraged his wife to take a shot at the seat. She did—and won. But her political victory was accompanied by personal reservations, Richards said. "In my heart of hearts I thought, if I go off and assume public office and David is left with a lot of the management and responsibility of this house, he isn't going to like it very much."

Her instincts were right. The couple soon began to drift apart and eventually divorced after twenty-two years of marriage. To this day, Richards feels the impact of that traumatic experience. "When you have two people who have lived together for a long time," she said, "you develop a pattern, and when that pattern is dramatically altered, as our was, it is very, very difficult to make the adjustment. There were other ingredients involved, but that was the beginning of our going our separate ways."

Plainly put, Richards wanted a life in politics, her husband did not. "It was the most difficult and sad thing that's ever happened in my life," she said. "And I certainly have regrets, but I've gained a lot personally—insights not just about myself but about life in general. I've learned to accept myself for who I am. I'm more centered; I have my feet more firmly on the ground than I did when I was married. I was a very dependent wife; I really looked to my husband for what I thought."

But even as her marriage was falling apart, Richards maintained the semblance of perfection, winning over an all-male road crew and introducing more human services to Travis County, such as an infant-parent training program for families with Down syndrome children, a rape crisis center, and a foundation for women's resources. In many ways, she has modeled herself after Eleanor Roosevelt; the former first lady has been her lifelong heroine because, Richards said, "She saw the human needs."

Richards also has been recognized for her good works. In 1981, the Texas Women's Political Caucus named her "Woman of the Year."

But privately, Richards was having dark moments and doubts about her life. Always able to "drink with the boys," she began to down four or five martinis every night—just to relax after work. Concerned about her increased alcohol intake, she consulted her doctor, who assured her he drank as much himself.

"I was screaming for someone to rescue me," she said. "I don't know what from. I couldn't hear it, but I was saying, 'I'm so afraid and desperate and I can't keep up.'"

Eventually her drinking got so out-of-hand that friends and family decided to come to the rescue by confronting her in an "intervention." It's one episode in her life that Richards reveals with absolute candor: "A friend asked me to come to her house and help her with something. I walked in and there, assembled in the living room, were some of my family and a lot of my friends."

"I was frightened at first," she continued, "because I thought something awful had happened to one of the children. Then I felt this anger at everyone kind of ganging up. You feel some are being hypocrites because they drink as much as you do. Then you are so overwhelmed that there's this feeling of devastation. But it was not long—within the first week—before I realized how much these people must love me to have put themselves through that kind of pain and anxiety."

The tactic worked. That day, she checked into St. Mary's Hospital, a rehabilitation center in Minneapolis. She hasn't had a drink since her month-long stay at the center, although thirteen years later, she continues to attend Alcoholics Anonymous meetings.

In 1982, Richards was elected state treasurer in an unusually ugly campaign. The issue of her alcoholism surfaced publicly for the first time—and to her credit, Richards reacted with characteristic candor. She did not remain unshaken during the whole ordeal; at one point she even canceled a public appearance scheduled after a dentist appointment because she didn't want to risk the raised eyebrows her slurred speech might incur. Another campaign issue she had to confront was the question of qualifications and the fact she had no financial or economic background. Her response: "I raised a family and ran a household," she said, explaining that the job of a traditional homemaker requires many management skills.

Having won the election, Richards soon had her hands full. The office she inherited was notoriously inefficient and out-of-date. She quickly automated operations by installing computers and check-encoding machines.

Her efforts earned the state of Texas millions of dollars in extra interest by reducing the time between receipt and deposit of a check; it went from 36 hours down to 90 minutes. She also introduced flexible work schedules and eliminated the notion that Texas politics is a bastion for white males only. By the end of her tenure, her staff in the treasurer's office was 57 percent white, 13 percent black, 28 percent Hispanic, and 60 percent female.

Richards' adeptness at performing the job and skill in making people feel at ease won her high praise—and a second term in office, since no one dared run against her. With the 1986 election, she became the first woman to serve two consecutive statewide terms in Texas history. Only the year before, she'd hit another milestone when she was named to the Texas Women's Hall of Fame for public service.

This silver-haired dynamo found herself back on the campaign trail in 1990—this time for governor. Again, the campaign was unnecessarily ugly and again, her opponent used her alcoholism as his most potent weapon. The Democratic primary was so close that a runoff election was necessary. Richards won by a narrow margin and then upset the Republican nominee, Texas oil man Clayton Williams, by an even slimmer 51 percent to 49 percent margin in the general election.

Today Richards is enjoying an unusually long "honeymoon" in her new job. She's focused on setting an activist agenda by tackling such issues as hazardous waste disposal, insurance regulation, and lobbying ethics. As for her continuing popularity, Steven D. Wolens, a Democratic state representative from Dallas, offers this explanation: "She's not only hands-on, she gets her hands dirty. No governor has done that in a long time and that's why she was able to set the agenda." Charles Elliot, a professor at East Texas State University, has a slightly different take. "It's not business as usual," he said of Richards' administration. "The old business and oil elite that dominated Texas politics is at least temporarily out of the saddle, or perhaps more accurately, they're having to share power with other people."

That Richards has changed Texas is obvious. But she's also changed herself. Aside from years of political learning and cajoling, she attributes this change to living without alcohol. "Not drinking changed my life dramatically," she said. "I allow myself to fail now. I don't expect to be perfect and I'm not judgmental anymore. I don't put people on a scale and find them wanting. I've learned that I must allow people to run their own lives."

This is a stark contrast to the way she used to managed her

life. "Before it was, 'You got a problem? Bring it to me!' There was nothing I loved more than solving others' problems," Richards said. "If you're in there 'helping' your children, your friends, their friends, then you're needed—and the more you take on, the more you're needed. I cannot tell you how much letting go meant to me."

While the value of this transformation cannot be underestimated, Richards' staying power has much to do with the lessons she learned as a little girl: the love of hard work, the capacity for compassion, and the power of a good laugh.

Martha Sloan

∼Hang in there! Things are getting better,
even though not as fast as we'd like.

When Martha Sloan attended college, women were not allowed to wear slacks to classes. For most co-eds, this was just an inconvenience; but for Sloan, it meant she couldn't pursue her education without embarrassment.

As the only woman majoring in engineering in her 1961 class at Stanford University, Sloan had her first taste of breaking gender barriers that threatened her success. Now at the height of her profession, Sloan's career climb has been lonely at times—because this stubborn optimist isn't about to walk away from a challenge when she believes something she can say or do will make a difference for women in the future. Among her many accomplishments, she is the first woman president of the 108-year-old Institute of Electrical and Electronics Engineers; the first female professor of electrical engineering at Michigan Technological University; and a recipient of the ASEE Frederick Emmons Termon Award for outstanding young electrical engineering educator.

But as a freshman at Stanford, Sloan dutifully followed the rules, wearing skirts to classes—until she took hydrolics, a course requiring students to scale metal scaffolding, which meant that men walking below could easily look under Sloan's skirt.

"I had to get permission to wear pants in hydrolics," said Sloan, who describes herself as a veteran feminist (she was a working mom long before it became fashionable). Although committed to the cause of equal rights, she is more realistic than angry that the women's movement has not yet achieved its goals. Maybe it's because at fifty-three, she has lived long enough to see that struggle metes out change with an eye dropper to appreciate how far women have come since the days when she needed permission to climb scaffolding in comfort—like men.

Being the only freshman female engineering major meant that all eyes were on Sloan. "At first it was sort of scary," she recalled. But having a high profile wasn't all bad: "By the second class, every professor knew my name, even if he knew no one else's."

Sloan struggled with feelings of isolation that first year. As a woman, she didn't fit in with the other engineering majors; as an engineering major, she didn't fit in with other women. At the time, few women chose to major in math or science. But that actually worked to Sloan's advantage, because it meant those students shared the same basic course requirements with engineering students. Sloan began studying with the other women in her classes, which helped allay her feelings of being different.

Eventually she became active at the student radio station and once again, Sloan found herself the only woman in a previously all-male environment. But for the first time, she made friends with male science types and engineers and learned an important lesson about bonding—men would accept her, as long as she entered their world.

Considering the obstacles Sloan faced, one can't help but wonder how she strayed so far from the female track, especially in an era when society had clearly defined what a woman could and could not do. "I was daddy's little girl," said Sloan, explaining that her father was an obstetrician who encouraged her to excel in math and science.

Raised in Aurora, Illinois, Sloan describes her childhood as typical for the times: She and her younger brother grew up in a home with both parents. Sloan, however, was not an average child. Recognizing their daughter's abilities early on, her parents arranged for Sloan to take an I.Q. test when she was in fifth grade.

She scored high, but it would be many years before Sloan fully comprehended the impact those results had on her life. "After the test, teachers started giving me books on things like nuclear

Martha Sloan   Photo by Pach Bros., NY

energy," Sloan recalled. "They saw I had ability and gave me material that challenged me." Today, she is awed by their efforts to enrich the intellectual curiosity of a girl.

Sloan didn't inherit her scientific ability entirely from her father. Her mother almost completed a college degree in chemistry, but then changed her major to English.

"My mother would have preferred a more traditional daughter," said Sloan. "One that was more into femininity than scholastics. I wasn't the daughter she expected." Sloan now realizes her mother's concerns were probably more about ensuring her daughter's happiness than about forcing her to conform. But it wasn't until Sloan was in her thirties that her mother resolved those concerns and accepted that her daughter was leading a full life.

When Sloan was in high school, she seriously considered choosing physics as her college major. But her father suggested she study engineering. They had a meeting of the minds after Sloan participated in a summer engineering program at Northwestern University and loved it.

A career in engineering appealed to Sloan for several reasons. One, she already knew she had a talent for the field. Previously she'd taken a day-long series of aptitude tests that indicated she should become an architect because she was good at spatial relationships. But Sloan also believed she might face less discrimination in the engineering profession because "women were a tiny part of it." Her hunch proved true: there simply weren't enough women around at the time for men to be exclusive.

Two years before graduation, Sloan felt sufficiently committed to the profession to join the IEEE. At the time, women made up less than one percent of the membership (today it's roughly six percent female). She also joined the Society of Women Engineers, often attending their functions because she found members were willing to offer guidance; in particular, Sloan was seeking insights on companies that treated women fairly.

"A man in my generation grew up thinking he owned the earth," said Sloan, who at the time believed women needed to find a niche in the working world. Being the only female engineering student in her graduating class was enough—Sloan wasn't ready to be the first female at a firm that traditionally hadn't hired women. "I didn't want to be a ground breaker," she explained.

So fellow Society members steered her to the Lockheed Corporation, a company that had a reputation for treating men and women equally in their hiring and salary practices. Simply put, the company used a formula that involved computing grade-point averages against a rating of an applicant's college, then adding work experience plus other well-defined factors. At Lockheed, salaries had nothing to do with sex—it was simply a number-crunching operation—and Sloan liked that idea.

She accepted a job working on satellite communication systems at Lockheed Research and Development Laboratories. At first Sloan relished delving into the engineering problems they gave her. After hours of library research and analytical thinking, she would present her supervisors with solutions.

But it was a lonely pursuit. "My interpersonal needs were not met," Sloan said of her years at Lockheed. Still, her commitment to engineering was solid, so she began working part time on a master's degree.

Then Sloan married a man in the Army, and accompanied him to Germany, where he was assigned. She became a seventh- and eighth-grade math and science instructor, and for the first time, experienced the joy of teaching.

Again, she liked her job initially, when everything was new. But by the second year, when she had her lesson plans down pat, Sloan began to feel she was in a rut and sensed the problem was a lack of focus in her career.

After her husband was discharged from the Army, the couple moved to Alaska. By then, they had a little girl, and Sloan settled into substitute teaching. But eventually the couple divorced, and a year later, Sloan moved to Michigan, where her career at last began to take shape.

In 1969, Sloan joined the faculty of Michigan Technological University. "I really found myself in teaching college," she said. Unlike junior high school, where the subject matter rarely changes, college engineering courses are never static. To ensure that her students are on the cutting edge of their field, Sloan must constantly learn new things herself.

"It is perfect for me," she said. Now a full professor at MTU, Sloan is more enthusiastic than ever about her work because it combines her two passions, engineering and working with people. Asked what she enjoys most about teaching Sloan cites two reasons. "The first is dealing with students," she said. "The second is the sheer challenge of ideas." Being surrounded by an ongoing parade of young people with quick minds and plenty of questions makes her job exhilirating, Sloan said.

Yet there is one part of teaching she would just as soon do without: grading. "You work all quarter long with students, like a coach," she said, "and at the end, it all comes down to a letter you have to put on their cards."

While training the next generation of engineers, Sloan has continued her own career climb. In 1971, she began a doctoral residency; in 1973, Stanford University awarded her a Ph.D. in engineering.

Having reached the pinnacle of her profession, Sloan's one wish is that more women would become engineers—and she's doing her part to see that happens. For example, she's been involved in research, funded by the National Science Foundation, which is designed to introduce seventh graders to mini-engineering projects that will expose them to the profession.

She has also worked on summer programs, inviting some one hundred high school junior and senior girls to perform scientific experiments at the university. The girls, Sloan proudly points out, have excelled in advanced math and science. "There's so much talent out there," she said.

Maybe even more important than the experiments is the exchange that occurs between the students and women already in the profession. In order to give the girls a feel for this career, a group of female engineers in their twenties and thirties talk to the students about their professional experiences, as well as marriage, having children, and what combining family and a career entails. "It's the best way to make a career decision," said Sloan.

As for her own career, Sloan continues to push ahead. Her most recent and perhaps most significant accomplishment occurred in 1993 when she was elected the first female president of the Institute of Electrical and Electronics Engineers. Once again, Sloan broke barriers in a highly visible fashion, for the IEEE is the largest technical professional society in the world, with 320,000 members in 150 countries. Among its wide-ranging functions, the Institute runs job fairs and lobbies Congress on issues concerning its membership, such as the outcome of pension bills or the promotion of technology relevant to engineering.

Sloan's election as president of the IEEE was hardly a series of green lights—she had to buck the male establishment just to get her name on the ballot.

Like others interested in the presidency, Sloan gave a speech outlining her ideas; from there, the Institute nominates candidates. During this process, Sloan heard rumors that she was initially slated to be on the ballot, but then her name was removed. When she began to question why, one colleague explained it this way: "Martha, you gave a superb talk," he said. "But you have to understand, men have vision and women are good at detail work."

But Sloan didn't understand—because her speech had specifically mentioned vision three times—and she suspected discrimination. "After that, I figured I had to run," she said.

Friends offered to draw up a petition to get her name on the ballot, but Sloan was determined to take matters in her own hands because, she said, "I had to show that I could do things." She distributed her own petition with the help of friends, eventually gathering signatures from 2,700 members who supported her nomination. The rest is history, said Sloan, who claims that since she assumed leadership at the Institute, people of both sexes have been cooperative.

Though she's had a stellar career, Sloan's idea of success is not limited to professional achievements. She believes a wholesome family life is an equally important part of the equation. "It's a classic thing from Freud," she said, referring to his theory of combining love and work. The goal is to find a balance between a job that is fulfilling while striving for a family in which everyone is valued and feels part of the unit.

Sloan has put this theory into practice in her own life. After moving to Michigan, she married again and when her daughter was eleven, she gave birth to a son. But even in this, she was a woman ahead of her time: Sloan was a working mom a good fifteen years before women starting going to work in droves and the issue of balancing work and family became a hot topic.

That she succeeded in having both a thriving career and a happy home life is a result of choices Sloan made about where to work and how to handle childcare. For example, she said, the academic life is perfect for a working mom because it offers flexibility. (She was able to breastfeed her son for fifteen months.)

Likewise, she said, "I had really good luck in finding daycare. And I had the same baby sitter for my son from birth until he was six." But it was more than luck. Sloan wisely chose to pay more than the going rate for childcare because she wanted to ensure her children's caretaker was competent and lasting. At the time, she said, other women boasted of paying rock-bottom salaries—but they always had problems. "Having the right baby sitter has an impact on family happiness," said Sloan.

Always one to go her own way—even when her choices run contrary to conventional wisdom—Sloan believes that stubbornness, a quality she inherited from both parents, has helped her cope with life's challenges. But her style of stubbornness is more like perseverance than pig-headedness. "I would like to feel that I'm not unreasonable," said Sloan, laughing. "In balance, I think my stubbornness is a strength."

She has needed that strength to face the past four years as a widow. Being on her own again has been an adjustment, but Sloan hardly has time to be lonely. As IEEE president, she travels around the country and the globe giving speeches. Three times a year, she attends week-long meetings, presiding over board and executive meetings.

Her current presidential lifestyle hasn't helped Sloan deal with the one thing she'd like to change about herself. "I've had a lifelong weight problem," she said. With straight brown hair, a friendly smile, and a cherubic face, Sloan is far from obese. But like so many women today, she'd love to shed some pounds. Yet dieting is harder than ever because of her constant traveling, and in that respect, she looks forward to the end of her IEEE term so she'll be able to stay in one place long enough to eat regularly.

On top of all her professional activities, Sloan is active politically. She's held various positions in the League of Women Voters and intermittently served on a local Michigan board. (Eventually she'd like to run for office, perhaps at the state level.) On campus, she's been involved in an academic women's caucus that meets weekly to discuss relevant social issues. Sloan encourages women to become involved politically, because she said, "It's the only way that change will be made for women."

Though she has no real regrets about her life, Sloan admits, "I wish I'd impressed patience on my daughter. Unlike my generation, hers expected that all the problems were solved and that women would be treated fairly."

Sloan said her daughter, who's now twenty-nine, had sailed through life without facing gender roadblocks. But while working on her Ph.D, she hit some flagrant discrimination and understood for the first time why her mother has been involved in feminist politics all these years. "I've been striving for continual improvement," said Sloan, explaining that impatience is good if it motivates change, but bad if it promotes expectations that the world will change overnight.

Sloan gives her daughter the same encouraging message she shares from the podium when speaking to young women who aspire to be engineers: "Hang in there! Things are getting better, even though not as fast as we'd like."

Marcy Syms

*⌒At the end of the day, it is your character, not
your résumé that successful career choices should
be building. Do something because you believe
in it. Not for the résumé. Not for the paychecks.
You have to trust your own judgment about
what is right for you, regardless of the trends
or the pressure.*

Fifteen-year-old Marcy Syms felt as if she were living a dream
come true when her family moved to a spacious Colonial home
in Bronxville, an affluent suburb of New York City. Finally, the
family of eight was going to have more than one bathroom.
Finally, she would have a bedroom to herself.

But the dream ended as abruptly as a good night's sleep inter-
rupted by an insistent alarm clock. When she started school,
Syms found herself in unfamiliar and sometimes hostile terri-
tory—a brunette in a world of blue-eyed blondes, the only
Jewish girl in Bronxville High.

She was taunted by older boys and watched her brothers come
home from school covered with bruises. She made girlfriends,
but none of the boys would ask her out. "I really did feel like an
outcast," Syms recalled. "I didn't care if I had my own bathroom—there were no parties for me to get dressed up for."

But the teenager did not retreat to a corner in the school cafeteria. She lost weight, changed her hairstyle, and joined the student government. She worked on the school paper and starred

in school plays. "I actually made the cheerleading squad," she said, "but it didn't help—my 'untouchable' status remained."

Those were painful years for Syms, but she did not allow the unhappiness to overwhelm her. Instead, she took action, and in the process, gained important skills. "I learned how not to be a quitter, and I learned how to tolerate not being popular, and I learned how to deal with disappointment," she said.

As a teenager, Syms came to understand that pain can bring gain and that inner strength is earned from problems confronted head-on. "I have tried to extract from the legacy of my childhood the ability to think positively," she said, "to win something positive from every experience, whether trying or joyous."

Syms has become a pro at using problems to her advantage—and she's proved on more than one occasion that she knows how to live life as a winner. In 1983, when she was only thirty-two, she became president of Syms Corp, the chain of off-price clothing stores founded by her father. The move made her one of the youngest female presidents of a New York Stock Exchange company. Today, as the corporation's president and chief operating officer, she presides over a chain of 35 stores operating in 14 states and employing more than 2,000 people.

Syms was born in Brooklyn in 1951, the oldest of six children. Her father, Sy, started out as a sportscaster. But realizing he needed a steadier income to support his family, Sy went to work in the clothing store his older brother had inherited from their father. In 1959, Sy opened his own store.

Syms' parents took a traditional view of family life. "It was always assumed that my three brothers would join the business and that I would be a teacher or something like that," Syms recalled. "At least that's what my mother thought. Her logic was straightforward: 'A grade school teacher can be home in time to take care of her husband and children.'"

But young Syms was curious about the world of work, the world outside their home that her father went off to every day. "I wasn't exactly sure what he got out of going to work," she said, "but I knew it offered more of the exotic and the unknown than my mother's world."

Syms' grandmother, who had come to the United States from

Romania by herself when she was only six years old, believed that a woman should have a career. "She never tired of telling me that a woman's most prized possession was her independence," Syms said. "To substantiate this, she often said that she only ended her career as the assistant manager of a small shoe store in Philadelphia in order to get married and have children. But should anything happen to grandpa, she always knew she'd be okay because she'd had her own career."

Her grandmother became Syms' first mentor, nurturing her sense of self-worth and self-reliance. When she was sixteen, she found another: the doctor who diagnosed and cured the skin disease that put her in the hospital and threatened her life. A distinguished Englishman in his seventies, the doctor visited Syms every day in the hospital.

"We talked about the world," Syms recalled. "I idolized him." The doctor introduced her to classic English literature, which she later made her college major. But, most important, Syms said, "He was the first person, who I believed, to tell me I was smart and that I had something unique to offer."

With the doctor's help, Syms began to develop what is perhaps a young woman's most useful possession—a belief in herself and her own capabilities.

Thus armed, Syms went to Finch College, where she earned a bachelor's degree, then it was on to Boston University for a graduate degree in public relations. After a stint as a paralegal, she decided to follow a long-time interest—and her father's footsteps—by pursuing a career in broadcasting.

Syms worked as an assistant to the president of Straus Broadcasting, then landed a job as associate producer for a television talk show. She liked the work, but she wanted a career ladder to climb, and she couldn't help but notice that women weren't moving beyond broadcasting's first rungs.

"I looked to see who the decision-makers at television and radio stations were," she said, "and I saw only a few token women at the vice-president level."

One day while working with the talk-show host whose show she was producing, Syms received an unnerving assignment: He wanted her to rub his back. It almost seemed as if he were telling

Marcy Syms

her that a woman's place in the industry was not in the executive suite. "When I declined," Syms recalled, "he said I should reconsider because it was the most important contribution I could make to the success of his show."

Before she could make a decision about her next career move, Syms became a victim of corporate cost-cutting and found herself without a job. She was doing freelance market research when, one night in 1977, she had dinner with her father and found another opportunity to follow in his footsteps.

By this time, Sy Syms had a growing, prosperous business. In the mid-1960s, he had tried the concept of "off-price" buying and selling—buying goods for less than wholesale and selling them at lower-than-normal retail prices. Sales increased, and Sy was able to open five smaller stores near the original.

Then, in the 1970s, the former sportscaster put himself in his own radio and television commercials, and told his audience, "An educated consumer is our best customer." Sales increased again as consumers responded to the message—and the straight-talking, unpretentious messenger.

Sy was ready to expand the business once more when he and his daughter met for the dinner that was to change her career. This time Sy wanted to move the company beyond New York. He'd chosen a site just outside Washington, D.C.

"It seemed natural for me to offer to go to Washington and work with him preparing an advertising and media plan," Syms recalled.

By the time she finished the project, Syms knew where her career was moving. "I was thoroughly enmeshed in the business of Syms," she said. "When I returned from Washington, and Sy asked me what my plans were, I had my answer ready: 'I'd like to work at Syms full time.'"

The timing was right all the way around. The company was poised for growth and Syms, who had proven herself outside the family business, had valuable skills and experience to offer. "I was very fond of my father and admired him tremendously," she said. "I wanted to help him, and I thought I could learn something from him."

In some ways, her move into the company was as inevitable as her transition from high school to college. After all, she'd grown up with the business. Before she was thirteen, she had worked as one of the store's cashiers and also had spent some school vacations learning how to arrange stock.

"I see much of my personal development as a seamless continuum from my early days to now," she said.

Still, her early days with the company were far from easy. "I was very sensitive about my actual contribution to the business and unsure about my own identity," Syms recalled. "I made a lot of wrong decisions as I learned the business."

In typical fashion, Syms didn't give in to her insecurities. She got to know the business from the switchboard up, using the tough times to learn and grow, just as she had at Bronxville High. "I really think it was during those dark days that I grew the most," she said. "And as time went on, I developed the nerve to take a really hard, analytic look at a mistake in judgment—that's when you can learn exponentially."

She may have made mistakes, but they were overshadowed by her successes. In Boston, for example, she engineered the simultaneous opening of two stores, allowing the company to get double the bang for its marketing buck. It became clear that Syms was a natural manager.

She believes those skills too can be traced to her childhood: "I know that I learned management and caretaking skills growing up. The oldest of six children, especially if the child is a girl, has to; it's expected of her by everyone."

Sy Syms recognized his oldest daughter's talents. One night while they were driving home from work together, he told her, "I'm going to be putting this in writing, but if something should happen to me, you'll be responsible."

Syms remembers being "quite simply overwhelmed" by the news. To begin with, she was not the obvious successor. A son would have been the traditional choice—and her three brothers were working in the business. But Sy saw things differently. Granted, he held some traditional views of women, but he'd also grown up with six older sisters and was accustomed to heeding the advice of females. Most important, he respected his daughter's strength and determination, and trusted her sense of morality.

When Syms was named president officially in 1983, her brothers were outraged. "All hell broke loose," she said. "My brothers saw me as the usurper of their birthright. How dare I! They were the sons."

Amidst painful family feuding, two brothers resigned from the company. Syms was distraught with mixed emotions. On one hand, she was delighted to be running the business. But, she said, "I would often think what it had cost me in peace of mind and wonder if it had been worth it."

Syms struggled with other family problems as well. She had to learn how to be both daughter and employee and how to deal with the occasional rebuke from a chief executive officer who was also her dad. At times, her close relationship with her father caused problems with her mother who, now divorced from Sy, felt hurt and abandoned.

"When I joined the family business I didn't realize how many demons I would have to face," Syms said. "I often felt confused by my dual role."

True to form, Syms did active battle with her demons. She found a therapist to help her understand her family relationships so that she could more effectively handle her roles in both the family and the business. And she decided to find out about other family-run businesses and how their management balanced professional and personal concerns.

"I believed then, as I do now, that the more I knew about processes within other family concerns, the more effective I would be at Syms," she said.

Syms read everything she could find on the subject, went to seminars and workshops, and talked to consultants. Through groups like the Young Presidents' Organization, where forty percent of the members are presidents of family-controlled businesses, and Women in Family Owned Businesses, Syms found people who were struggling with the same issues that preoccupied her.

Her involvement with these groups enabled Syms to develop a support network. "I had a lot of heart-to-heart discussions with my peers," she said.

The talks piqued Syms' curiosity still further. She wanted to learn more about what made family businesses work. "I wanted to talk with the mothers and fathers who had brought their children into the business and had made it work," Syms said. "How did they deal with such issues as succession, separation of home and work, in-laws, sibling rivalry, and twenty-four-hour accountability?"

What started out as a modest survey of people involved in family businesses eventually yielded a book's worth of information. Syms analyzed her respondents' experiences and wrote

Mind Your Own Business: And Keep It in the Family, incorporating the lessons that she and others had learned in running family businesses. The book was published in 1992 by MasterMedia.

Today Syms is a columnist for *Family Business* magazine and a frequent speaker on the subject. The process she began to help herself has evolved into an opportunity to help others.

Syms also is active in women's organizations and willingly offers the benefit of her particular experience. "Choosing to work in the business my father started was very much influenced by my being a woman," she explained. "I wanted to be a stakeholder, not an outsider. I figured my father would be less likely to inhibit my ambitions than other bosses, and fortunately for me, I turned out to be right."

She can tell the other side of the story as well. "Meshing both family and business every workday has been a continuing challenge and being a woman hasn't made either role any easier," she said. "My father came from a traditional European background with all the old attitudes toward women that implies."

In some ways, being a daughter helped Syms establish a successful working relationship with her father—because there was no competition between the two. As Syms puts it, "We're not going in there with the same equipment, so to speak. Over the years, we have grown to respect and nurture our unique talents and thrive on our differences. My father and I bring out the best in each other. As Sy says, 'We egg each other on.'"

Eventually Syms also came to terms with her brothers. As a sister and as the company's president, she said, "I tried to reassure them that I had their best interests at heart."

Now three of Sy's children work in the business, and the equilibrium that was upset when Syms was named president has been restored. "We all see ourselves as part of the management team," Syms said. "I think the comment of my brother, Stephen—the oldest male child—says it for all of us: 'Fortunately, it's a growing company and there's plenty of room for everyone to feel important, regardless of titles.'"

Syms believes traditions and stories play an important role in shaping the identity and character of a family business. The defining Syms story involves Sy's battle with U.S. Steel. The giant corporation wanted to build a skyscraper on the site of one of his stores. Sy refused a settlement and stayed in his store until his lease was up.

The incident illustrates the values that Sy passed on to his children. "My family story is not about size or strength but of courage, stamina, and moral influence," Syms said.

That no doubt explains why Marcy Syms prizes her integrity and inner strength above her title or even financial success. "At the end of the day, it is your character, not your résumé that successful career choices should be building," she said. "Do something because you believe in it. Not for the résumé. Not for the paychecks. You have to trust your own judgment about what is right for you, regardless of the trends or the pressure. Seeing your judgment validated will keep you moving toward your goal and make the getting there worthwhile."

Syms, who is single and lives in Manhattan, balances her hectic work life with twice-a-month weekend retreats to her country hideaway. During the week, she unwinds in front of the VCR. "I am a movie fanatic," she said. She also enjoys the theater and socializing with friends.

"I genuinely like and enjoy people," Syms said. And she considers this an important ingredient in her success, although certainly her sense of purpose, perseverance, and commitment to excellence were essential to the mix.

Although she joined a family business, Syms found no shortcut to success. She suffered her share of self-doubt and disappointment, inner turmoil, and close relationships gone bad. But she tackled each problem, dealt with each setback, and never felt sorrow for the hard times. After all, she mastered that lesson at Bronxville High.

"I believe that you really do learn through adversity," she said. "I wouldn't change a thing that contributed to my becoming the person I am today. I feel lucky to be living the life I have."

Silvia Unzueta

*⌒Culturally, you have a double whammy: The
system makes you choose if you're a woman
or a Hispanic. I happen to be all of it.
I don't want to be dissected into pieces.*

When Silvia Unzueta was growing up in a poor Cuban neighborhood in Miami, a few empty soda bottles could mean the difference between eating and going hungry.

Unzueta arrived in Miami in 1961 at the age of thirteen, alone and with little more than the clothes on her back. In her homeland of Cuba, her family was very wealthy and could afford to give her all the luxuries of life. But after Fidel Castro took power, her parents feared she would be sent to Russia along with other Catholic school children. So they spirited her away to the United States to live with acquaintances.

Eventually Unzueta would earn a degree from Harvard and become a leading voice for women and Hispanics in Dade County. But growing up in a Miami ghetto, far from the people who loved her, she easily could have chosen a much different path. She remembers scrounging for bottles to get enough money to pay for her lunch. Once, a man chased her when she took five bottles from his garage. The bottles meant 10 cents to her—a fortune. "I have never run faster in my life," she recalled. "But he never got me."

Unzueta shares this particular episode from her childhood because, she said, "It's sort of an example of how difficult things were....You had a certain rhythm that was guided by lack of money but also by purpose. You knew that internally there is a security that comes from having had. You never do see yourself as second class. I never assumed that I was less than anybody."

These days, Unzueta lives in Coral Gables, Florida, an affluent municipality not far from the Cuban neighborhood known as Little Havana, but a world away from the life she once knew. She has kept in touch with her culture even as she rose through the ranks of the mainstream bureaucracy.

As superintendent of the South and Cultural Affairs Division for the Metropolitan Dade County Park and Recreation Department, Unzueta, now forty-five, oversees the management of performing arts facilities and coordinates special programs, such as Women's History Month celebrations, as well as major events like the pope's visit. She also is responsible for the operation of numerous parks and other recreational facilities.

But Unzueta's official title "doesn't begin to describe her range of activism and quiet influence," said Liz Balmaseda, a columnist for the *Miami Herald.* "She is ubiquitous in matters of women and minorities, and not very good at keeping her distance from issues that affect them."

For example, Unzueta organized the first federation of Hispanic employees working in Dade County government, and designed and implemented the county's first affirmative action program in the late seventies. More recently, she was influential in planning The Women's Park, which honors the contributions of women of all races. And she's worked extensively with refugees and migrant farm workers. Many of her efforts, however, have been directed toward helping young people who, like her, have had to overcome the obstacles of poverty and prejudice.

Growing up in Havana, Cuba, Unzueta had everything a child could wish for: loving parents, a beautiful home, and her own horse to ride whenever she pleased. Her father, Horacio, came to Cuba from Spain at the age of fifteen and learned the craft of furniture making. He eventually became one of Havana's best furniture makers and interior designers, and he often took his inquisitive daughter along when visiting his wealthy clients. "I have since loved the smell of wood," Unzueta said. "He was a very hard-working role model. So I am a workaholic, I guess. Me and my brother."

Horacio Unzueta Jr. was a few years older than his sister and a model student. Silvia decided that since her brother was so good in academics, she would forge her own path and become "the light, funny one. I would get away with murder and he wouldn't." When Horacio was sixteen, however, he was accused of placing a bomb in a communist-controlled facility. If found guilty, he could have been executed by a firing squad, Unzueta said.

To escape prosecution, Horacio was sent to live on an uncle's farm in Spain. The following year, Silvia's parents obtained a visa for her to leave Cuba as well. If asked, she was told to say that she was going to visit her grandmother in the United States for a few days. (Her grandmother, whom Silvia had never met, had died in Spain years before.) She remembers riding her horse for the last time: "My eyes were watering because I knew I was going; I would never see my horse again."

Her parents chose to remain in Cuba to safeguard their business and property, hoping that Castro soon would be overthrown and their family could be reunited. Eventually Horacio Unzueta's business was taken by the communist government, and he was sent to work on a farm. It would be thirteen years before Silvia saw her parents again. By then she was a grown woman and had convinced her parents to give up their vigil and join her in the United States. She never returned to her homeland, although her greatest wish is to see democracy restored there someday.

In the United States, where Silvia was granted political asylum, she soon realized that her life would never be the same. "I aged the moment I stepped off that plane," she said. "I stopped being a pampered little brat and became an adult at age thirteen." The people who took her in were kind but had very little money to spare. She received a check for $33 each month from the state of Florida. From that she had to pay for her school lunches, buy clothes, and call her parents regularly in Havana. "That was as important as eating," she said.

By the middle of most months, the money was gone. Rather than apply for free lunches—to which she was entitled but which her foster parents were too proud to accept—the resourceful

Silvia Unzueta

young Unzueta would gather up cartons of untouched milk in the cafeteria. Still, she refused to think of herself as second class. Whenever a well-meaning acquaintance would introduce her as "poor Silvia from Cuba," Unzueta would become angry. "I said, 'I'll be damned if I'm going to take that reading of my soul. I've got two hands, a head, and a good brain.'"

But it would take more than a feisty spirit to make it in a country where she barely spoke the language and where she was considered inferior simply because of the color of her skin. Because of her poor English, Unzueta struggled in school. She was bright but bored, and her teachers labeled her "dumb." She was ashamed of the colorful "Third World" dresses she had brought with her from Cuba. She wanted to fit in with American girls, who wore conservative blouses and tailored skirts. But her culture kept her separate in so many ways. When she gathered with other Cuban immigrants on the sidewalks, people would yell at them and call them "spics."

Unzueta had been in the United States only a few years when her foster father was offered a job in the Canary Islands, near the northwest coast of Africa. Since she was considered a ward of the state, the family had to sneak her out of Miami. Finding herself once again in a strange new country, Unzueta turned to books for company. She began reading all the classics, especially Russian literature. Suddenly she discovered that she enjoyed learning and excelled in school. A nun named Sister Gloria became her teacher and her lifelong friend.

"She knew there was something either difficult or painful about my life and wanted in some way to be part of it and help me. She allowed me to thrive," Unzueta said.

After high school, Unzueta got a job with a real estate development company and continued her education at night. She was promoted quickly and was making good money. She had a boyfriend. Her friends, many of whom still were being cared for by their parents, admired her independence. But she secretly envied their family life. She loved her foster parents, but she never felt like an important part of their household. And she rebelled against their protectiveness. "I grew up like a wild weed," she said.

When she turned twenty, her brother decided to immigrate to the United States and asked her to join him. She had mixed feelings—because it was in America that she had encountered prejudice for the first time. But she also knew that America offered opportunities she couldn't find elsewhere. Once there, she became determined to help others find those opportunities too. While attending college full time, Unzueta went to work for

Protestant Social Services and soon was placed in charge of services to migrant workers in south Dade County.

"A different world opened up for me," she said. "I began to realize this was a community that really didn't know what to do with Hispanics. We had to make the transition between recent arrivals and contributing partners in the wealth of the community."

In 1975, Unzueta was hired by Dade County to design and implement a plan to recruit and train minorities to work in all aspects of county government. Later, she was named special projects administrator for refugee affairs. She supervised the initial stages of the Cuban Mariel boat lift and worked with Haitian refugees to obtain legal status and services. In 1986, after earning a master's degree in public administration from Harvard, she became the first woman and the first Hispanic to head a division within the Metro Dade Park and Recreation Department.

As superintendent of the South and Cultural Affairs Division, Unzueta says her goal is to make the county's parks and cultural facilities more open and responsive to the needs of all Dade County residents. For instance, in the wake of Hurricane Andrew, her division initiated the Metro Parks Mini-Fest Caravan. Touring tent cities set up in the aftermath of the disaster, the caravan provided family-oriented entertainment and activities for both victims and volunteers. The program has continued and the caravan now tours parks throughout the county.

Unzueta also organizes special festivals each year aimed at getting the city's youth involved in parks programs. She is particularly proud of the Metro Parks Jazz Band, a group of talented high school musicians who perform around the state; many of these young musicians receive scholarships to attend the nation's best colleges and universities.

The band "fits with my desire to reward excellence," Unzueta said. "You get a lot of attention if you kill somebody, if you do drugs. I want kids to get attention for doing things right."

Unzueta also is active in issues involving women. She has been named Woman of the Year by the Latin Business and Professional Women's Club and the Coalition of Hispanic-American Women, and she was a 1992 nominee for Florida's Women's Hall of Fame. For many years, she has hosted a monthly gathering of women professionals known as the "Agendaless." It is a chance for women to meet, share ideas, and forge alliances in an informal setting. Meetings typically take place in Unzueta's living room, where participants sip wine and listen to traditional Hispanic music. But more comes out of these meetings than social chit-chat.

It was here, for instance, that Dade County's family leave policy first gathered force. And it was here that the idea for The Women's Park first began to take shape. Believed to be the first of its kind in the nation, the park features a time capsule containing items that are meaningful to women of all races and backgrounds.

Unzueta feels the park sends an important message: "Women have a bond that transcends who we are and where we came from. Traditionally, feminism has been defined by American liberal white women. We need that translation and those voices to continue to be joined by women of color. That hasn't always happened because women of color have not trusted other women and have been too torn by their own cultural identities.

"Culturally, you have a double whammy," she continued. "The system makes you choose if you're a woman or a Hispanic. I happen to be all of it. I don't want to be dissected into pieces."

For Unzueta, cross-cultural cooperation among women can't begin soon enough. She has been involved with getting Hispanic mothers to enroll their daughters in mainstream organizations such as the Girl Scouts and the YWCA. (She has served on the national boards of both groups for many years.) She believes that young women need these opportunities to thrive and compete with one another. "By the time they hit the real world," she observed, "the men are already out there. They know how to work together. We have to come to the table having had an opportunity to have a little place where we can practice our skills."

Unzueta knows firsthand how important it is for women to have that chance to prove themselves. Growing up in a strange country without her parents to nurture her was difficult, but it also made her strong—and self-reliant.

"I am very grounded in where I come from; I don't forget it," she said. "I'm not embarrassed or ashamed of how I picked up my five bottles. I can detect kids who are in the process of finding their five bottles and I can help them....It all comes around."

Wendy Wasserstein

~I want to entertain, but I also want to use the theater to shake things up a bit. I want to make people think.

Wendy Wasserstein is a woman of many roles. She's the kid from Brooklyn who made it to Broadway writing funny, poignant plays about people with problems like yours. She's a commentator on the monumental changes in women's lives over the past three decades. And she is the voice of her generation: baby boomers born in the fifties and coming of age in the sixties, the first generation raised on television and rock 'n' roll.

Yet for all her success, Wasserstein has stayed surprisingly humble and human—she seems more like the girlfriend you'd trust with your most embarrassing secrets than one of the hottest playwrights in America. With a cherub's face framed by full, curly brown hair, Wasserstein is quick to giggle and make fun of herself. Like her characters, she is open and totally vulnerable. She's real. And professional concerns aside, the struggles in her life are comfortingly ordinary—her hair, her clothing, her mother, and men. The same things that plague other women. Wasserstein's been up and down with her weight. But then, who hasn't?

"No matter how successful I become as a playwright," she said, "my mother would be thrilled to hear me tell her I'd just lost twenty pounds, gotten married, and become a lawyer." A quintessential New Yorker, she is a lovable, witty, anxious, fortysomething, single Jewish woman. Yet underneath her humor, she's sometimes lonely, sometimes sad and disappointed. Her greatest strength is making light of her weaknesses, and she frequently taps her tortured adolescence, filling her plays with scenes and characters stolen from life with the family Wasserstein.

As a columnist for the now defunct *New York Woman*, Wasserstein contributed monthly first-person essays entitled "The Meaning of Life." Never reluctant to reveal herself, Wasserstein touched nerves by exploring topics such as a Jewish girl's memories of Christmas or by asking troubling questions about why so many of her friends couldn't conceive. Every time Wasserstein submitted an essay, she invariably received a call from her agitated editor, who would scream, "Wait a minute, you can't print that."

Besides having a gift for getting laughs from punchy one-liners, Wasserstein is an acute observer of life. She seems to remember everything that ever happened to her. And she expects a lot from people and situations. Even as a child watching TV comedies like the *Danny Thomas Show,* she'd think to herself, "I'm funnier than that." No wonder the families featured on the sitcoms were downright boring compared to the wacky Wassersteins.

Born the youngest of four children, Wasserstein describes her family as close and affectionate, if not a bit crazy. Her father, Morris, ran a thriving textile business. One incident that typifies her father was the shopping trip they took to an upscale store when she was in high school. "My father goes up to this Ultrasuede dress and starts feeling the fabric," she recalled. "He's hard of hearing, and he doesn't know he's shouting at the top of his lungs." Who else but a Wasserstein would announce to the whole store that he could get the same fabric for $3.98 a yard?

By contrast, her mother, Lola, was a theater lover and a tireless dance student; now in her seventies, she still takes four classes a day. Maybe that's why Wasserstein's chubbiness and "comfortable" attire have always been sore points. In an effort to instill poise in an awkward daughter whose socks were always falling down and who wore the same work shirt to school every day, Lola Wasserstein enrolled her daughter in the June Taylor School for Dance. She also sent her to Helena Rubinstein for "charm" lessons. There young Wasserstein learned the proper way to

Wendy Wasserstein   Photo by James Hamilton

enter and exit a cab—and mined enough material for several essays. Some of her best were collected and published in a book called *Bachelor Girls*.

The Wasserstein household had a rhythm all its own. Lola Wasserstein hated cleaning and never cooked, so there was rarely anything in the house to eat; mostly the family lived on meals from Cooky's, a local delicatessen. Even on Thanksgiving, Lola ordered from Cooky's, while boiling garlic to give their house the smell of homemade cooking. When she'd tell guests she'd slaved in the kitchen all day, the rest of her family cooperated by complimenting the food and pretending to exchange recipes. Still, the Wassersteins wondered why no one seemed to notice the obvious absence of dirty pots in the kitchen.

Wasserstein immortalized her mother in a collection of anecdotes that comprise the play *Isn't It Romantic*. At one point, the father in the play tells Janie, a character Wasserstein modeled after herself, "Believe me, you were born to order up." To this day, when Wasserstein visits her mother, she brings a bag with take-out coffee, which Lola daintily pours into china cups.

Wasserstein likens her mom to Auntie Mame because of her flair for dressing in stylish but flamboyant fashions. Take the time she introduced playwright Christopher Durang, her best friend from Yale Drama School, to her mother: Lola Wasserstein was dressed like Patty Hearst, sporting a beret and carrying a toy gun.

"I'm someone who's always tried to become normal—it's just never worked out," said Wasserstein, describing how her parents wanted their children exposed to culture of all kinds. "My parents would take us to see anything." As a child, she spent many an evening in nightclubs in the Catskills, listening to comedians compare matzo balls to women's anatomy.

For all their eccentricities, Morris and Lola Wasserstein believed their son and three daughters were destined for greatness or success, whichever came first. And they simply couldn't imagine less for their children—a theme that comes through in Wasserstein's newest play, *The Sisters Rosensweig*. Sara, the oldest of the sisters Rosensweig, talks about getting a ninety-nine on a test, only to have her mother ask, "What happened to the other point?" Funny thing, Wasserstein's sister, Sandy, had the same experience as a child.

Schooling began for Wasserstein in a Brooklyn yeshiva, a Jewish parochial school. She had her first theatrical experience in second grade when she played Queen Esther. Even then, people noticed her humor and ear for conversation.

When Wasserstein was twelve, her family moved to the affluent Upper East Side of New York City, during the period when she took tap and ballet lessons at June Taylor. As part of the family's Saturday ritual, her parents would pick up Wasserstein after class and they'd go to a Broadway matinee.

"I was a show business baby, born in a trunk," said Wasserstein. Her ideas about theater began taking shape while she was still a young girl. In particular, she remembers wondering why so few plays featured strong female characters. But she loved musicals—and quickly discovered that she could get excused from gym class at Calhoun School, the prep school she attended, by writing the musical revue for their annual mother-daughter luncheon. During high school, she'd amuse herself by sneaking to the restroom to read *Franny and Zooey*.

After graduation, Wasserstein majored in history at Mount Holyoke, one of the highly competitive Seven Sisters colleges for women. Undecided about a career, she toyed with making her mother happy by pursuing a law degree. But while studying to be a congressional intern, Wasserstein continually fell asleep over her books. Midway through college, at the suggestion of a friend, she took a summer play writing course at Smith College—because shopping was much better there than at Mount Holyoke. (This reasoning foreshadowed the career of a playwright whose characters often wrestle with traditional roles versus the goals they have set for themselves.)

Excited by her experience in the summer course, Wasserstein began performing in campus theatrical productions during her junior year, which was spent at Amherst College. "If you're shy, acting is a way of being someone else," Wasserstein said. "And theater creates a family, an environment that's very nice. What I didn't know at that point was that you could do something in life that you liked—so I thought I had to take the law boards, which I did every year for years."

After college, Wasserstein was still unsure about whether to follow her heart and head for the theater, or pursue a more secure career. So she returned to New York where she worked at odd jobs and studied play writing with Israel Horovitz and Joseph Heller. In 1973, her play *Any Woman Can't*, which she describes as "a girl who gives up and gets married after blowing an audition for tap dancing," opened Off-Broadway at Playwrights Horizons, a non-profit theater that nurtures promising young writers.

Wasserstein then received a master's degree from City College, and with some misgivings, enrolled at Yale University's School of Drama. Her parents gave their blessings "because it was Yale, and I could meet a doctor or a lawyer there," Wasserstein said. "I guess they thought I'd be writing plays in the library of the medical school." Her choice of Yale was complicated by the fact that Wasserstein had also been accepted at Columbia Business School. But she knew it wasn't for her. "I decided to take the risk of trying something I really wanted to do," she said. Years later, much to Wasserstein's delight, the dean of Columbia sent her a note saying, "You made the right choice!"

But at the time, she wasn't so sure. During her first few months at Yale, Wasserstein was frightened to death. "I felt like I was going from platform to platform, trying to catch the train to Moscow," she said. "I had no idea what I was doing at drama school." One reason she felt so lost was that everyone she knew was going to law school or marrying a lawyer.

Happily, Wasserstein soon got her bearings and thrived at Yale. But one question continued to haunt her as she studied her craft: where were the great roles for women? Even in 1973, Yale's curriculum didn't include any plays by women, any female playwrights as guest speakers, or any female directors.

So for her master's thesis, Wasserstein wrote *Uncommon Women and Others*, a one-act version of what eventually became her first successful play. "I started writing *Uncommon Women*," she said, "because we'd been reading all this Jacobean drama, and men were kissing the skulls of women and dropping dead from poison. And I thought, this is not familiar to me."

Uncommon Women takes place in an elite women's college in the early seventies, when feminism first challenged many assumptions about women's roles. Similar to Wasserstein's college experience, the five central characters struggle to realize their dreams and to forge lives in a rapidly changing world. They face the doubts and fears associated with decisions that must be balanced against the powerful pull to become a wife and mother.

Wasserstein clearly struck a controversial chord. At the first reading at Yale, she recalled, "this guy got up at the end of the first act and said 'I can't get into this, it's about girls.'"

Amazed that someone would make such a remark and not be embarrassed, Wasserstein was equally disgusted by his reaction. "I thought, I spent my life getting into *Hamlet* and *Lawrence of Arabia,* so why don't you try it," she said. "I was quite angry." But because she's as good-natured and likable as most of her characters, instead of lashing out at her critics, Wasserstein chose a more constructive course of action: "I made the play really good."

Her efforts paid off. Following her graduation in 1977, *Uncommon Women* was produced by the Phoenix Theatre in New York and featured Glenn Close and Jill Eikenberry. Later Meryl Streep joined the cast in a PBS television production of the play.

Wasserstein acknowledges that *Uncommon Women* is not a conventionally structured play. "It's like an odd sort of documentary. I am more interested in content than form. *Uncommon Women* is episodic. I don't know what actually happens in that play…They graduate."

Critics have occasionally found Wasserstein's unorthodox style problematic. Yet her plays never fail to arouse emotions in audiences. "I take my work very seriously," said Wasserstein, explaining that she matured when writing roles for women simply didn't exist. "In some cases, I created characters who hadn't been put on the stage, whose voices hadn't been heard. It always seemed so obvious to me that their stories should be told."

Her work explores the successes and failures of the women's movement, sometimes lightly, but sometimes painfully as feminism unravels. Observing social change from the sixties to the nineties, Wasserstein's musings often revolve around women who have traded in NOW values for Volvos and kiddie car seats.

A classic example is *The Heidi Chronicles,* the story of one feminist's roller coaster ride from college in the sixties to a career in the eighties, minus the trimmings of a husband and child. Heidi, who doesn't want to forgo motherhood while waiting for "Mr. Right," is a typical Wasserstein character in that she reflects the issues of a whole generation of women who are struggling toward self-definition amid ever-increasing expectations to be a wife and mother, to have a lucrative profession, and to do it all while looking as good as Meryl Streep.

Similarly, the characters in *The Sisters Rosensweig* struggle to put the pieces of modern womanhood together in some satisfying fashion. Pfeni's writing career takes shape as her relationship with a bisexual theater producer wavers. Gorgeous, the happily married mother of four, begins a career on talk radio because all she's missing is some "sparkle." And the twice-divorced international banker, Sara, resists the affections of Merv, who flips for her, flaws and all.

"These characters are part real, part made up," said Wasserstein, who admits once again to borrowing from her background. "But my play is fiction. Fiction! I'm not putting my sisters on stage."

Not that her mom would mind. Lola Wasserstein still wishes that her playwright daughter would find a "Merv," a loving man with whom she could settle down and have a family. But Wasserstein is skeptical about that aspect of her personal life, in part because she's achieved so much professionally. She's won a Pulitzer, a Tony, the New York Drama Critics Circle Prize, the Drama Desk Award, the Outer Critics Circle Award, and the Susan Smith Blackburn Prize.

"All that success intimidates a lot of men," she complained. "I wouldn't want to date a man who was intimidated by my success."

Though Wasserstein is happy for the awards that have come her way, she said, "Success is isolating because you don't have that many people who have had the same exact experience." Contemplating the prospect of a new relationship, she wonders out loud what it would be like meeting a man in a bar these days: "Hi there. I'm Wendy," she'd say. "I won the Pulitzer Prize. What do you do?"

After a series of disappointing love affairs, Wasserstein is aware that her future may never include a husband. Still, she has a soft spot for romance when it comes to writing. Her play *Isn't It Romantic* portrays a trim, aerobics-crazed mother, a silent, supportive father, and a smart, single daughter who is untidy and out of shape. And, as the title suggests, there's a love interest—the Russian taxi driver who the parents keep trying to fix up with their daughter.

"Drama and romance, in particular, are almost always presented in contemporary works by men," Wasserstein said. "Male playwrights still far outnumber their female counterparts, as the characters they create for the stage reveal."

Wasserstein's mission is to change things around. That's why the fiftyish Merv in *The Sisters Rosensweig* falls in love with a woman his same age—a scenario rarely presented in other scripts. "I want to entertain, but I also want to use the theater to shake things up a bit," said Wasserstein. "I want to make people think."

Claiming that she started writing to make order out of chaos, Wasserstein feels like "a perpetual graduate student who just gets older and older." She lives on the Upper West Side of New York with her cat, Ginger, and has a large, devoted circle of friends. "I don't know when she has time to write," said a girlfriend who's known Wasserstein since college. "Being a good friend takes time, and Wendy is one."

To know Wasserstein is to like her, acquaintances say, and people just naturally open up to her. As Wasserstein walks down Manhattan streets, ladies often call out her name, dodging city traffic as they race to meet her. Without prelude, these women launch into conversations about their daughters and their daughters' boyfriends, about their husbands and their own lives. Wasserstein listens, giving them a big hug as they depart. Yet when Wasserstein's companions ask who that lady was, she invariably says, "I've never met them before in my life."

But such fame hasn't changed Wasserstein one bit—she's the same outgoing, down-to-earth, comfortable-to-be-with person she was before the whole world got to know her as a playwright. Recently Wasserstein felt she was socializing too much and accepting too many speaking engagements. She was doing too many things besides writing plays. While some of this activity helps her gather material, it can quickly become an evasion—a way of avoiding the necessary confrontation with the blank first page of a script. When that happens, Wasserstein knows she needs to pull back, that she's seen too much of the world for awhile.

"I guess I've discovered that that's who I am," she said. "I'd rather be in a tiny garage writing a play than going out to dinner parties or making speeches." After all, one of the reasons she became a writer was to remove herself from the day-to-day fray most people face. As she puts it, "Can you think of any other job where you can work all day in a flannel nightgown and slippers?"

Edith Weiner

*⟶My life and the world I live in are mine
to make, to live, to affect.*

Do you ever wonder why people shop in retail stores, now that
flea markets, warehouse outlets, mail-order catalogues, and tele-
vision-shopping networks are taking over?

Questions like this occur to Edith Weiner all the time. She is a
futurist and she makes it her business to think ahead. Analyzing
what's happening now, she predicts events to come.

But Weiner is not a fortuneteller; she's a specialist, selling
advice to major corporations, research and consulting firms,
trade and professional associations, and the government. Her
many clients have included Avon, NYNEX, American Express,
Owens-Corning, the Southern Baptist Sunday School Board,
J.C. Penney, and even the U.S. Congress.

Seeing retailers losing out to cheaper, more convenient shopping outlets, Weiner advises them to adapt or face extinction.
She believes that dressing rooms are the main reason customers
will continue to shop for clothing in stores—because people
want to try on some kinds of clothes, and you can't do that with
catalogues, TV home shopping, flea markets, or buying clubs.

Having made that prediction, Weiner doesn't quit looking
ahead or asking questions: If dressing rooms are becoming the
main attraction of retail fashion stores, then why are they still as
dinky and dark as they were twenty-five years ago? And why do
stores limit the amount of merchandise customers can take

inside? Why not make dressing rooms large and luxurious? Why not furnish them with chairs, so that women can see how far skirts hike up when they sit down? And why not improve lighting to show clothing in typical day and evening settings?

Such questions form the foundation of a futurist's work, explained Weiner, who is president of Weiner, Edrich, Brown, Inc. People today are in a constant state of flux; nothing is permanent. Her voice is soothing as she cautions against hysteria over the demise of most department stores, the bulwark of shopping past. But she also points out that shoring them up is a waste of time, since similar trends are happening in every field.

"Distribution channels are changing for automobiles, insurance, paintings, clothing—even for lawyers and doctors," she said. For instance, lawyers now face competition not only from paraprofessionals offering wills or divorces at cut-rate fees, but from potential clients who are opting to do their own legal work.

Likewise, the public no longer views doctors with awe, now that there are so many healthcare options—"doc in a box" clinics, homeopaths, nutritionists, and acupuncturists. Even so, the profession keeps patching and repairing out-of-date systems, instead of letting go and rebuilding, Weiner said.

And that's a critical mistake for most industries, because the key to future planning is not learning—it's forgetting. "The forgetting curve is much harder to ascend than the learning curve," said Weiner. That's where her expertise comes in—Weiner has a talent for making insightful suggestions that help executives and their corporations stay flexible and on target.

Suggestion number one: Know the difference between a trend and a fad, advises Weiner, who dresses well enough to double as a model for executive women's fashion. A trend has staying power and is never totally out of style. A fad never lasts; once its time passes, a person clinging to it looks out of date. For example, wearing jeans is a long-term trend, but bell bottoms go in and out of fashion.

Yet every trend contains the seeds of its own countertrend. For instance, one trend today is combining technology with communication. Status comes to those with laptop computers, beepers, mobile telephones, and portable fax machines.

Edith Weiner

But eventually people will become overstimulated, Weiner said, and status will shift to those products and services that allow them to detach from the abuse of ready communication. She foresees a future where people will choose to vacation on islands or at resorts that have only one telephone and prohibit personal electronic equipment. One such resort already exists in the Florida Keys—proving there is often money to be made on a countertrend.

Moving ahead of, or away from, the pack can be a very effective strategy. However, trends do not work like pendulums, Weiner warned. It is misleading to think that anything will return to a fixed point, regaining its original popularity or profitability.

For instance, although marriage is once again on the rise, few brides and grooms today share their grandparents' vision of celebrating a golden anniversary. Thanks to changing attitudes and demographics, divorce and remarriage are now common, as are moms who never marry.

In planning for the future, sometimes ideas are discovered by accident, observed Weiner. When a major washing machine manufacturer designed a model with large print so that elderly customers could read the directions more easily, it turned out to be their best seller. Why?

"Because most people have their machines in the basement, where the lighting is poor and the large type was easier for everyone to read," said Weiner, claiming that experience often leads to complacency. "The more a person knows about anything, the less he or she can envision it being different."

So how does Weiner know so much?

She draws her amazing, yet accurate, conclusions from reading. Subscribing to more than fifty wide-ranging global publications, Weiner scans magazines and newspapers in search of anything that signals change. In particular, she's on the lookout for new meanings to current trends, as well as tidbits that seem to contradict the counsel she's been giving clients.

Weiner's not afraid to be wrong and she's a pro at connecting events that at first glance appear to have nothing in common. That's why fifteen years ago, when other observers thought the environmental movement had died because newspapers were silent on this issue, Weiner saw a regrouping on several fronts, including religious interests. Specifically, more people were interpreting Genesis to mean that humans did not have dominion over, but stewardship for, the earth and all its creatures. So she warned food and pharmaceutical clients to watch out. Just as she predicted, the animal rights movement gained strength and began pressuring drug companies to stop animal testing of their products.

Weiner has worked in the futures business for two decades. She proved herself a leader early on by directing the first industry-wide futures research program while she was still in her twenties. She started her career as a social researcher. "My first job allowed me to invent new ways of studying what was happening in the world," she said. It didn't take her long to discover that change was the major happening—change in lifestyles, values, technology, and economic conditions.

"So I gradually realized I would be unhappy studying or practicing just one thing," said Weiner. That first job not only exposed her to wide-ranging subjects, it introduced her to the two great mentors of her career—Arnold Brown and Hal Edrich, who later became her business partners.

Together she and Brown put their theories into two books: *Supermanaging,* which advises executives on how to manage in the changing worlds of business and society; and *Office Biology: Or Why Tuesday Is Your Most Productive Day & Other Relevant Facts for Survival in the Workplace.*

Why is Tuesday best? Because on Monday, everyone is sleepy and in transition from the weekend. In fact, the wee hours of Monday morning are when the highest percentage of strokes and heart attacks occur—because facing the stress of the work-week is something our bodies must fight against. On Tuesday, people rally and are fully focused on work. By Wednesday, mid-week fatigue sets in. On Thursday, people rally again, but never reach Tuesday's pitch. And by Friday, they're slumping, preparing to unwind for another weekend.

Biology is destiny in the workplace, opine the authors. And while such observations might at first sound glib, the business world is becoming increasingly aware of the relationship between office conditions and biology, which has everything to do with worker productivity and the bottom line. For example, if office lighting is poor, eye strain and headaches result, causing a slowdown in performance. One study estimated that for every dollar saved by reduced lighting, $160 of productivity was lost.

Weiner also has studied the effects of scent. Leading fragrance producers believe that certain scents have the potential to make people eat less, work harder, drive safer, and sleep more soundly. In the future, corporations may tap fragrances to their advantage. Kajima, a Tokyo corporation, is already using them to affect mood and output among office workers by sending different aromas into their environment over the course of the day. For instance, in the morning, the invigorating scent of lemon is pumped into offices to wake up workers. Just before noon, the scent of roses is substituted, offering a calming effect for their enjoyment of lunch. In the afternoon, when energy tends to flag, the woodsy odor of tree-trunk oils is used to pep up workers whose productivity may be slackening.

The fact that Weiner has trained her mind to constantly think in the future is understandable, since her past would have slowed down a less determined person. Born in Brooklyn, New York, to a warm and loving family, Weiner was the second of three children. She remembers her parents as people who were full of fun and a bit zany. But their lives were torn apart after Weiner's mother contracted multiple sclerosis when Weiner was not yet two years old.

"I grew up in foster homes, where I was only valued as an income-producing property by the people I lived with," said Weiner, explaining that she had loved camp, but was not allowed to become a counselor since the work would have taken her out of her foster home, thus depriving her guardians of two months' income. And she was not allowed to accept a scholarship in journalism from a major out-of-town university, because her foster family would not have received a stipend if she was away.

Such slights were characteristic of a painful childhood that Weiner survived with charm and a remarkable sense of self-esteem. "They told me that I was unattractive and that I would never amount to anything," said Weiner, whose chic brown hair sets off a face with large sparkling eyes and dramatic bone structure. "None of my foster parents gave me any encouragement to succeed. I was always told I was a problem child."

Their criticism was all the more cruel considering Weiner maintained a straight-A average, had plenty of friends, and took the initiative in helping out with household chores. Even though she was an excellent athlete, she was never encouraged to become a track star.

Nor was she encouraged to become a doctor, or a weather forecaster, or a marine biologist. "So I never had career goals," said Weiner. "That left me totally open to follow whatever I was interested in and felt I could excel at."

As a child, Weiner learned to look within for the strength to believe in herself. "My philosophy of life has always been that I am everything and I am nothing," she said. "Nothing, because in the vast scheme of things, no one really amounts to anything." This philosophy helps Weiner keep everyday problems in perspective. At the same time, she also believes "I am everything— because if I die, my whole world dies with me. So my life and the world I live in is mine to make, to live, to affect." This philosophy is both humbling and uplifting, which is why she's a go-getter who never became conceited.

After such a childhood, Weiner was destined to either crumble or become a leader. She always knew that in spite of hardship, she could make something of herself through perseverance. And she's proven that repeatedly in her life. In addition to writing books, Weiner has published a stream of articles without the benefit of journalism school. And despite having only a bachelor's degree from the City College of New York, she has been a guest lecturer at Harvard, Wharton, Brown, and other major universities.

Early in her career, hard work paid off with recognition. At twenty-six, she chaired a panel for the U.S. Congress on the future of health and welfare. A year later, she was chosen as one of ten business leaders to participate in the National Science Foundation Bicentennial Program. At twenty-nine, she became the youngest woman ever elected to the board of directors of a major financial institution when she joined the board of Union Mutual Life Insurance Company, now known as UNUM Corporation.

In addition to striving for personal achievement, Weiner has always believed in reaching out to others in need of a boost. In 1985, she founded and chaired the BUDDY Awards (Bringing Up Daughters Differently) for the NOW Legal Defense and

Education Fund. And in 1992, she founded and chaired the NAFFY Awards (Nurturing the Aspirations of Females for the Future) for the National Association for Female Executives. Proceeds from this event fund a program called Esteem Teams that Weiner created to pair underprivileged girls with executive women who have volunteered to serve as mentors.

The Esteem Teams provide each girl with a network of resources—tutoring, role models, friends, social workshops, plus exposure to the professional world—throughout their adolescence. "It's a very exciting program," said Weiner, whose aim is to enrich lives by providing these girls with hope for the future.

A dance lover, Weiner also is on the board of the Jose Limon Dance Foundation. "But my real passion," she said, "is helping people, especially helping young girls develop inner strength." More than anything, she wants them to believe in their abilities and to feel that, no matter what, they can earn a living and be proud of who they are—because in today's world, it's important for girls, as they mature, to learn how to take charge, explained Weiner.

As more women step into positions of importance, they should know how to lead in their own style, not by traditional standards. "Leadership resides in you and only you," advised Weiner, who believes that women have something unique to offer. "The next time you are at work, at church, with your friends, or with your associates—you suggest a challenge, you outline the work, you put the resources together. You make things happen."

In the midst of a life that gathered momentum early, Weiner married at twenty, promising herself that she would never forgo family life for a career. Nine years later, when she was ready for a baby, she knew she wanted to raise the child with her husband—not with a nanny. So Weiner started her own business, "because I knew no employer would give me the family latitude I wanted." And she has never regretted a minute spent with her son, Jared. By taking the initiative, Weiner has seamlessly woven together motherhood and career.

When asked to name her most important achievement, Weiner is quick to respond: "Becoming pregnant when it was totally unfashionable for executive women." Since there weren't any decent maternity clothes for businesswomen before 1980, Weiner had to struggle to piece together a wardrobe appropriate for her many roles—a business owner meeting clients, corporate board member, and public speaker.

But she believes her pregnancy opened the way for future executive women who wanted to be working moms. "I have always tried to be a role model for others who are less comfortable than I am in breaking the stereotypes and the molds," said Weiner, proving that time after time, both professionally and personally, she has reached for the future, watched it become the present, only to break future boundaries again.

About the Authors

Currently at Harvard working on an M.B.A., Lindsey Johnson has been involved in politics and public service as an advocate for women since 1976.

After graduating from the University of Chicago, where she earned a degree in international relations, Johnson ventured into professional politics. During the next few years, Lindsey served as campaign manager for several congressional campaigns and also worked on numerous state and local races. (She was first exposed to politics as a teenager, when she helped her mom, Congresswoman Nancy L. Johnson, win her first election on a local Connecticut board.)

In 1985, Johnson was named the director of legislative affairs for the Washington, D.C.-based law firm Verner, Liipfert, Bernhard, McPherson & Hand. There she specialized in employee benefits and health care, domestic and international trade, contracting and transportation issues.

In 1988, she joined the Bush presidential campaign as the national director of the Coalition for Women. In this position, she was responsible for creating and implementing special projects related to women and women in business. She also helped develop a policy strategy to support women entrepreneurs. After the election, she worked with a transition team given the responsibility of recruiting women for the new administration.

In 1989, at age twenty-nine, Johnson was selected as the director of the Office of Women's Business Ownership with the U.S. Small Business Administration. In her role as an advocate for the nation's five million women business owners in the public and private sectors, Johnson was responsible for wide-ranging programs and projects, chief among them a $7.5 million demonstration project to establish long-term training and counseling centers for women entrepreneurs throughout the country. She also oversaw a nationwide mentor program designed to link experienced female CEOs with women business owners ready for expansion.

During that time, Johnson was frequently asked to speak at conferences and to associations on behalf of the nearly five million women entrepreneurs in this country. She is also credited with implementing the Women's Business Ownership Act of 1988 and the Women's Business Development Act of 1991.

Johnson's interest in small business, particularly women entrepreneurs, continues to grow. After completing her studies at Harvard, she plans to launch a public service career that will involve linking private sources of funding with small business owners seeking capital for expansion.

Johnson lives in Boston.

Three-time Olympic gold medalist Jackie Joyner-Kersee may be widely regarded as a champion athlete, but she'd rather be remembered as a role model for future generations.

Growing up in East St. Louis, Illinois, she demonstrated her athletic ability and ambitions early. When she was nine, she began running track and dreaming of being recognized on television as the world's greatest track star. She proved herself a star at Lincoln High School and later at the University of California at Los Angeles, where she was on the basketball and track teams.

She won her first Olympic title while still in college. In the 1984 games in Los Angeles, Joyner won the silver medal in the heptathlon, a two-day, seven-event competition that includes running, long jumping and javelin throwing.

By the time the 1988 Olympic Games rolled around, she had graduated from college and married her coach, Bob Kersee, who she met at UCLA. At the games in Seoul, Korea, she claimed two gold medals and set world records for the same event.

Joyner-Kersee successfully defended her Olympic heptathlon

championship in the 1992 games in Barcelona, Spain. As she came off the field after winning her second straight heptathlon, Joyner-Kersee was greeted by Bruce Jenner, the famed 1976 decathlon champion, who proclaimed her "the greatest athlete in the world."

Despite suffering from asthma since 1982, the thirty-one-year-old superstar continues to pile up world records—currently Joyner-Kersee holds the six highest records in heptathlon history. And she's already preparing for the 1996 Olympics in Atlanta.

But between training, she devotes much of her energy to the Jackie Joyner-Kersee Community Foundation, which sponsors education and recreation programs for disadvantaged youngsters. She has said the foundation is her way of reaching back to her hometown for the support she received there when she was growing up.

Besides her work on behalf of the foundation, Joyner-Kersee is known for her spontaneous acts of generosity. For example, when she won an *Essence* magazine award in 1988, she gave $1,000 to one of the other awardees, a ten-year-old girl, so she could further her education. She did the same thing for the anti-drug abuse organization New Start in Santa Monica, California. On another occasion, when a Belleville, Illinois, group that desperately wanted her for a keynote speaker ran into scheduling problems, Joyner-Kersee graciously suggested they hold the event on her birthday, because that was the one day she had free.

Joyner-Kersee often visits schools to talk with young people, knowing that her status as a star athlete may just make the kids sit up and take notice of the lessons she wants to teach them about staying on track in life. "I do feel what you stand for should be more important than athletics," she says. "Young people look at me as a role model, but I'm just a human being. I say emulate me as a person, not an athlete."

Joyner-Kersee and her husband make their home in St. Louis.

Additional copies of *A Woman's Place Is Everywhere* may be ordered by sending $9.95 to MasterMedia Limited, 17 East 89th Street, New York, NY 10128. Or call (800) 334-8232 or fax (212) 546-7638. Be sure to include $2 for postage and handling of the first copy, and $1 for each additional copy.

Other MasterMedia Books

At bookstores, or call (800) 334-8232 to place a credit card order.

AGING PARENTS AND YOU: A Complete Handbook to Help You Help Your Elders Maintain a Healthy, Productive, Independent Life, by Eugenia Anderson-Ellis, is a complete guide to providing care to aging relatives. It features practical advice and resources for adults helping their elders lead productive lives. Revised and updated. ($9.95 paperbound)

BALANCING ACTS! Juggling Love, Work, Family, and Recreation, by Susan Schiffer Stautberg and Marcia L. Worthing, provides strategies to achieve a balanced life by reordering priorities and setting realistic goals. ($12.95 paperbound)

BEATING THE AGE GAME, Redefining Retirement, by Jack and Phoebe Ballard, debunks the myth that retirement means sitting out the rest of the game. The years between 55 and 80 can be your best, say the authors, who provide ample examples of people successfully using retirement to reinvent their lives. ($12.95 paperbound)

BEYOND SUCCESS: How Volunteer Service Can Help You Begin Making a Life Instead of Just a Living, by John J. Raynolds III and Eleanor Raynolds, C.B.E., is a unique how-to book targeted at business and professional people considering volunteer work, senior citizens who wish to fill leisure time meaningfully, and students trying out career options. ($9.95 paperbound, $19.95 hardbound)

THE BIG APPLE BUSINESS AND PLEASURE GUIDE: 501 Ways To Work Smarter, Play Harder, and Live Better in New York City, by Muriel

Siebert and Susan Kleinman, offers visitors and New Yorkers alike advice on how to do business in the city as well as how to enjoy its attractions. ($9.95 paperbound)

BREATHING SPACE: Living and Working at a Comfortable Pace in a Sped-up Society, by Jeff Davidson, helps readers to handle information and activity overload, in order to gain greater control over their lives. ($10.95 paperbound)

CITIES OF OPPORTUNITY: Finding the Best Way to Work, Live, and Prosper in the 1990s and Beyond, by Dr. John Tepper Martin, explores the job and living options for the next decade and into the next century. This consumer guide and handbook, written by one of the world's experts on cities, selects and features forty-six American cities and metropolitan areas. ($13.95 paperbound, $24.95 hardbound)

THE CONFIDENCE FACTOR: How Self-Esteem Can Change Your Life, by Dr. Judith Briles, is based on a nationwide survey of six thousand men and women. Briles explores why women so often feel a lack of self-confidence and have a poor opinion of themselves. She offers step-by-step advice on becoming the person you want to be. ($12.95 paperbound, $18.95 hardbound)

DARE TO CONFRONT! How To Intervene When Someone You Care About Has a Drug or Alcohol Problem, by Bob Wright and Deborah George Wright, shows the reader how to use the step-by-step methods of professional interventionists to motivate drug-dependent people to accept help they need. ($17.95 hardbound)

THE DOLLARS AND SENSE OF DIVORCE: The Financial Guide for Women, by Dr. Judith Briles, is the first book to combine the legal hurdles by planning finances before, during, and after divorce. ($10.95 paperbound)

THE ENVIRONMENTAL GARDENER: The Solution to Pollution for Lawns and Gardens, by Laurence Sombke, focuses on what each of us can do to protect our endangered plant life. A practical source book and shopping guide. ($8.95 paperbound)

FINANCIAL SAVVY FOR WOMEN: A Money Book for Women of All Ages, by Dr. Judith Briles, divides a woman's monetary life span into six phases, discusses specific issues to be addressed at each stage, and demonstrates how to create a sound money plan. ($15.00 paperbound)

FLIGHT PLAN FOR LIVING: The Art of Self-Encouragement, by Patrick O'Dooley, is a life guide organized like a pilot's checklist, to ensure you'll be flying "clear on top" throughout your life. ($17.95 hardbound)

GLORIOUS ROOTS: Recipes for Healthy, Tasty Vegetables, by Laurence Sombke, celebrates the taste, texture, and versatility of root vegetables. Contains recipes for appetizers, soups, stews, and baked, broiled, and stir-fried dishes—even desserts. ($12.95 paperbound)

HOT HEALTH-CARE CAREERS, by Margaret T. McNally, R.N., and Phyllis Schneider, provides readers everything they need to know about training for and getting jobs in a rewarding field where professionals are always in demand. ($10.95 paperbound)

HOW TO GET WHAT YOU WANT FROM ALMOST ANYBODY, by T. Scott Gross, shows how to get great service, negotiate better prices, and always get what you pay for. ($9.95 paperbound)

KIDS WHO MAKE A DIFFERENCE, by Joyce M. Roché and Marie Rodriguez, is an inspiring document of how today's toughest challenges are being met by teenagers and kids, whose courage and creativity enables them to find practical solutions! ($8.95 paperbound, with photos)

THE LIVING HEART BRAND NAME SHOPPER'S GUIDE, by Michael E. DeBakey, M.D., Antonio M. Gotto, Jr., M.D., Lynne W. Scott, M.A., R.D./L.D., and John P. Foreyt, Ph.D., lists brand name products low in fat, saturated fatty acids, and cholesterol. Revised edition. ($14.95 paperbound)

THE LIVING HEART GUIDE TO EATING OUT, by Michael E. DeBakey, Antonio M. Gotto, Jr., and Lynne W. Scott, is an essential handbook for people who want to maintain a health-conscious diet when dining in all types of restaurants. ($9.95 paperbound)

THE LOYALTY FACTOR: Building Trust in Today's Workplace, by Carol Kinsey Goman, Ph.D., offers techniques for restoring commitment and loyalty in the workplace. ($9.95 paperbound)

MAKING YOUR DREAMS COME TRUE: A Plan For Easily Discovering and Achieving the Life You Want, by Marcia Wieder, introduces an easy, unique, and practical technique for defining, pursuing, and realizing your career and life interests. Filled with stories of real people and helpful exercises, plus a personal workbook. ($9.95 paperbound)

MANAGING IT ALL: Time-Saving Ideas for Career, Family, Relationships, and Self, by Beverly Benz Treuille and Susan Schiffer Stautberg, is written for women juggling careers and families. With interviews of more than two hundred career women (ranging from a TV anchorwoman to an investment banker), this book contains many humorous anecdotes on saving time and improving the quality of life. ($9.95 paperbound)

MANAGING YOUR CHILD'S DIABETES, by Robert Wood Johnson IV, Sale Johnson, Casey Johnson, and Susan Kleinman, brings help to families trying to understand diabetes and control its effects. ($10.95 paperbound)

MANAGING YOUR PSORIASIS, by Nicholas J. Lowe, M.D., is an innovative manual that couples scientific research and encouraging support, with an emphasis on how patients can take charge of their health. ($10.95 paperbound, $17.95 hardbound)

MANN FOR ALL SEASONS: Wit and Wisdom from The Washington Post's *Judy Mann,* shows the columnist at her best as she writes about women, families, and the impact and politics of the women's revolution. ($9.95 paperbound, $19.95 hardbound)

MIND YOUR OWN BUSINESS: And Keep it in the Family, by Marcy Syms, CEO of Syms Corp, is an effective guide for any organization facing the toughest step in managing a family business—making the transition to the new generation. ($12.95 paperbound, $18.95 hardbound)

OFFICE BIOLOGY: Why Tuesday Is the Most Productive Day and Other Relevant Facts for Survival in the Workplace, by Edith Weiner and Arnold Brown, teaches how in the '90s and beyond we will be expected to work smarter, take better control of our health, adapt to advancing technology, and improve our lives in ways that are not too costly or resource-intensive. ($12.95 paperbound, $21.95 hardbound)

ON TARGET: Enhance Your Life and Advance Your Career, by Jeri Sedlar and Rick Miners, is a neatly woven tapestry of insights on career and life issues gathered from audiences across the country. This feedback has been crystallized into a highly readable guide for exploring who you are and how to go about getting what you want. ($11.95 paperbound)

OUT THE ORGANIZATION: New Career Opportunities for the 1990s, by Robert and Madeleine Swain, is written for the millions of Americans whose jobs are no longer safe, whose companies are not loyal, and who face futures of uncertainty, provides advice on finding a new job or starting your own business. (Revised $12.95 paperbound, $17.95 hardbound)

THE OUTDOOR WOMAN: A Handbook to Adventure, by Patricia Hubbard and Stan Wass, details the lives of adventurous women and offers their ideas on how you can incorporate exciting outdoor experiences into your life. ($14.95 paperbound)

PAIN RELIEF: How to Say No to Acute and Chronic Pain, by Dr. Jane Cowles, offers a step-by-step plan for assessing pain and communicating it to your doctor, and explains the importance of having a pain plan before undergoing any medical or surgical treatment; includes "The Pain Patient's Bill of Rights," and a reusable pain assessment chart. ($22.95 paperbound)

POSITIVELY OUTRAGEOUS SERVICE: New and Easy Ways To Win Customers for Life, by T. Scott Gross, identifies what '90s consumers really want and how business can develop effective marketing strategies to answer those needs. ($14.95 paperbound)

POSITIVELY OUTRAGEOUS SERVICE AND SHOWMANSHIP, by T. Scott Gross, reveals the secrets of adding personality to any product or service and offers a wealth of nontraditional marketing techniques employed by top showmen, from car dealers to restaurateurs, amusement park operators to evangelists. ($12.95 paperbound)

THE PREGNANCY AND MOTHERHOOD DIARY: Planning the First Year of Your Second Career, by Susan Schiffer Stautberg, is only undated appointment diary that shows how to manage pregnancy and career. ($12.95 spiralbound)

REAL BEAUTY...REAL WOMEN: A Handbook for Making the Best of Your Own Good Looks, by Kathleen Walas, International Beauty and Fashion Director of Avon Products, Inc., offers expert advice on beauty and fashion for women of all ages and ethnic backgrounds. ($19.95 paperbound)

REAL LIFE 101: The Graduate's Guide To Survival, by Susan Kleinman, supplies welcome advice to those facing "real life" for the first time, focusing on work, money, health, and how to deal with freedom and responsibility. Revised. ($9.95 paperbound)

ROSEY GRIER'S ALL-AMERICAN HEROES: Multicultural Success Stories, by Roosevelt "Rosey" Grier, is a candid collection of profiles of prominent African Americans, Latins, Asians, and Native Americans who revealed how they achieved public acclaim and personal success. ($9.95 paperbound, with photos)

SELLING YOURSELF: How To Be the Competent, Confident Person You Really Are! by Kathy Thebo and Joyce Newman, is an inspirational primer for anyone seeking to project a positive image. Drawing on experience, their own and others', these entrepreneurs offer simple techniques that can add up to big successes. ($11.95 paperbound)

SHOCKWAVES:The Global Impact of Sexual Harassment, by Susan L. Webb, examines the problem of sexual harassment today in every kind of workplace around the world. Practical and well-researched, this manual provides the most recent information available, including legal changes in progress. ($11.95 paperbound, $19.95 hardbound)

SIDE-BY-SIDE STRATEGIES: How Two-Career Couples Can Thrive in the '90s, by Jane Hershey Cuozzo and S. Diane Graham, describes how to learn the difference between competing with a spouse and become a supportive power partner. Published in hardcover as *Power Partners.* ($10.95 paperbound, $19.95 hardbound)

THE SOLUTION TO POLLUTION: 101 Things You Can Do To Clean Up Your Environment, by Laurence Sombke, offers step-by-step techniques on how to conserve more energy, start a recycling center, choose a biodegradable product, and even proceed with individual clean-up projects. ($7.95 paperbound)

THE SOLUTION TO POLLUTION IN THE WORKPLACE, by Laurence Sombke, Terry M. Robertson, and Elliot M. Kaplan, offers everything employees need to know about cleaning up their workplace, including recycling, using energy efficiently, conserving water, and buying nontoxic supplies. ($9.95 paperbound)

SOMEONE ELSE'S SON, by Alan A. Winter, explores the parent-child bond in a contemporary novel of lost identities, family secrets, and relationships gone awry. Eighteen years after bringing their first son home from the hospital, Trish and Brad Hunter discover they are not his biological parents. ($18.95 hardbound)

STEP FORWARD: Sexual Harassment in the Workplace, by Susan L. Webb, presents the facts for dealing with sexual harassment on the job. ($9.95 paperbound)

THE STEPPARENT CHALLENGE: A Primer For Making It Work, by Stephen J. Williams, Ph.D., offers insight into the many aspects of step relationships—from financial issues to lifestyle changes to differences in race or religion that affect the whole family. ($13.95 paperbound)

STRAIGHT TALK ON WOMEN'S HEALTH: How to Get the Health Care You Deserve, by Janice Teal, Ph.D., and Phyllis Schneider, is destined to become a health-care "bible." Devoid of confusing medical jargon, it offers a wealth of resources, including contact lists of healthlines and women's medical centers. ($14.95 paperbound)

TAKING CONTROL OF YOUR LIFE: The Secrets of Successful Enterprising Women, by Gail Blanke and Kathleen Walas, is based on the authors' professional experience with Avon Products' Women of Enterprise Awards, given each year to outstanding female entrepreneurs; offers a plan to help you gain control over your life, plus business tips as well as beauty and lifestyle information. ($17.95 hardbound)

TEAMBUILT: Making Teamwork Work, by Mark Sanborn, teaches businesses how to increase productivity, without increasing resources or expenses, by building teamwork among employees. ($12.95 paperbound, $19.95 hardbound)

A TEEN'S GUIDE TO BUSINESS: The Secrets to a Successful Enterprise, by Linda Menzies, Oren S. Jenkins, and Rick R. Fisher, provides solid information about starting your own business or working for one. ($7.95 paperbound)

TWENTYSOMETHING: Managing & Motivating Today's New Work Force, by Lawrence J. Bradford, Ph.D., and Claire Raines, M.A., examines the work orientation of the younger generation and offers managers practical advice for understanding and supervising their young employees. ($12.95 paperbound, $22.95 hardbound)

WHAT KIDS LIKE TO DO, by Edward Stautberg, Gail Wubbenhorst, Atiya Easterling, and Phyllis Schneider, is a handy guide for parents, grandparents, and baby sitters. Written by kids for kids, this is an easy-to-read, generously illustrated primer for teaching families how to make every day more fun. ($7.95 paperbound)